Corporations and Partnerships in Ireland

Corporations and Partnerships in Ireland

Second Edition

Irene Lynch Fannon

with contribution from
Karole Cuddihy

This book was originally published as a monograph in the International Encyclopaedia of Laws/Corporations and Partnerships.

General Editors: Roger Blanpain, Frank Hendrickx
Volume Editor: Koen Geens

Wolters Kluwer

Published by:
Kluwer Law International B.V.
PO Box 316
2400 AH Alphen aan den Rijn
The Netherlands
Website: www.wklawbusiness.com

Sold and distributed in North, Central and South America by:
Wolters Kluwer Legal & Regulatory U.S.
7201 McKinney Circle
Frederick, MD 21704
United States of America
Email: customer.service@wolterskluwer.com

Sold and distributed in all other countries by:
Turpin Distribution Services Ltd.
Stratton Business Park
Pegasus Drive, Biggleswade
Bedfordshire SG18 8TQ
United Kingdom
Email: kluwerlaw@turpin-distribution.com

ISBN 978-90-411-6853-5

This title is available on www.kluwerlawonline.com

The Authors

Professor Dr Irene Lynch Fannon is a graduate of *University College Dublin, Oxford University* and the *University of Virginia*. She practices as a Consultant Solicitor specializing in the law relating to corporate insolvency, restructuring and rescue in Ireland. She has taught Company Law, Corporate Insolvency Law and Corporate Law Theory in the School of Law, at *University College Cork* since 1987. She is the author (with the Gerard Murphy BL) of *Corporate Insolvency and Rescue* (Second Edition, Bloomsbury, Dublin 2012), having authored the first edition with Rory O'Ferrall and Jane Marshall in 1996. She has published articles in a range of journals on corporate law, corporate insolvency and corporate governance. She served on the Audit Review Committee established by the Irish Government in 2000 following the Public Accounts Committee Enquiry into DIRT and other financial irregularities. This Committee issued its report in 2000, which led, *inter alia*, to the passing of the Companies (Auditing and Accounts) Act 2003. She was a member of the Business Regulation Forum established by the Irish Minister for Enterprise and Employment in 2005, which issued its report in April 2007, and she was then a member of The High Level Group on Business Regulation established by the Minister in July 2007 until she resigned in 2011. She was a Visiting Professor at Cleveland Marshall College of Law at Cleveland State University in 2002 and held the Baker Hostetler Chair at that law school for the academic year 2003/2004. She was a Visiting Academic at Oxford Law Faculty in 2014. She was an External Examiner in Company Law and other legal subjects for Dublin City University and was an internal examiner in Company Law for the Honourable Society of the Kings Inns. She is External Examiner for the Quinn School of Business at University College Dublin. She was appointed Head of the Department of Law for the period 1999–2002. She was elected Dean of the Faculty of Law 2000–2002 and between 2008 and 2013 she occupied a senior management position as the Head of the College of Business and Law at *University College Cork*.

The Authors

Karole Cuddihy is a practising solicitor at Maples and Calder, Dublin. He is a graduate of University College Cork (BCL, LLM) and the King's Inns (BL). He was in practice at the Bar of Ireland between 2008 and 2013. As well as completing his Master's thesis at university under the supervision of Professor Lynch-Fannon, he has subsequently collaborated with Professor Lynch-Fannon on several company law and insolvency projects.

Table of Contents

List of Abbreviations

ADR	American Depository Receipts
ADS	American Depository Securities
AGM	Annual General Meeting
AIM	Alternative Investment Market
CLEA	Company Law Enforcement Act
CLRG	Company Law Review Group
CPT	Cuideachta Phoibli Theoranta
CRO	Companies Registration office
CSO	Central Statistics Office, Ireland.
DAC	Designated Activity Company
ECHR	European Convention on Human Rights
ECJ	European Court of Justice
EEA	European Economic Area
EEIG	European Economic Interest Grouping
EGM	Extraordinary General Meeting
ESRI	Economic and Social Research Institute (Ireland)
EU	European Union
FDI	Foreign Direct Investment
GDP	Gross Domestic Product
GNP	Gross National Product
IDA	Industrial Development Authority
IEX	Irish Enterprise Exchange
IFSRA	Irish Financial Services and Regulatory Authority
ILP	Investment Limited Partnership
ISA	International Standards on Auditing
LTD	Private Company Limited by Shares
NAMA	National Asset Management Agency

List of Abbreviations

ODCE	Office of the Director of Corporate Enforcement
OECD	Organisation of Economic Co-operation and Development
PLC	Public Limited Company.
PRSI	Pay Related Social Insurance
SAP	Summary Approval Procedure
UCITS	Undertakings for Collective Investment in Transferable Securities
VAT	Value Added Tax

General Introduction

§1. The General Background of the Country

I. Geography

1. The island of Ireland is situated in the extreme north-west of Europe between 51.5 and 55.5 degrees north latitude and between 5.5 and 10.5 degrees west longitude. The total area of the island of Ireland is 84,421 km2 (32,595 sq. mi) with the Republic of Ireland covering 70,282 km2 (27,136 sq. mi) and Northern Ireland, 14,139 km2 (5,459 sq. mi). The greatest length (N/S) is 486 km (302 mi), the greatest width (E/W) is 275 km (171 mi), and the total coastline measures 3,172 km (1,970 mi). The island comprises a large central lowland of limestone with a relief of hills surrounded by a discontinuous border of coastal mountains that vary greatly in geological structure. Influenced by the Gulf Stream and with the prevailing winds predominantly from the south-west, the climate is equable and temperatures are fairly uniform over the whole country. The coldest months are typically January and February, with mean daily air temperatures of between 4°C and 7°C, while July and August are the warmest (18°C–20°C on average inland). Extremes of air temperature, below –10°C or above 30°C, have rarely been recorded. Average annual rainfall in the lowlands varies between 750 mm and 1,250 mm, with higher figures (up to 2,000 mm). The *State* of Ireland is not coterminous with the *island* of Ireland, in that one-sixth of the territory (in the north-east corner) is known as Northern Ireland and is part of the United Kingdom.[1] In effect there four different legal jurisdictions in the British Isles – the Republic of Ireland (the *State* of Ireland), Northern Ireland, Scotland and finally, England and Wales. In relation to the Republic of Ireland (the *State* of Ireland) there is a completely separate legislative framework and court system whereas this is not the case in relation to all matters within the United Kingdom.

II. Population and Vital Statistics

2. As of 2011, (the date of the most recent census) the island of Ireland had a population of slightly over 6 million, with figures for the separate populations of the

1. Unless the context indicates the contrary, all information in this monograph concerns the *State* of Ireland, described in cases of ambiguity as the *Republic of Ireland*, although its official name is *Ireland*. ('The name of the state in English is Ireland and is *Éire* in the Irish language … ' *Bunreacht na hÉireann* (Constitution of Ireland), Art. 4).

Republic and the North at 4, 588, 252[2] and 1,742,000,[3] respectively. In the Census of 2011 figures show that the population of the Republic grew strongly in the intercensal period from 2006–2011 increasing by 348, 404, a population growth of 8.2% in this period. This growth was driven primarily by very high birth rates combined with a fall in deaths. Total births between 2006 and 2011 were 365,000, leading to a natural population increase of 225,000 which is described by the CSO 'as the highest ever for an intercensal period'.[4] Net migration into Ireland for 2011 stood at 125,000 which fell from a high of 192,000 in 2006. The number of Irish residents born outside Ireland increased by 25% from 2006 to a figure of 766,770 in 2011 which amounts to 17% of the population. 65% of the population lived in urban areas in 2011 compared with 46.4% 50 years ago. The average age of the population was 36.1.

III. Cultural Composition

3. Under the Constitution (*Bunreacht na hÉireann*), '[t]he Irish language as the national language is the first official language. The English language is recognised as a second official language'.[5] The predominantly spoken first language is English. As of 2011, 1.77 million people said they could speak Irish, but just 77,185 persons spoke Irish daily outside the education system.[6] Most interesting, however, is that in Census 2011, 11% of Irish residents reported speaking a language other than English or Irish at home, the principal languages being Polish, French (in some cases spoken by persons born in African countries), Lithuanian and Latvian.

4. The Constitution of Ireland guarantees '[f]reedom of conscience and the free profession and practice of religion', subject to public order and morality, to every citizen, and guarantees that the State will neither 'endow any religion' nor 'impose any disabilities nor make any discrimination on the ground of religious profession, belief or status'.[7] The stated religion of most people in Ireland (Republic) is Roman Catholic. According to the 2011 census, 84.1% of the population were Roman Catholics. There was an increase in the actual number of Roman Catholics which was derived from the non-Irish (immigrant) communities. The remainder were members of the Church of Ireland (Anglican), which represented an increase of 6.4% in actual figures from 2006, Presbyterian, Methodist, Jewish, Muslim or other faith, along with minorities who either stated they had no religion or declined to

2. Central Statistics Office, This is Ireland, Highlights from Census 2011 Part 1 (CS0, Government of Ireland, March 2012). All further statistical information solely concerns the Republic, unless the context indicates the contrary. All subsequent population statistics are taken from, and available on, the website of the Central Statistics Office, with particular focus on the information gained from Census 2011, unless otherwise stated.
3. Northern Ireland Statistics and Research Agency (23 Oct. 2007).
4. This is Ireland, Highlights from Census 2011, Part 1. p. 10.
5. *Bunreacht na hÉireann* (Constitution of Ireland), Art. 8.
6. *Supra* n. 4 p. 10.
7. *Bunreacht na hÉireann* (Constitution of Ireland), Art. 44.2.

say.[8] The number of persons who identified as Muslim increased by 51.2% which led the CSO to identify the Muslim religion as the most significant 'non-Christian' religion in the State.

IV. Political System

A. *The Constitutional Framework*

5. Ireland is a parliamentary democracy, and as such, operates under the second constitution passed since independence, namely the 1937 Constitution (*Bunreacht na hÉireann*). The national parliament (in the Irish language, *Oireachtas*) consists of the President (*an tUachtarán*) and two Houses: a House of Representatives (*Dáil Éireann*) and a Senate (*Seanad Éireann*). In October 2013 a referendum was held which considered abolishing the second house i.e., the Senate (*Seanad Éireann*) but this was rejected by the population. The executive power of the State is 'subject to the provisions of [the] Constitution,' exercised 'by or on the authority of the Government', which is to consist of not less than seven and not more than fifteen members.[9] The Prime Minister (*Taoiseach*), Deputy Prime Minister (*Tánaiste*) and Minister for Finance must be members of the Dáil. The other members of the Government may be members of the Dáil or Seanad, but not more than two may be members of the Seanad. The Government acts collectively and is responsible to the Dáil. The Taoiseach is appointed by the President on the nomination of the Dáil. He or she must resign on ceasing to retain the support of a majority in the Dáil. The Taoiseach nominates one member of the Government to be Tánaiste. The Tánaiste acts in place of the Taoiseach, if the Taoiseach is temporarily absent or becomes incapacitated.

6. The Attorney General is 'the adviser to the Government in matters of law and legal opinion', and, though s/he 'shall not be a member of the Government', may (and in practice does) attend Cabinet meetings.[10] The Attorney General's tenure of office is normally coterminous with that of the Taoiseach. The Taoiseach assembles a Government and assigns Departments of State to Ministers. Usually, each member of the Government heads one Department, but occasionally a Minister is responsible for more than one Department. Ministers of State, or 'junior ministers', who are not members of the Government, assist Government Ministers in their Parliamentary and Departmental work. The maximum number of Ministers of State is fixed by law at twenty.

8. Census 2011, *supra* n. 4. p. 10.
9. *Bunreacht na hÉireann* (Constitution of Ireland), Art. 28.2 and 28.1, respectively. The rest of this paragraph is a brief summary of Art. 28.
10. *Bunreacht na hÉireann* (Constitution of Ireland), Art. 30.

B. Political Parties

7. Ireland is a constitutional democracy. Elections are based on a system of voting known as proportional representation. At the time of writing (early 2015), the Government was composed of a coalition between *Fine Gael* (loosely translated from Irish as 'tribe of the Irish') and the *Labour Party*. The opposition parties are currently *Fianna Fáil* (which, loosely translated, means 'Soldiers of Destiny'), and *Sinn Féin* ('ourselves alone'), together with a range of independent members of parliament. All elected members of parliament are referred to as TDs, an abbreviation of the Irish term, *Teachta Dála*. Some of the independent members of parliament who are without party affiliation have come together in a loose coalition referred to as the 'Technical Group'. Before the election in 2011, the Green Party had been a member of a coalition government but was all but eliminated as a political force in Irish politics at that time. In relation to the Green Party and the Labour Party, their political identity and mission would be apparent to the reader from the party titles. However, the other parties, Fine Gael, Sinn Féin and Fianna Fáil, have their historical roots in the armed struggle for Irish independence and in the stance taken by these parties in relation to republicanism and later the Anglo-Irish Treaty of 1921, the subsequent Civil War and the establishment of the Free State in 1922 pursuant to the Treaty. Generally speaking, Fianna Fáil would be regarded as more conservative on social issues than Fine Gael and Sinn Féin. Fianna Fáil and Fine Gael are often similarly positioned on fiscal issues, although the latter are generally regarded as more fiscally conservative, with Sinn Féin a more socialist party on issues such as distributive justice. Following the global financial crisis and subsequent economic crash in Ireland which began in 2008, the 2011 general election heralded a period of significant political change with the then dominant party Fianna Fail suffering considerably from populist opinion which blamed the government for continuing with policies which contributed to a period of economic crisis. Consequently, the current government (consisting of a Fine Gael/Labour coalition) was returned with a significant majority. During its period of office there has been some growth in support for the more socialist and left leaning parties in opposition to 'austerity' programmes. Among these is Sinn Fein, but this party remains somewhat controversial (because of its association with the IRA and the violent activities of the latter in Northern Ireland, the United Kingdom and indeed, the Republic of Ireland from the 1970s–1990s). In that political context there have been calls for, and attempts made, to create additional political parties in Ireland.

V. Economy

8. Ireland is a member of the Eurozone, joining the EU currency system in 1999. Since 2008, Ireland has witnessed a significant period of economic change following the global financial crisis. Ireland is a small, modern, trade-dependent, open economy that experienced unprecedented economic growth between 1994 and 2004. However, by 2006 there was a groundswell of opinion, albeit a minority, to the effect the continued economic growth was over reliant on the construction industry and an unsustainable property boom. By summer 2008, Ireland, along with other western democracies was plunged into a financial crisis linked to various banking practises and into recession. However, by the end of the following summer, in 2009, it became clear that Ireland's problems were not linked to the global financial crisis alone and that the economic downturn would be more serious and more sustained in Ireland. Effectively, the Irish banking sector had become overexposed to the property market during this period with significant risks emerging that the banking sector would collapse. In response, the Government executed a bank guarantee in 2008, effectively turning a banking crisis into a sovereign debt crisis.[11] The Committee of Inquiry into the Banking Crisis, colloquially known as the Banking Inquiry, is a joint committee of the Houses of the Oireachtas. It was formally established in November 2014 under the Houses of the Oireachtas (Inquiries, Privileges and Procedures) Act 2013. The purpose of the Inquiry is to inquire into the reasons Ireland experienced a systemic banking crisis, including the political, economic, social, cultural, financial and behavioural factors and policies which impacted on, or contributed to, the crisis and the preventative reforms implemented in the wake of the crisis.[12]

9. These events led to an austerity programme over seen by the IMF, the European Central Bank and the European Commission which provided funds to Ireland to support the guarantee. The effects of the austerity programme are still in evidence, although during the current year (2015) there are signs of significant recovery. Nevertheless a significant personal debt problem, again linked to the property bubble, is still problematic.

10. Growth in Ireland's GDP in the decade from 1996 to 2006 averaged about 9% year on year with a turning point around the year 2000, but, thereafter, the economy averaged growth of around 4% from 2000 to 2005. A consequence of this was rapid convergence with the EU average of output per capita: Indeed, per capita GDP at that time was about 40% above the EU 25[13] average and 10% above the average of the four biggest European economies. The Organization of Economic Co-operation and Development (OECD) estimated that in terms of GDP per capita, based on Purchasing Power Parities, Ireland was ranked fifth in the world. In 2005 Ireland's GDP growth rate averaged 5% for that year but in 2009, within a period

---

11. There have been a number of preliminary investigations in the Irish Banking Crisis including the following:

    The Irish Banking Crisis: Regulatory and Financial Stability Policy 2003–2008 (The Honohan Report May 2010). Klaus Regling & Max Watson: A Preliminary Report on the Irish Banking Crisis (May 2010). Misjudging risk: Causes of the Systemic Banking Crisis in Ireland: Report of The Commission of Investigation into The Banking Sector in Ireland (The Nyberg Report March 2011).

12. http://inquiries.oireachtas.ie/banking/. See also www.bankinginquiry.ie. This is now completed as of January 2016.
13. The twenty-five Member States of the EU for the period between the accession of ten new Member States on 1 May 2004 and the accession of Romania and Bulgaria on 1 Jan. 2007.

of four years, the GDP rate of decline averaged -9%. In the Euro 15 zone the figures for the same years are just under 2% growth rate in 2005 and -4% decline in 2009 showing a much less significant 'swing' than that of Ireland. In 2010 the Euro Zone 15 showed a small overall growth rate, whereas the figures were still negative for Ireland for 2010. Household indebtedness, as a percentage of gross disposable income, also began to grow remarkably from 2002 and has continued to grow every year since then. During the 'boom period' the rate of unemployment dropped from more than 15% in 1993 to 6% in 2000; with a further decline for each of the years 2000–2007, when the unemployment rate was approximately 4%–5%. Sadly, by 2011 the unemployment rate had risen to 14.6% and in real numbers this meant that over 317,000 Irish people were on the live register. By 2014, these figures stabilized at around 11.3% and continue to remain at this figure for early 2015. Numbers on the live register dropped to their lowest levels since 2009 in March 2015. Unemployment for March 2015 was 10%. Unemployment levels have been under 10% since May 2015.

11. When considered in the overall European context, the figures from 2005 to those most recently available illustrate that Ireland has experienced significant changes during the last decade in terms of GDP growth and subsequent decline, compared even with its closest European neighbours.

12. One factor which has remained constant throughout the cycle of boom and bust is that agriculture, once the most important sector, is now dwarfed by industry and services. Industry accounts for 46% of GDP and about 80% of exports and employs 28% of the labour force. The food industry is however an important sector. The Census figures for 2011 show that there has been a significant move to urban areas.

13. The period of apparently spectacular economic growth between the mid 1990s and the beginning of the economic crisis, was preceded by periods of stagnation that, on balance, commentators are now agreed should not have occurred. For example, during the period 1977–1984 the Government pursued fiscal and economic policies that had a damaging effect on overall economic performance.[14] In addition, Ireland's relatively poor economic performance in the 1950s and particularly in the 1960s[15] meant that some part of this growth involved an element of catch-up with its European neighbours, although commentators are divided as to the significance of this catch-up point. In relation to factors that fed into the period of growth, and relying on information available from government agencies such as the Economic and Social Research Institute (ESRI),[16] there is a broad consensus as to the factors that contributed to economic success, namely:

14. B. Nolan et al., *Bust to Boom? The Irish Experience of Growth and Inequality* (Institute of Public Administration 2000); Kieran A. Kennedy et al. *The Economic Development of Ireland in the Twentieth Century*, 87–90 (Routledge 1988).
15. J. Lee, *Ireland, 1912–1985: Politics and Society* (Cambridge University Press 1989).
16. Economic and Social Research Institute. 'www.esri.ie'.

- pursuit of pragmatic and innovative government policies;
- an emphasis on education and technological innovation;
- a youthful population and rapidly expanding labour supply;
- an openness to international trade in goods and services and to new ideas;
- substantial inward investment inflows, encouraged by (among other factors) a low rate of corporation tax and the work of agencies such as Enterprise Ireland[17] and the Industrial Development Authority (IDA);[18]
- the strategic deployment of EU Structural and Cohesion Funds; and
- a 'social partnership' approach to economic development.

These factors continue to be present in the Irish economic and political framework and so it is more than likely that such factors will contribute to the recovery.

14. In 2014, Ireland's ratio of combined exports and imports of goods to Gross Domestic Product (GDP) was just over 200%. In 2014, GDP grew by 4.8%, exports increased 10.5%, while domestic demand a key driver of jobs growth rose 3.5%. Gross National Product (GNP), which strips out the effect of multinational companies, grew by 5.2%. The latest quarterly summary from the ESRI forecasts GDP growth for Ireland of 6% for 2015.

§2. The Historical Background to Corporations and Partnerships

I. The Development of the Common Law

15. Ireland was part of the British Empire until the declaration of independence in 1916 and the subsequent establishment of the Irish Free State in 1922. The Irish law of companies and partnerships reflects that history, and as a consequence, this body of law shares the same historical provenance as the law of England and Wales and many other common law countries. In understanding the regulatory framework it is important to recognize that Irish company law is still today a combination of statute law and judicially developed principles derived both from common law and equity. For example, two fundamental principles underpinning the success and significance of the limited liability corporation are the concepts of limited liability, a statutory invention, and the concept that the corporation or company is a separate legal person, a judicial doctrine developed and refined in case law.[19] Thus, statute and judicial doctrine continue to combine to create the body of Irish company law.

16. The Partnership Act of 1890, is still the primary relevant legislation, concerning Irish partnership law. However, the 1890 Act was itself a distillation of pre-existing principles developed by the courts at common law and in equity. These

17. www.enterprise-ireland.com.
18. www.idaireland.com.
19. These are discussed in detail *infra* Part 1, Ch. 1 §2.

principles continue in force to the extent that they are not inconsistent with, the 1890 Act.[20]

II. The Genesis of Company Law

A. The Common Law Period

17. The limited liability company is a relatively recent legal invention that came into existence toward the end of the nineteenth century as a result of statutory intervention. Until 1844, there were only two means by which a company could be legally incorporated. First, the Crown granted charters and letters patent authorizing the creation of companies, often for purposes related to overseas colonies (e.g., facilitating trade with these colonies).[21] Second, private Acts of Parliament were enacted, creating companies for specific objects or purposes, such as the completion of infrastructure projects, sometimes with a lifespan limited in time or by the particular project.[22] These early 'joint-stock companies' had several of the attributes of modern companies, including perpetual succession and power to act and transact in the corporate name (including in litigation). However, Royal Charters, letters patent and private Acts of Parliament were difficult and expensive to obtain. Over time it became clear that there was greater demand for the corporate form amongst business people: 'the privilege of limited liability was precisely that of which [practical men] were most desirous, and without which mere incorporation was of little importance'.[23]

18. In 1844 and 1855, Parliament moved to provide an alternative legal structure to facilitate the operation of businesses and, in particular, to facilitate groups of merchants investing in a collective business scheme. Statutes enacted in those years laid the foundations of modern company law in Ireland and in England and Wales.[24] Considerable similarities remain between these jurisdictions. The result

20. See *infra* Part II on Partnerships.
21. The East India Company ('the grandest society of merchants in the universe') is a well-known example. Elizabeth I granted its charter in 1600, initially allowing the company a twenty-one-year monopoly on trade in the East Indies. Over time, the company acquired auxiliary governmental and military functions, and for a time (ending in 1858) virtually ruled India and several other Asian colonies.
22. Many examples of the latter type of companies are immortalized in the case law, including *Hutton v. West Cork Railway Company* (1883) 23 Ch D 654; *Bagshaw v. Eastern Union Railway Co.* (1849) 7 Hare 114, 68 ER 46; and *Preston v. Grand Collier Dock Company* (1840) 10 L.J.Ch. 73, 11 Sim. 327, 59 ER 900. On the formation of companies by Royal Charter and Letters Patent, see F.W. Clark, *A Treatise on the Law of Partnership and Joint-Stock Companies, According to the Law of Scotland* 96–102 (books.google.com 1866), and on the railway companies, see *ibid.*, 801–808.
23. F.W. Clark, *A Treatise on the Law of Partnership and Joint-Stock Companies*, 1, 76 (Forgotten Books 2013).
24. See the Companies Act 1844 (7 & 8 Vict. c.110) and the Limited Liability Act 1855 (18 & 19 Vict. c. 133), respectively.

was that investors were now free, firstly, to incorporate companies for their own purposes (subject to registration with a State official), and, secondly, to limit their liability to the amount of their investment. The introduction of these concepts – incorporation by registration and limited liability – provided the foundations of a framework for the modern company, which, though consolidated on several occasions,[25] has remained in place ever since. At the time, the idea of limited liability was received with distaste by some commentators, who feared it would amount to 'a rogue's charter'.[26] This concern, surviving in various degrees, has led over the ensuing century and a half to the accretion of a body of statutory law aimed at minimizing abuse or misuse of limited liability – to reduce the rogue's freedom to do harm or, as the economist would say, to reduce externalities.[27] The mid-Victorian legislatures that enacted these reforms appear to have maintained a distinction between partnerships and companies on the basis of the number of members. Thus, the 1844 Act provided that, where twenty-five or more persons associated together for the purpose of business, they could not form a partnership, only a company. The 1855 Act then provided that twenty-five persons was the minimum number of members required before a limited liability company could be incorporated. Today this numerical framework of minimum and maximum members has more or less vanished from the law. The 1856 Act reduced the minimum number of members in a limited liability company to seven, the Companies Act 1963 reduced this number to two, and in 1989 the Member States of the European Community agreed to permit the creation of single-member companies in a Directive that was transposed into Irish law in 1994.[28] This is now re-enacted in the Companies Act 2014. This result had, of course, been substantially achieved a century before, due to the decision of the House of Lords in *Salomon v. Salomon & Co.* (interpreting the 1862 Act, which had maintained the seven-member minimum) that a sole trader could validly incorporate his business, along with six bare nominees (in that instance, the appellant's wife and children, who took no part in his boot and shoe business). The House of Lords refused to imply into the statute a legislative requirement that all seven members need to take an active part in the affairs of the company.[29] More importantly, the number of directors required in an Irish company had been reduced to two and is now further reduced to one by virtue of section 128 of the new Companies Act 2014.

25. The Joint Stock Companies Act 1856 (19 & 20 Vict. c. 47), the Companies Act 1862 (25 & 26 Vict. c. 89) and the Companies (Consolidation) Act 1908 were the chief instances applicable to pre-independent Ireland. Palmer described the 1862 Act as 'the *Magna Carta* of co-operative enterprise'. G. Morse et al., *Palmer's Company Law*, 1 (25th edn., Sweet & Maxwell 1992).
26. (1854) 24 *Law Times* 142; (1855) 25 *Law Times* 116 and 210. Others saw the 1855 Act rather differently: 'This Act was no sooner in operation, than it gave great and general satisfaction, and the prognostications made by the opponents of limited liability were found to have been purely imaginary.' (Clark, *Treatise on the Law of Partnership*, 9).
27. These statutory developments are considered *infra*; see para. 60.
28. EC Directive 89/667, [1989] O.J. L395/40 (transposed into Irish law by the European Communities (Single-Member Private Limited Companies) Regulations of 1994 (S. I. 275 of 1994)). Note that the UK Parliament had moved to this position earlier: Companies Act 1985, s. 1(3A).
29. *Salomon v. Salomon & Co.* [1897] AC 22. Lord Halsbury remarked that the legislature had 'enact[ed] nothing as to the extent or degree of interest which may be held by each of the seven [members] or as to the proportion of interest or influence possessed by one or the majority over the others'.

19. It is clear that recognition of the benefits of what are sometimes termed the 'privileges' of limited liability and corporate personality must be counterbalanced by the need for regulation to prevent abuse of these doctrines. In modern Ireland, as in other jurisdictions, debate continues as to the proper balance to be struck in this regard. Recent changes to the regulatory structure have been of sufficient significance to have raised the question as to whether the burden of legal compliance is now too heavy (see *infra* for relevant statistics). This concept of incorporation as a privilege has a clear historical provenance, in that, as noted above, prior to the general availability of incorporation to all kinds of businesses, only certain kinds of business ventures were granted the privilege of incorporation. The grand trading companies such as the English East India Company were early examples. In the nineteenth century, railways were granted corporate status, but they were tightly controlled by the State granting the privilege; the corporation was confined to specific objects and purposes, such as infrastructural projects, and often confined to survival for a specified lifespan. Although corporation is today readily available to all kinds of business people, this availability has historically been coupled with a desire on the part of the courts and legislature to address excesses.

B. Post-1937 Constitution

20. Following the passage in 1937 of *Bunreacht na hÉireann* (the Constitution of Ireland) and the establishment of independent Irish courts, development of an independent Irish corporation and partnership legal framework began in earnest. The original legislation was the 1908 Companies Act. In 1963, the Companies Act was passed, which up until 2014 was referred to as the 'Principal Act'. Significant amendments and changes to the 1963 legal framework were made in subsequent legislation from the 1980s onward. Most noteworthy of these legal enactments were the two pieces of legislation passed in 1990, the 1990 Companies Act and the 1990 Companies (Amendment) Act. This latter Act introduced a statutory corporate rescue process known as 'examinership'.[30] In addition, the 2001 Company Law Enforcement Act made a significant difference to the enforcement of and compliance with company law 1 in Ireland.[31]

21. However, following a major process of review and consolidation of all existing company law conducted under the auspices of the Company Law Review Group (CRLG),a draft Companies Consolidation Bill, which would consolidate and update all prior company law legislation was published in 2007.[32] Following extensive consultation and debate this legislation was passed by the legislature in late 2014, signed into law by the President on 23 December 2014 and was, in large part, commenced in June 2015. It is the largest single statute passed in the history of the State

30. See *infra*, Part I, Ch. 1 §5, IV.
31. See *infra*, Part I, Ch. 1 §4, III, F.
32. See www.clrg.org.

and is designed to present the body of Irish company law in a 'single comprehensible code.' This monograph has been written to take account of these developments and has been updated accordingly.

III. Development of Irish Company Law and Membership of the EU

A. *Introduction*

22. Since accession to the European Union (EU), Ireland has enacted all major European Company Law Directives. Ireland acceded to the European Community in 1972 and since that time has enacted Directives in the legislation indicated *infra*. In terms of affecting the landscape of Irish law, some of the EU Directives have had more impact than others, in particular the Directives concerning minimum capital requirements and accounting and the Directives in relation to the regulation of the capital markets, such as the Directives on Prospectuses, Insider Dealing and Market Manipulation. In all cases, the process of harmonization of company law at EU level is marked by a notable difference between the common law origins of Irish and UK company law and the civil law origins of the corporation systems of other Member States. The significance of the legislative changes deriving from Europe are summarized below:

- The First Company Law Directive (68/15/EEC) was enacted through the European Communities (Companies) Regulations 1973, which provided a statutory notification framework regarding officers and others with the authority to deal on behalf of the company and a notification framework regarding the filing of other company documents. The most significant change emanating from this legislation, ameliorating the doctrine of constructive notice regarding outsiders dealing with the company had previously been addressed in section 8 of the 1963 Companies Act. Nevertheless an additional Regulation was passed providing for the obligation to deal in good faith which is imposed on third parties dealing with the company and providing for a system of registration of those authorized to bind the company.[33] These provisions are now contained in sections 39 and 40 of the Companies Act 2014.
- The Second Directive (77/91/EEC) regarding the formation of Public Limited Companies (PLCs), minimum capital requirements for PLCs, and important capital maintenance and alteration rules was enacted by the Companies (Amendment) Act 1983, which also set out the requirements that private limited companies would be denominated by the term 'Limited' or 'Ltd' or the Irish language equivalent 'Teoranta' or 'Teo'. For PLCs the term used is PLC or in Irish 'cuideachta phoibli theoranta' (CPT); see further Directive 2006/68/EC, which amends these provisions. Under the Companies Act 2014 these provisions are now contained in Part 17. The abbreviation PLC or CPT is retained for public limited companies, but private companies limited by shares are now categorized into LTD or DAC, depending on whether the private company limited by shares

33. Regulation 6(3) of EC Regulations 1973, (S.I. 163 of 1973).

has opted to have no specific designated activity or has opted for a designated activity structure.[34]

- The Third Directive (78/855/EEC), which dealt with the mergers of public companies, and the complementary Sixth Directive (82/891/EEC) on demergers were enacted in Ireland by the European Communities (Mergers and Divisions of Companies) Regulations 1987. Now enacted as Regulation 5 of the European Communities (Mergers and Division of Companies) (Amendment) Regulations 2011 (S.I. No. 306 of 2011).[35]
- The Fourth Directive (78/660/EEC) related to the preparation of annual accounts and was enacted by the Companies (Amendment) Act 1986. In enacting the legislation, the Irish Government provided for the inclusion of the exemptions available in the Directive to small and medium-sized private companies. These companies can accordingly present their accounts in an abbreviated format. These provisions are now contained in Part 6 of the Companies Act 2014.
- The Seventh Directive (83/349/EEC) provided for the preparation of consolidated accounts in the group context and was enacted in Ireland by the European Communities (Companies) (Group Accounts) Regulations 1992 (S.I. 201 of 1992). See also the European Communities (Accounts) Regulations 1993 (S.I. 369 of 1993) and the European Communities (International Financial Reporting Standards and Miscellaneous Amendments) Regulations 2005 (S.I. 116 of 2005).

Directive 2006/46/EC consolidates and amends these Directives. These provisions are now contained in Part 6 of the Companies Act 2014:

- The Eighth Directive (84/253/EEC) deals with the qualifications, professional standing and independence of Auditors. This was implemented by Part X of the 1990 Companies Act. See further the Companies (Auditing and Accounting) Act 2003 passed following the Report of the Audit Review Group in 2000. These provisions are now amended and contained in Part 6 of the Companies Act 2014.
- The Prospectus Directives – 80/390/EEC, 79/279/EEC and 82/121/EEC, – which have now been consolidated in Directive 2003/58/EC, were transposed in the Investment Funds, Companies and Miscellaneous Provisions Act 2005 and 2006. These provisions are now amended and contained in Part 23 of the Companies Act 2014.
- The European Economic Interest Grouping (EEIG) Regulation (EEC/2137/85) was further implemented by the European Community (EEIG) Regulations 1989 (S.I. 191 of 1989).
- The Twelfth Directive (89/667/EEC), which provided for the single-member private company, was enacted as mentioned by the European Communities (Single-Member Private Limited Companies) Regulations of 1994 (S.I. 275 of 1994). These provisions are now amended and contained in Part 4 of the Companies Act 2014.

---

34. See Companies Act 2014, Part 2 s. 38, Part 16 ss 972, 973.
35. Considered *infra* Part 1, Ch. 1 §6, III.

- The Takeover Directive (2004/25/EC) was implemented in Ireland by the European Communities (Takeover Bids Directive) Regulations 2006 (S.I. 225 of 2006).
- In light of the increased interest in contributing to the liquidity of capital markets within the European Union in recent years, a number of Directives have been passed addressing the preservation of the integrity of such capital markets. These include Directive 2004/109/EC (the Transparency Directive), Directive 2004/39/EC (Markets in Financial Instruments Directive) and Directive 2003/6/EC (the Market Abuse Directive). These were implemented in the Investment Funds, Companies and Miscellaneous Provisions Acts of 2005 and 2006, as well as the Market Abuse (Directive 2003/6/EC) Regulations 2005 (S.I. 342 of 2005). These provisions are now amended and contained in Part 23 of the Companies Act 2014.
- Finally, the, EC Council Regulation 1346/2000 on cross-border insolvencies is an important development in the recognition of insolvency processes and orders among the Member States of the European Union. This matter has become of increasing relevance in recent years in Ireland. Current reforms are being considered by the EU.[36]

B. Choice of Law

23. In terms of choice of law, the importance of the European Court of Justice (ECJ) decisions in the *Centros, Überseering* and *Inspire Art* cases cannot be underestimated (see *infra*, paragraph 45). The freedom for nationals of different Member States to form and establish companies in any country of the EU has had a significant impact on the importance of Ireland, along with the UK and the Netherlands, as a desirable place of incorporation. A supportive tax structure is considered to be a significant advantage (see *infra* Part I Chapter 1, §8) Given the growth of company formation in Ireland and some concerns regarding abuse of the corporate form during the period of economic growth, some specific control measures were put in place to ensure the 'authenticity' of business incorporating in Ireland. These include:

(i) a requirement that at least one of the directors must be resident in Ireland which was provided for in section 43 of the Companies (Amendment No. 2) Act 1999. This has been re-enacted in section 137 of the 2014 Act as a requirement that at least one director must be resident in an EEA state;

(ii) a limitation was imposed by section 45 of the same Act on the number of directorships that any one particular individual may hold. Section 142 of the 2014 Act provides that a person shall not at any particular time be a director of more than twenty-five private companies limited by shares, or in the case of other types of companies, twenty-five in total;

(iii) a requirement that an Irish registered company must carry on an activity in the state under section 44 of the same Act (now section 18 of the 2014 Act).

36. *Infra.*

IV. The Modern Period

24. 1998 was a significant year in Irish Company Law with the publication of the McDowell Report on Company Law Compliance. This report found that more than 60% of registered Irish companies were non-compliant with many provisions of company law. As a consequence, significant efforts were made to increase enforcement with the enactment of the Company Law Enforcement Act 2001, which accomplished two major initiatives: establishing the Office of the Director of Corporate Enforcement (ODCE, <www.odce.ie>) and establishing the Company Law Review Group (CRLG, <www.clrg.org>), charged with continuously monitoring company law developments. Since 2001, detection and enforcement of breaches of company law in Ireland has significantly improved, due largely to the efforts of the ODCE and the Companies Registration Office (CRO, <www.cro.ie>). Provisions of the 2001 Act have been re-enacted as Part 15 of the Companies Act 2014. Chapter 3 effectively re-enacts sections 7–18 of the Company Law Enforcement Act 2001, which outlines the powers of the ODCE. Chapter 4 deals with the Company Law Review Group and re-enacts sections 67–71 of the CLEA 2001.

V. Reform Proposals for Irish Company Law

25. Once established the Company Law Review Group engaged in a significant consolidation and codification process in addition to reforming certain key areas of Irish company law. In 2007, the CRLG published a draft Companies Consolidation Bill, which was designed to consolidate and update all existing Irish company law legislation. The thematic drivers of this reform project were stated by the CLRG in its 2007 report (Chapter 3) to be as follows:

- to promote enterprise;
- facilitate commerce;
- simplify the operation of the Companies Acts;
- enhance corporate governance; and
- encourage commercial probity.

The Bill has now been passed and enacted as the Companies Act 2014 and has been commenced (i.e., put into force) in large part since June 2015. The Companies Act 2014 replaces and consolidates all existing Companies Acts from 1963 to 2013. It also introduces a number of reforms which will be described in this text.[37] Since the beginning of the original review process the idea of 'Think Small First' (possibly inspired by a similar approach in the UK) has been adopted and in fact this latter theme has refocused the legislation on the private company limited by shares, as distinct from the public limited company. Accordingly the structure of the new Act is to provide for the regulation of the private company limited by shares in Parts 1–15, with the public limited company being provided for in Part 17. Part 17 begins

37. See generally Courtney (gen. ed.), *Bloomsbury Professional's Guide to the Companies Act* (Bloomsbury Professional, Dublin, 2015).

by providing a Table of relevant sections which are disapplied or altered as they apply to the PLC.[38] Further parts deal with other kinds of companies. For example, Part 16 of the Companies Act 2014 deals with what are called Designated Activity Companies, which are private companies limited by shares with stated activities.[39] Part 18 deals with Guarantee Companies and so on.

VI. The Role of Partnership Law

26. In Ireland, the formation of a limited liability company is relatively cheap because of the fact that, unlike most European countries, there is no minimum capital requirement and formation costs are likewise low. Because of the cheap availability of the limited liability corporate form, there has been a decline in interest among most business people in the types of partnership structures available. As far as partnerships go, the regulatory framework is based on the Partnership Act 1890, the Limited Partnerships Act 1907 and the Limited Partnership Act 1994, which has contributed a significant statutory framework in relation to the development of investment funds and the investment fund industry in Ireland. Over 30% of the global hedge fund industry is based in Dublin Ireland. Dublin is now a world administration centre for hedge funds.[40]

§3. Definitions of Corporations, Companies and Partnerships

I. Different Forms of Companies

27. Several different kinds of corporate form are available under Irish law. In relation to companies that acquire the privilege of limited liability, companies can be limited by shares or by guarantee. However, private companies limited by shares are the most popular type of incorporated limited companies. It is also possible to incorporate with unlimited liability, which is a popular corporate form used as a holding company in a group situation, particularly where the corporate group is privately held. The advantages of this form of incorporation lie in reduced disclosure obligations under the legislation as compared with disclosure obligations imposed on limited liability companies. Incorporation is also attractive to nonprofit businesses such as charitable corporations.

28. Partnerships are more commonly used in relation to the operation of particular professions, such as the legal and accounting professions. A statutory impediment imposed on legal firms in Ireland still prevents them from forming private

38. See Companies Act 2014, s. 1002 and the Table contained therein.
39. See Part 1, Ch. 2, ss §1 and §2.
40. Figures from the Irish Funds Industry Association show that in August 2015 over 6,000 different funds were registered in Ireland with net assets valued at just over EUR 1.8 billion. www.irishfunds.ie.

companies. The introduction of the Limited Partnership Act in 1994 added significantly to the range of options in Ireland.

A. *Limited Company*

29. There are four types of limited company:

(1) *A private company limited by shares*: In the event that the company is wound up, the members' liability, is limited to the amount, if any, unpaid on the shares they hold. There is no minimum capital requirement in Ireland for private companies, and so it is possible to form a limited liability company cheaply on payment of the registration fee of approximately EUR 100. The usual number of shareholders is two, but it is possible, to form a single-member company, under section 175(3) and 175(4) of the Companies Act 2014. The maximum number of members for a private company is 149. The single member private company was introduced as a business form pursuant to an EC Directive of 1989,[41] which was transposed into Irish law in 1994. Originally, even where there was only one shareholder, the company was obliged to have at least two directors and a secretary. This is no longer the case under the Companies Act 2014[42] where these companies are permitted to have only one director. The sole member company was permitted to dispense with the holding of general meetings, including Annual General Meetings (AGMs). This exemption still pertains but has been extended under the Companies Act 2014 to other companies in certain circumstances.[43] Accounts and reports that would normally be laid before the AGM of a company still need to be prepared, forwarded to the member(s) and filed in the normal way.[44]

The Companies Act 2014 recognizes two different types of private company limited by shares. The first type are LTDs – a private company limited by shares with no specified activities in its constitution. These companies have full capacity to engage in any activity. The second type of private company limited by shares are DACs-designated activity companies, where companies either opt for specifying particular activities in their Constitution or where, in certain cases, the company is obliged to specify an activity. This latter obligation usually arises only in relation to companies which are seeking to trade in debt securities on a market. The Companies Act 2014 requires that where a company wants to list debt securities on a stock exchange or has debt securities listed on a stock exchange, it must register as a DAC.[45] Subject to compliance with the Central Bank requirements where a company is operating as a credit institution or insurance undertaking it will be registered as a DAC.

---

41. EC Directive 89/667, [1989] O.J. L395/40 (transposed into Irish law by the European Communities (Single-Member Private Limited Companies) Regulations of 1994 (S.I. 275 of 1994)).
42. Companies Act 2014, s. 128.
43. *Infra*. Part 1 Ch. 1, §4, II.
44. Companies Act 2014, s. 175.
45. Companies Act 2014, ss 56, 68.

As regards DACs these companies are confined to acting within specified purposes. It should be emphasized however, that the specification of activities does not raise any issue of legal capacity in terms of the old *ultra vires* rule.[46] DACs must be registered with at least two directors.[47]

(2) *A company limited by guarantee not having a share capital*: In the event that this kind of company is wound up, the members' liability is limited to the amount they have undertaken to contribute to the assets of the company, not exceeding the amount specified in the memorandum. If a guarantee company does not have a share capital, the members are not required to buy any shares in the company. Many charitable and professional bodies find this form of company to be a suitable vehicle as they wish to secure the benefits of separate legal personality and of limited liability but do not necessarily require any working capital and therefore do not generally raise funds from the members. These companies are now governed by Part 18 of the Companies Act 2014.

(3) *A company limited by guarantee having a share capital*: The members have liability under two headings: firstly, the amount, if any, that is unpaid on the shares they hold, and, secondly, the amount they have undertaken to contribute to the assets of the company, in the event it is wound up. These are now governed by Part 18 of the Companies Act 2014.

(4) *A public company limited by shares*: This company type must have a minimum of seven members. The liability of the shareholders is limited to the amount, if any, unpaid on shares held by them. It should be noted that it is unlawful to issue any form of prospectus except in compliance with the Companies Act 2014. The nominal value of the company's allotted share capital must not be less than EUR 25,000,[48] at least 25% of which must be fully paid up before the company commences business or exercises any borrowing powers, as provided for by the Companies Act 2014. This amount has been reduced from previous legislation. This can be changed by Ministerial order (usually by what is referred to as a Statutory Instrument). The essential difference between a private limited company and a PLC is that the shares of the latter must be traded on a public market. Irish PLCs are quoted on the Irish Stock Exchange <www.ise.ie>, which provides for full listing but also has a market for smaller companies, the Irish Enterprise Exchange (IEX); the IEX is equivalent to the UK alternative investments market (AIM). It is possible to have a dual IEX and AIM listing. Several Irish PLCs are also quoted on the London Stock Exchange and in New York. PLCs are now governed by Parts 1–14 and Part 17 of the Companies Act 2014.

B. *Unlimited Company*

30. In an unlimited company, no limit is placed on the liability of the members. Recourse may be had by creditors to the shareholders in respect of any liabilities owed by the company that the company has failed to discharge. Such companies

46. *Infra*. Part 1, Ch. 2, §2, III.
47. Companies Act 2014, s. 985(1).
48. Companies Act 2014, s. 1000(1)(a).

must have a minimum of two shareholders. In Irish commercial practice it is common to convert the holding company of a group into an unlimited company due to the less rigorous disclosure requirements applicable under the accounting provisions. The shareholders may, and often will be, companies with limited liability. These companies are now governed by Parts 1–14 and 19 of the Companies Act 2014.

II. Other Forms of Business Organization

A. *Undertakings for Collective Investment in Transferable Securities (UCITS)*

31. A UCITS is a type of PLC formed under European Communities (UCITS) Regulations of 1989 and 1999, and the Companies Act 2014. The sole object of a UCITS is the collective investment in transferable securities of capital raised from the public that operates on the principle of risk spreading. The competent authority, which must approve all registrations of UCITS that wish to carry on activities within the State, is the Central Bank of Ireland.

B. *European Economic Interest Grouping*

32. The European Economic Interest Grouping (EEIG) is a mechanism through which businesses within the EU can engage in cross-border commerce. This was created as an entity by virtue of the EEIG Regulation (EEC/2137/85), which was implemented in Ireland by the European Community (EEIG) Regulations 1989 (S.I. 191 of 1989). The purpose of an EEIG is to facilitate or develop the economic activities of its members on a cross-border, non-profit model. For example, it could be used to facilitate the development of research or products. An EEIG must have from two to twenty members, who may be companies or natural persons, from different Member States. The manager of an EEIG may be a natural person or a body corporate.

C. *Societas Europaea*

33. A Societas Europaea (SE) is a European public limited liability company formed under EC Council Regulation 2157/2001 and the European Communities (European Public Limited Liability Company) Regulations 2007 (S.I. 21 of 2007). An SE can be formed by merger, as a holding or subsidiary SE or by conversion of a PLC. An SE must have members from different Member States. As there is no pan-European registration system, the SE must be registered in a particular Member State. An interesting feature of this form is that an accompanying Directive (2001/86/EC) provides a model for the involvement of worker representatives on management boards. This has caused some controversy over the period of harmonization of European company law, such as in regard to the proposed Fifth Directive on worker representation, which was never enacted. The Societas Europaea is to be regarded as a PLC for the purposes of the Companies Act 2014 and is governed by Part 17 of that Act.[49]

D. *Registration of a Business Name*

34. It is obligatory to register a business name in Ireland. When individuals or partnerships carry on a business under a name other than their own true names, this business name must be registered with the CRO. This applies to all business formats from sole trader to partnerships to companies where the business name is different from the actual name of the company.[50]

III. Partnerships

A. *Traditional Partnerships*

35. The partnership, is a traditional form of business dating back centuries, and is defined in section 1 of the Partnership Act 1890 as 'the relation which subsists between persons carrying on a business in common with a view of profit'. It is an alternative form of business organization to a sole tradership or incorporation. Several factors differentiate a traditional partnership from a limited liability company. A partnership is not a separate entity but merely refers to the relationship between partners. In addition, partners, unlike shareholders in a limited liability company, are liable beyond their capital investment to the full extent of the debts owned by the partnership. (Limited partnerships are a more recent statutory creation; see *infra.*) Certain kinds of businesses are not permitted under Irish law to form limited liability companies and usually conduct their business as a partnership, for example those practicing as Solicitors (lawyers).[51]

The law of partnerships is considered in more detail in Part II, Chapters 1 and 2.

B. *Limited Partnerships*

36. This business form is quite popular, particularly in the investment fund, private equity and venture capital sector in Ireland. As of the end of 2014, there were 1049 limited partnerships registered with the CRO.[52] The relevant legislation includes the Limited Partnership Act 1907 and rules made under that, the Limited Partnership Rules (S.I. 1020 of 1907), and the Investment Limited Partnership Act 1994 and subsequent rules (S.I. 402 of 1994 and S.I. 570 of 2001).

49. Companies Act 2014, s. 1003.
50. Registration of Business Names Act 1963; www.cro.ie.
51. Solicitors Act 1954 (as amended).
52. Companies Registration Office Report 2014.

IV. Statistics

37. As of 1 June 2015, a total of 189,703 companies were on the register maintained by the Registrar of Companies (CRO): There were 168,232 private companies limited by shares and of these 61 were registered as Designated Activity Companies. In addition there were 1,642 companies registered as PLCs, 4,458 unlimited companies and 15,310 companies limited by guarantee.[53] Thus, it can be seen that private limited companies made up 88.68% of the total, as compared to only 0.86% for PLCs.

§4. Sources and Hierarchy of Laws

I. The Development of the Common Law Approach

38. The influence of English company law principles (both statute and case law) and the approach of English courts and legislatures to company law matters is significant in relation to the development of Irish company law. This is a more accurate observation than might be made in relation to other areas of law that are of a more recent vintage, such as employment law or environmental law. Thus, the principles of Irish company law are still very similar to those of English company law and give expression to what could be described as an Anglo-American or common law approach to company law, as distinguished from the European approach taken in the civil law countries of continental Europe. Irish company law is therefore first and foremost a common law system of company law and, as such, is in the first instance derived from a large body of case law. However, at this point in time there is a significant statutory framework. The passing of the Companies Act 2014 is a significant development in this context, representing both consolidation and some reform. Many of the cases setting out the principles followed in Irish company law were decided by English Chancery courts, sometimes stretching back to the Victorian period, relating to issues such as capital maintenance,[54] directors' duties'[55] and separate corporate personality.[56] Ireland achieved its independence in 1922, and the current legal system is now based on the 1937 Constitution, *Bunreacht na hÉireann.* Since that time, the development of company law, as with any common law system, continues to rely to a great extent on the decisions of chancery courts. Since 1922, decisions of the English courts are of only persuasive authority before the Irish courts, in the same way as decisions of other common law jurisdictions, including the courts of Northern Ireland,[57] Australia[58] and

53. https://www.cro.ie/About-CRO/Contact-Us/Whats-New.
54. *Trevor v. Whitworth* (1887) 12 App Cases. 407.
55. *Regal (Hastings) v. Gulliver* [1942] All ER 378; IDC *Ltd v. Cooley* [1972] 2 All ER 162.
56. *Salomon v. Salomon & Co. Ltd* [1897] AC 22.
57. *In Re Armagh Shoes Ltd* [1982] NI 59 (cited in, for example, *Re Keenan Brothers Ltd* [1985] IR 401).
58. *Kinsley v. Russell Kinsela Pty Ltd* (1986) 10 ACLR 395; *Walker v. Wimbourne* (1976) CLR 1 (cited in *Re Frederick Inns Ltd* [1991] ILRM 582).

New Zealand.[59] In addition to the persuasive authority of these cases, Irish courts follow doctrines of precedent in the same way as other common law jurisdictions, and so the hierarchy of the court system is also important. (*Infra*).

II. The Court System in Ireland

39. Following an armed struggle for independence the Anglo-Irish Treaty was agreed on 6 December 1921. Subsequently, the Irish Free State (Constitution) Act 1922 was passed by the Westminster (British) Parliament. The Dáil, the Irish Parliament, then enacted the Irish Free State (*Saorstát Éireann*) Act 1922 implementing the Irish Free State Constitution, which was based on the terms of the Treaty. The Constitution followed the separation of powers model between the executive, legislative and judicial branches of government. The judicial branch consisted of a Supreme Court, High Court, and lower courts of local and limited jurisdiction with rights of appeal and a final right of appeal from the Irish Courts to the Judicial Committee of the Privy Council in London. Prior to this, two court systems had been in operation since 1920, the original court system established during British rule in Ireland and a Dáil court system. Following the signing of the Anglo-Irish Treaty, the Dáil courts were wound up and later the courts established under the Irish Free State Constitution held all decisions of the Dáil courts to be void.[60]

40. The Courts of Justice Act 1924 established the court system that has been replicated in the Constitution of 1937 and again followed in the Courts (Establishment and Constitution) Act 1961 pursuant to Article 34 of the 1937 Constitution. Articles 34–37 of the Constitution contain the provision relating to the administration of justice. The Constitution provides for a Supreme Court as a final Court of Appeal and courts of first instance, including the High Court, which has full jurisdiction in civil and criminal matters, as well as courts of limited and local jurisdiction, including the Circuit Court and the District Court. A new Court of Appeal which will hear appeals from the High Court was established in 2014. Further amendment to the Constitution provides for the supremacy of the law of the EU and as such recognizes the jurisdiction of the ECJ in relation to the legal framework and laws emanating from the institutions of the EU.

41. The High Court currently consists of a President and thirty-six ordinary judges. This court has full original jurisdiction to determine all matters of law and fact in civil and criminal matters. It also has jurisdiction to review the validity of laws and executive actions having regard to the provisions of the Constitution. It has an appellate jurisdiction from decisions of the Circuit Court and various tribunals and may give rulings on questions of law from the District Court. Matters of

59. *Nicholson v. Permakraft (NZ) Ltd (in liq)* [1985] 1 NZLR 242 (cited in *Re Frederick Inns Ltd* [1991] ILRM 582).
60. *R (Kelly) v. Maguire* [1923] 2 IR 58.

company law are usually heard in the High Court,[61] from which an appeal could, in the past be brought to the Supreme Court. The appeal structure has changed recently following legislation passed in 2014 discussed *infra* in paragraph 42. Additionally, there are some exceptions to the original jurisdiction of the High Court in company law matters, including a recent attempt to facilitate the rescue of more SMEs by giving jurisdiction over certain kinds of examinerships to the Circuit Court.[62] The primary motivation of this change was to reduce the costs of rescue. Overall, there has not been a significant effect arising from this change. Accordingly, all references to 'the Court' herein in regard to companies should be interpreted as referring to the High Court unless otherwise stated. In 2004 the Rules of the Superior Courts[63] were amended to provide for the transfer of certain kinds of High Court proceedings to a dedicated Commercial List, with a view to expedited resolution of such matters as are admitted to that List. This is particularly important for company and commercial law matters. Applications for transfer to the High Court Commercial List may be made in respect of proceedings instituted on or after the 12 January 2004 in accordance with the Practice Directions emanating from the High Court and the revised Order 63A of the Rules of the Superior Courts.[64] The judge dealing with the List has discretion as to which cases may be admitted, but a minimum EUR 1 million value threshold must be met.

42. Finally, a significant change was made in late 2014 with the establishment of a Court of Appeal.[65] This court occupies an appellate jurisdiction between the High Court and the Supreme Court. The Court of Appeal is composed of a President and nine ordinary judges. This is designed to reserve cases concerning important points of law to the Supreme Court and to allow ordinary appeals from the High Court which would hitherto have been heard by the Supreme Court to be heard in the Court of Appeal. Exceptions are those cases in which the Supreme Court has permitted an appeal to it on being satisfied that the appeal meets the threshold set out in Article 34.5.4° of the Constitution. The Chief Justice and the President of the High Court are ex officio judges of the Court of Appeal. The Court may sit in divisions of three judges. Some interlocutory and procedural applications may be heard

61. Companies Act 12014, s. 2. The definition of court is more involved in this new Act. In particular the prosecution of offences under the Companies Act 2014 may under this definition be pursued in the District Court.
62. This change was originally contained in the Companies Act 2013 but has now been reconsolidated in Part 10 of the Companies Act 2014.
63. Order 63A of the Rules of the Superior Courts (S.I. No. 2 of 2004).
64. Order 63A provides for a definition of commercial proceedings to enable facilitation of the removal of certain kinds of cases from the High Court list to the High Court Commercial List. Interestingly, the rules do not refer specifically to matters arising under the Companies Acts 1963–2006, but refer to matters arising in relation to the operation of stock, share or other investment markets and also gives discretion to the Judge of the High Court Commercial List to approve other cases for entry to the list (Ord. 63A(b)).
65. The Court of Appeal was established on 28 Oct. 2014 under the Court of Appeal Act 2014 which was passed following a referendum approving the 33rd amendment to the 1937 Constitution which provided for the creation of this court. Following the establishment of the Court of Appeal specified appeals pending in the Supreme Court which had been initiated before the establishment day and had not been fully or partly heard by that court were directed by the Chief Justice to be heard and determined by the Court of Appeal.

by the President alone or by another judge nominated by the President. The Court has full jurisdiction including jurisdiction to hear appeals from the High Court on Constitutional law matters. Under the Court of Appeal Act 2014, the Court of Appeal was given the appellate jurisdiction previously exercised by the Court of Criminal Appeal. Appeals by the Director of Public Prosecutions against an acquittal or against a decision not to order a retrial also lie to the Court of Appeal. The decision of the Court of Appeal is final unless the Supreme Court permits an appeal under Article 34.5.3 of the Constitution. Questions of law which could previously be referred by the Circuit Court to the Supreme Court for determination (a 'case stated') are now determinable by the Court of Appeal.

III. The Role of Legislation

43. Increasingly in Ireland, as with other common law jurisdictions, the role of legislation has become significant in the area of company and commercial law. For many years, the 1963 Companies Act, was the principal piece of legislation, but as explained above this and all other legislation enacted up to 2013 has now been consolidated in a major statute, the Companies Act 2014.[66] This Act now contains all the statutory principles relevant to company law in Ireland. In addition to this consolidation exercise, there are some reforms made, and additionally certain matters, for example directors' duties have been codified for the first time.[67] Where the 1963 Act had provided a standard form set of Articles of Association for different types of companies, (essentially rules for the conduct of internal affairs that companies were required to create and that bound companies and their members) the 2014 Companies Act provides for the Constitution of a company. Many of the provisions which had hitherto been contained in the 'standard-form articles' are now statutory provisions, for example the rule regarding the delegation of management powers from the shareholders to the board previously contained in Article 80 of the old Articles of Association is now provided for in section 158 of the 2014 Act.[68] These statutory provisions are either mandatory or optional and will be discussed in more detail in the text as they arise.

44. Since the late 1970s, a number of factors have contributed to a significant growth in company legislation. The first of these is membership of the EU. The extent and scope of the influence of the European harmonization project has been discussed earlier.[69] The second is the modernization of the Irish economy, beginning with a period in the late 1980s when it became apparent that with an increase in economic activity, there were serious issues to be addressed in relation to awareness of and compliance with, even the most basic of company law provisions. A third significant factor was the spectacular growth in the Irish economy during the

66. See further Courtney, (gen. ed.), *Bloomsbury's Professional Guide to the Companies Act 2014* (Bloomsbury 2015).
67. Companies Act 2014, ss 227, 228.
68. *Infra* Part 1 Ch. 1, §4.
69. *Supra.* Introduction, section §2 III – *Development of European Company Law and Membership of the EU.*

'Celtic Tiger' years (late 1990s–2005). This led to an increased awareness of the importance of ensuring adequate regulatory standards, but in addition it also led to an awareness of the potential for company law and related areas of legislative activity to be enabling in some ways. This concept became particularly important in relation to the developing financial services industry, which along with biotechnology and information technology were and continue to be significant factors in the continued economic performance of Ireland. Thus in relation to aspects of the financial services industry that interface with company law we have seen the enactment of legislation that supports and regulates this kind of activity. This is particularly true of certain aspects of financial services activity such as the funds industry and the development of private equity investment vehicles.

45. As a result of the global financial crisis and the significance of the economic and banking crisis in Ireland, a 'bad bank' of sorts was created to take over the operation of a significant number of non-performing loans from a range of Irish banks. The National Asset Management Agency was created by the NAMA Act of 2009.[70] It was considered as the best possible option available to address the collapse of the Irish property market and the consequent significance of this collapse for the domestic Irish banking sector which was heavily exposed to the construction and property sector. The purpose of the legislation was to provide a structure whereby 'bad' banking loans could be transferred from the banks to the National Agency together with all security rights and other rights and liabilities attaching to these loans. The purpose was to provide some sort of liquidity in terms of payments for these loans to the banks and to allow the stable part of domestic banking activity to proceed in a normal way whilst the Agency would, over time, seek to sort out the financial consequences of the exposure of the banks to the construction and property sectors:

> NAMA is, first and foremost, an asset management agency, established with the aim of transferring certain higher risk property-related exposures from the balance sheets of the participating financial institutions in return for Government guaranteed securities. We will manage these loans with the aim of achieving the best possible return for the taxpayer over a 7–10 year timeframe. Replacing these property-related loans with Government Guaranteed Securities will help remove uncertainty about the soundness of banks' balance sheets, provide the institutions with much needed liquidity and should make it easier for the institutions over time to access capital (for some) and liquidity (for all) in the international capital markets.[71]

70. See further Lynch Fannon & Murphy, *Corporate Insolvency and Rescue* (2nd edn, Bloomsbury Professional 2012). Ch. 1.

71. As stated by Brendan McDonagh, Chief Executive of the Agency to the Committee of Public Accounts in November 2010. For a very complete treatment of the provisions of this legislation please refer to H. Byrne & L. McEntaggart, *The National Asset Management Agency Act 2009: Annotations and Commentary* (Bloomsbury Professional 2010) and M.R Whelan, M. Kennedy & F. O'Raghallaigh, *The National Asset Management Agency Act 2009* (Gill and MacMillan 2011).

46. Significant features of this legislation include very extensive powers provided to the State in relation to the operation, management of the loans taken over from the banks and the underlying securities. The powers therefore accorded to the relevant Minister, in this case the Minister for Finance were commented on from the outset. For example, in the McKillen case[72] the High Court described the 'general powers of NAMA' as being 'manifold'. In short, that section provides that NAMA 'has all the powers necessary or expedient for, or incidental to, the achievement of its purposes and performances of its functions.' These powers included for example a right to the state agency to act a receiver in relation to property with a broad range of powers. It is important to note therefore that in certain circumstances that company law is affected by provisions of the Act where one is dealing with assets and transactions arising from the operation of provisions of that Act.[73]

IV. The Constitution: *Bunreacht Na Héireann*

47. All company law principles, whether derived from common law or from legislation, are subject to the provisions of the Irish Constitution, which includes provisions relating to separation of powers and guaranteeing fundamental rights and freedoms. All positive laws are subject to judicial review against these fundamental provisions in the same way that in the United States, acts of Congress or of Government are subject to review by the courts. Accordingly, provisions of the Companies Acts have from time to time been challenged as being unconstitutional,[74] as have actions of the Government through its agencies in enforcing company law provisions. The constitutionality of provisions of company law is potentially difficult, particularly in the area of enforcement.[75]

V. European Sources

48. The development of Irish company law following accession to the European Community in 1972 has been documented above (see *supra* paragraphs 20 ff.). As sources of law, it is important to note that as with other Member States, the passing of a Directive requires implementation into domestic legislation, normally with some provisions in the Directives being a matter of choice for the particular jurisdiction. On the other hand, Regulations emanating from the EU have direct effect. In this context, it would be fair to characterize Irish company law as being more permissive than other European jurisdictions and, in this respect is more similar to the neighbouring UK jurisdictions, in particular to the approach taken to company law regulation and theory in England and Wales. It is worth mentioning that failure to implement a particular Directive in a proper and timely manner may lead to the

72. *Dellway Investments and Ors v. NAMA and the Attorney General* [2011] IESC 364.
73. See further Lynch Fannon & Murphy, *Corporate Insolvency and Rescue* (2nd edn., Bloomsbury Professional 2012) Ch. 1 for further discussion of the caselaw.
74. For example, *Desmond v. Glackin* (No. 2) [1993] 3 IR 67 where the provision was successfully challenged; *O'Keeffe v. Ferris* where the challenge was unsuccessful. [1993] 3 IR 165.
75. For example, *Re Tralee Beef and Lamb Ltd (In Liquidation); Kavanagh v. Delaney* [2008] 3 IR 347.

possibility of its provisions being directly enforceable against that Member State.[76] In addition, once implemented, Directives may be relied upon and enforced by individuals against public bodies; this is known as the 'vertical direct effect' of EU law.[77] It is usually the case that Directives, unlike Treaty provisions[78] and regulations, cannot be directly enforced as between private litigant parties; this concept is known as 'horizontal direct effect'.[79]

VI. International Sources

49. Under the provisions of the Irish Constitution (*Bunreacht na hÉireann*) of 1937, the force of international law and Ireland's obligations under internationally agreed treaties is recognized. Of particular interest in this context is that Ireland is a signatory to the European Convention on Human Rights (ECHR) and accordingly recognizes the decisions of the European Court of Human Rights; decisions of that court have in recent years acceded to the notion that corporations may be entitled to the protection of at least some of the rights accorded under that Convention.[80] This viewpoint has met with some resistance on the domestic front in relation to constitutionally protected rights.[81] Quite apart from the ECHR, however, Ireland is a Member State of the EU and Communities, and the Constitution of Ireland has been amended to recognize the doctrine of supremacy enunciated in the case law of the ECJ. That is, Ireland is bound to apply the laws and regulations necessitated by such membership, even when these are contrary to current or preexisting domestic law.[82] Accordingly, compliance with EU law is of paramount importance in the hierarchy of sources of Irish law.

§5. Private International Law (Conflict of Laws)

I. The General Rules

50. A person, whether artificial (as a company is) or real, can be sued in Ireland if, in the case of a natural person, he or she is present, as the common law rules determining jurisdiction depend on the idea of service on a person. For companies, the place of registration is taken as a location that represents the company for the

76. *Francovich v. Italy* (Cases C-6 and C-9/90) [1991] ECR I-5357.
77. *Marleasing S.A. v. La Commercial International de Alimnetacion S.A.* (Case C-106/89) [1991] ECR I-4135.
78. *Defrenne v. Sabena* (No. 2) (Case C-43/75) [1976] ECR 455.
79. *Marshall v. Southampton and South-West Hampshire Area Health Authority* (Case 152/84) [1986] ECR 723.
80. *Pine Valley Developments Ltd v. Ireland* (1992) 14 EHRR 319; *National & Provincial Building Society v. UK* (1997) 25 EHRR 127.
81. See *infra*, paras 90–91 and 92–93.
82. *Bunreacht na hÉireann* (Constitution of Ireland), Art. 29.4.10.

purpose of service. Suing the partnership in the firm name is now possible, and this represents a change in the law in which each partner had to be named individually.

II. Choice of Forum

A. *EC Regulation 44/2001*

51. Regulation (EU) 1215/2012 on jurisdiction and the recognition and enforcement of judgments in civil and commercial matters (recast) ('the Recast Regulation') came into effect in Ireland on 10 January 2015. The Recast Regulation replaces Regulation 44/2001 ('the Brussels Regulation'):

(a) Both Regulation 44/2001[83] and, in turn the most recent Regulation 1215/2012 replace the Brussels Convention on jurisdiction and the enforcement of judgments in civil and commercial law matters. The Regulation applies to all proceedings commenced after the date of commencement of the Regulation. Under the Regulations, the general rule is that persons shall be sued in the courts of the Member State in which they are domiciled. In those circumstances, therefore, the preliminary issue will be where the company is domiciled. Under Irish law, as with English law, the domicile of a corporation is determined by its place of incorporation as neither Irish nor English law apply the concept of 'real seat'. Irish registered companies are considered to be domiciled in Ireland under Irish law, regardless of the scope and extent of their activities overseas. In the case of partnerships the domicile of the principal partner or partners is the relevant criteria. More detailed provisions regarding the enforcement of contracts is provided for in the Regulation. Thus the Regulation provides that the relevant forum in matters relating to a contract, is the courts of the place of performance of the obligation in question;

   and goes on to clarify that

(b) for the purpose of this provision and unless otherwise agreed, the place of performance of the obligation in question shall be:
   - in the case of the sale of goods, the place in a Member State where, under the contract, the goods were delivered, or should have been delivered;
   - in the case of the provision of services, the place in a Member State where, under the contract, the services were provided or should have been provided.

Article 5(1) of the Brussels Convention contained a similar provision, and the interpretation of this provision has been the subject of much litigation before the ECJ. The Convention provision was amended by the addition of paragraph 1(b) of Article 5, quoted above.

83. Council Regulation (EC) No. 44/2001 on jurisdiction and the recognition and enforcement of judgments in civil and commercial matters (O.J. L012/1 16 Jan. 2001).

B. Council Regulation 848/2015

52. The Council Regulation on insolvency proceedings is of real importance in the corporate law context. As stated above, under Irish law, the jurisdiction issue (as it relates to companies) will generally begin by reference to the place of incorporation of the company. Council Regulation 1346/2000 on Insolvency Proceedings which has now been updated and replaced by Council Regulation 848/2015 refers to the 'centre of main interest' as being the determinant of jurisdiction in relation to a corporation or individual involved in insolvency proceedings. In turn the 'centre of main interests' is determined by reference to the place of incorporation of the debtor company, but, as with the previous Regulation, this presumption in favour of the place of incorporation as the determinative factor can be displaced by reference to an enquiry as to where the debtor 'conducts the administration of its interests on a regular basis and is therefore ascertainable by third parties'. The Insolvency Regulation and its more recent replacement continues to provide a compromise between the 'place of incorporation' theory regarding corporate domicile and the 'real seat' theory more prevalent in continental European jurisdictions.[84] The recent regulation applies to all insolvency proceedings, including proceedings which concern restructuring of corporate entities. However, the Regulation does not apply to restructuring processes which are derived from company law. The latter will include English Schemes of Arrangements and the similar provisions in Irish company law, now re-enacted in Chapter 1 of Part 9 of the Companies Act 2014.[85]

III. Choice of Law

53. In Ireland, as in England, the place of registration of companies is deemed to be paramount in determining the domicile of companies and accordingly the jurisdictional law that applies to their affairs. This is very different from the position applicable in most European countries and therefore allows for the registration of companies in Ireland and England that may operate in other jurisdictions of the EU. In tandem with decisions of the ECJ holding that restraints on the adoption of nationals of other Member States of incorporation in Ireland or England are in breach of the right to freedom of establishment, this approach provides for a 'Delaware effect'. The possibilities of this competition for corporate business were finally brought into immediate focus in the significant decisions of the ECJ in the *Centros*,[86]

84. See further Moss, Fletcher & Isaacs, *The EC Regulation on Insolvency Proceedings: A Commentary and Annotated Guide* (2nd edn., OUP 2002, 2009). Moss & Wessels, *EU Banking and Insurance Insolvency* (OUP 2006) and see also Wessels, B. Markel, B.A. Judge & J. Kilborn, *International Co-operatioin in Bankruptcy and Insolvency Matters* (Oxford University Press 2009). See also Lynch Fannon & Murphy, *Corporate Insolvency and Rescue* (2nd edn., Bloomsbury Professional 2012) Ch. 1.

85. Discussed *infra*. Part 1, Chapter 1, §6.

86. *Centros Ltd v. Erhvervs-Og Selskabstyrelsen* (Case C-212/97) [1999] ECR 1459.

Uberseering[87] and *Inspire Art*[88] cases. In these cases, the ECJ held that no prima facie restrictions could be placed on the ability of individuals who were nationals of EU Member States to incorporate companies in other jurisdictions in the Union. There are a number of different aspects to the establishment of freedom to incorporate throughout the EU, but the dismantling of barriers relates primarily to the sidelining of the 'real seat' theory that prevails in a number of EU jurisdictions and to the dismantling of additional restrictions placed on foreign-registered companies before being permitted to operate in a particular jurisdiction. The 'real seat' theory, which is certainly alien to the common law countries of Ireland and the UK, prevents the incorporation of a company in the relevant jurisdiction, such as France, when its main activities are to take place outside France; it also provides that when a French company moves its main operations outside France, it will be wound up or liquidated. (Interestingly, *Centros* concerned a Danish couple wishing to avoid the minimum capital requirements imposed in Denmark described above by incorporating in the UK and setting up a branch of the company in Denmark while never engaging in any trading activity in the UK). These decisions have given rise to considerable debate about the desirability of the Delaware effect. While the debate has raged, some States – notably the UK, Ireland and, it would seem, the Netherlands – have continued to benefit from this phenomenon.[89] As the globalization of economic activity continues to occur, it is possible that courts, other than Irish courts, may choose to apply Irish law. In the United States, it is common for courts to consider detailed argument on two distinct questions, the first pertaining to choice of forum and the second to choice of law. In *Tomran Inc. v. William M. Passano, Jr et al.*, for example, Matricciani J. accepted jurisdiction in relation to certain matters involving an Irish banking corporation, but also decided that the applicable law was Irish company law and proceeded to decide the case on that basis.[90]

IV. Overseas Companies

54. Companies from outside Ireland wishing to trade in Ireland may set up a subsidiary, and the subsidiary will be treated as an Irish company arising from its registration in Ireland. It is also possible for the overseas company to establish a branch, which will not be considered to be a separate entity. Under the Companies Act 2014 Part 21 deals with External Companies. Here a distinction is made between a 'branch' of an external company and a 'place of business' of an external company. This distinction determines registration and filing obligations of the related enterprise, so that only a branch of a foreign registered company must be registered in Ireland under sections 1300–1302 of the Companies Act 2014.

---

87. *Uberseering BV v. Nordic Construction Company Baumanagement GmbH* (Case C-208/00) [2002] ECR 9919.
88. *Kamer van Koophandel en Fabrieken voor Amsterdam v. Inspire Art Ltd* (Case C-167/01) [2003] ECR 10155. See further A. Looijestijn-Clearie, *Have the Dikes Collapsed? Inspire Art a Further Breakthrough in the Freedom of Establishment of Companies?*, 5 Eur. Bus. Org. L. Rev. 389 (2004).
89. See further I. Lynch-Fannon, *The Luck of the Irish or Just Plain Old Tax and Regulatory Planning? The Success of Venture Capitalism in Ireland*, 2 Entrep. Bus. L.J., 1–35 (2006).
90. Baltimore City Circuit Case N: 24–C–02–002561.

§6. THE LABOUR LAW CONNECTION

55. De minimis classification of corporate governance systems would identify two categories of governance structures. The first, the 'arms length financial model' of corporate governance, relies significantly on the capital markets as an accountability and monitoring device. This model is also described as an 'outsider' model with the emphasis on shareholders, on the shareholder-management relationship and on the market as a monitoring device.[91] This is the US model. In contrast is the 'relational finance' model relying on close internally constructed relationships between the corporation and the providers of capital, including both shareholders and bankers or other financial institutions. This model is also described as an 'insider' model as it gives internal recognition through, for example, representative board membership for stakeholders in addition to shareholders. Such stakeholders include creditors (financiers) and employees. This type of model is exemplified both by the Japanese experience and in continental Europe.[92] Whereas many corporate governance scholars regard the 'arms length financial model' as being *Anglo*-American in character with the common law being identified as its legal progenitor, this classification ignores the significant shift in understanding of the appropriate corporate response to employees as stakeholders that has taken place in the United Kingdom and Ireland since the beginning of the last century and accelerated as a result of membership of the EU since 1972.[93] Furthermore, it underestimates significant local variations even in apparently similar corporate law rules governing, for example, the rights of minority shareholders.[94] Similarly, within the broad category of relational finance models, there are also significant local variations of these governance systems. This is true of continental European countries where differences are found as between Member States of the EU in relation to the recognition of workers' interests and rights, in relation to recognition of minority shareholder rights,[95] and in relation to the recognition of the rights of creditors.[96] Under European Social Policy, which applies obviously throughout the entire EU, the corporation is seen as the appropriate subject of State regulation, where the object of this regulation is to achieve broad-based social, employment or economic policies as distinct from simply delivering an acceptable level of corporate behaviour. Such

91. Armen A. Alchian & H. Demsetz, *Production, Information, Costs and Economic Organisations*, 62 Am. Econ. Rev. 777–783 (1972) for a consideration of agency problems and costs in this kind of organization. See further Eugene F. Fama, *Agency Problems and the Theory of the Firm*, 88 J. Pol. Economy, 288 (1988) and *Efficient Capital Markets*, 46 J. of Fin., 1575 (1991) for a description of how capital markets address some of these agency problems (in theory, at least).
92. Ronald J. Gilson & Mark J. Roe, *Understanding the Japanese Keiretsu: Overlaps between Corporate Governance and Industrial Organisation*, 102 Yale L. J. 871 (1993); Rafael La Porta et al., *Legal Determinants of External Finance*, 52 J. Fin. 1131 (1997); *Law and Finance*, 106 J. Pol. Economy, 1113 (1998); *Corporate Ownership Around the World*, 54 J. Fin., 471 (1999).
93. Kraakman et al., *The Anatomy of Corporate Law* (2nd edn., OUP 2009). I. Lynch-Fannon, *Employees as Corporate Stakeholders: Theory and Reality in a Transatlantic Context*, 27 J. Corp. L. Stud., 155 (2004).
94. I. Lynch-Fannon, *A Transatlantic Case: The Derivative Action as a Corporate Governance Tool*, 27 Dublin U. L. J. 1 (2005); R. Nolan, *Indirect Investors: A Greater Say in the Company?*, 3 J. Corp. L. Stud. 73 (2003).
95. COM (2003) 284/final; MARKT/13.05.2005.
96. COM (2003) 284 final.

policies and subsequent legislation can include legislation designed to facilitate investment in job creation and growth; legislation designed to assist in the elimination of social exclusion or poverty, such as legislation facilitating and supporting part-time workers to increase labour market participation;[97] initiatives to support a better work-life balance for employees;[98] or legislation ensuring environmental protection and sustainable development. From the European perspective the corporation is seen as one of a number of social partners, all of whom have a role to play in contributing to the planning of both macroeconomic and social outcomes. In addition the European approach considers it appropriate not only to regulate external corporate relationships with stakeholders such as employees or the community (environment) but also to regulate governance structures within the corporation. The aim of this regulation is to reinforce recognition of stakeholders' rights, specifically through mandated representation of stakeholders, creditors and/or employees on boards of management.[99] The latter is a feature of a number of continental European corporate governance structures. In contrast, in the United States this level of managed planning is not present. In addition, the 'free market' ideal militates against regarding the corporation as some sort of tool of state or government planning. Furthermore, the broader European concept of 'social partnership' inclusive of business and trade unions and other social groups is completely lacking. In theoretical terms, this has been described in earlier research by this author (Prof. Lynch Fannon) as a contrasting view from both sides of the Atlantic of the corporation as a public or private actor, and some examination of the significant philosophical and political theories underlying these particularly different approaches has been carried out.[100] Thus, the corporate governance systems of both Ireland and the UK provide an interesting bridge between these two models of governance, particularly concerning the labour law dimension.

97. Directives 97/81/EC O.J. (L 14) and 98/23/EC O.J. (L 131) on Part-Time and Fixed Term Workers.

98. Directives 92/85/EC O.J. (L 348) on Maternity Leave; Directive 96/34/EC O.J. (L 145) on Parental Leave; and Directive 93/104/EC, the Organization of Working Time Directive.

99. See Directive 2001/86/EC on worker representation on the board of the European company provided for under Council Regulation 2157/2001: The Statute for the European Company.

100. I. Lynch-Fannon, *Working within Two Kinds of Capitalism* (Hart Publications 2003). See also M.T. Moore, *Corporate Governance in the Shadow of the State* (Hart Publications, 2013).

Part I. Corporations

Chapter 1. The Public Company

§1. Introduction

56. The previous section [paragraph 29] described the different kinds of companies available under Irish law. As far as companies are concerned, by far the most popular type of incorporation format is that of the private company limited by shares. Within the limited liability company category, where this is a company limited by shares, the distinction between a public limited liability company and a private limited liability company is the most significant, with the private company limited by shares predominating as the corporate form registered in Ireland. The main distinguishing feature is that in a public company shares can normally be traded on a public market. Much of the regulation of limited liability companies in Ireland is now statute based under the provisions of the Companies Acts 2014.[101] Nevertheless, a considerable body of case law sets out fundamental principles of company law and offers interpretation by the judiciary of this legislation. Many of the modern decisions are available on the website of the Irish Courts service[102] or alternatively on the BAILII website.[103] Despite the prevalence of the private limited liability company, orthodox analysis of company law in Ireland, as with English jurisprudence, assumes that the rules apply to both private and public companies, with variations being highlighted where appropriate. Indeed the structure of this work reflects that traditional emphasis on the public company as being centre stage with this first chapter of Part 1 describing the provisions as they apply to public companies, and the second chapter of Part 1 describing the law as it relates to private companies. The new Irish Companies Act 2014 reverses this emphasis however, and focuses, in the first instance, on the private company limited by shares. The first 14 Parts of the legislation set out the rules relating to the private company limited by shares. Part 16 deals with Designated Activity Companies, (DACs) as a variation of this type of company. Part 17 then sets out the provisions which apply to public limited companies. Section 1002 provides a Table which shows which provisions do not apply to PLCs. In keeping with the approach taken by the publishers

101. A useful website in relation to Irish law in general is <www.irishstatutebook.ie>. For examples, for the principal legislation on Irish company law, the Companies Act of 2014.
102. www.courts.ie.
103. www.baillii.org.

of this series, this monograph will take the approach adopted in the first edition, outlining company law as it applies to both public and private companies and highlighting variations for the private company limited by shares in Chapter 2. It should be noted, however, that the structure of the Irish legislation adopts the latter company as the default business organization e with the public limited company being treated in one distinct Part of the legislation.

§2. Formation of a PLC

I. Incorporation: An Introduction

A. Incorporation and Registration

57. The Companies Act 2014 (the '2014 Act') has altered the previous position whereby it was necessary to register a memorandum and articles of association. The 2014 Act has different requirements for different types of company. For a private company limited by shares, the memorandum and articles have now been replaced by a single document, known simply as the 'constitution' of the company.[104] A public limited company ('PLC') shall continue to have a memorandum and articles of association, which shall together be referred to as a 'constitution'.[105] Whereas previously the 138 model articles of Table A were the basis for extensive articles of association, the substance of the former Table A has been incorporated into the 2014 Act and therefore there is no real need to have extensive articles of association in a private company limited by shares. The memorandum of association of a PLC must comply with the requirements set out in section 1006 of the 2014 Act.[106]

Registration of a limited liability company in Ireland is a relatively cheap affair. In an effort to encourage its uptake, the fee for registration online at <www.cro.ie> is EUR 50, half the cost of filing these documents the 'old-fashioned way'. At EUR 100 for the latter mode of filing and EUR 50 online, the privilege of incorporation and limited liability is much more readily available than in other European countries. PLCs must file a form requesting to commence business with the Companies Registration Office. The purpose of this form is primarily to confirm that the PLC has complied with the minimum capital requirements established for this business form.[107] The minimum capital requirement for a PLC in Ireland is currently set at EUR 25,000, of which one-quarter (25%) must be paid up before the company commences business,[108] and this must be stated in the memorandum.[109] A PLC may not reduce its company capital below the authorized minimum.[110]

104. Companies Act 2014, s. 21. The constitution shall comply with certain requirements set out in s. 19 of the 2014 Act.
105. Companies Act 2014, s. 1006.
106. In respect of a company which predated 1 Jun. 2015, the relevant provision is s. 1007 of the 2014 Act.
107. Companies Registration Office (Form A4/70).
108. Companies Act 2014, s. 1010.
109. Companies Act 2014, s. 1006.
110. Companies Act 2014, s. 1084.

B. Limited Liability and Corporate Personality

58. Limited liability is defined in section 655 of the Companies Act 2014, which deals with the issue of who is liable to contribute to the payment of a company's debts on winding up. Section 25(2) of the 2014 Act states that the subscribers and other members of the company will collectively become a 'body corporate' with the liability of the members to contribute to the assets in the event of a winding up to be described in the Act. Section 655(1) addresses the liability of past and present members of a range of different kinds of companies, including those limited by guarantee or companies that are unlimited. The section goes on in subsection 655(1)(d) to state that 'in the case of a company limited by shares, no contribution shall be required from any member exceeding the amount, if any, unpaid on the shares in respect of which he is liable as a present or past member'. In a PLC this amount is set as described above, but in most cases concerning private companies, there is no amount unpaid on the shares, the issued share capital being usually minimal and the amount paid up at the formation of the company. In relation to the shares in a public company, these must be tradeable on a public market. Limited liability is complemented in its effect by the doctrine of corporate personality, which was first considered in England in the case of *Salomon v. Salomon & Co. Ltd.*[111] The decision in that case, and the jurisprudence following from it, form part of Irish company law (see §2, IV, *infra*).

II. Registration Requirements

59. Registration requires the lodging of the 'constitution' of the company (which for a PLC will now contain a Memorandum of Association and Articles, drawn up with reference to the provisions of the Companies Act 2014) together with the relevant Companies Registration Office forms (Form A1 and A70). Details of a registered address to which all formal documents can be sent must be provided. It has been possible for a single member company to be formed in Ireland for some time and now under section 128 of the Companies Act 2014 it is possible for companies to have only one director. At least one of the directors of a company must be resident in an EEA State,[112] although it is possible for the company to be exempt from this provision if a bond is lodged to the value of EUR 25,000.00, which becomes payable to a person nominated by the Registrar of Companies or the Revenue Commissioners, as the case may be, for the purpose of discharging any fine imposed on the company.[113] There are statutory rules for assessing whether a director is resident

111. *Salomon v. Salomon & Co. Ltd* [1897] AC 22 (reversing *Broderip v. Salomon* [1985] 2 Ch. 232).
112. Companies Act 2014, s. 137(1).
113. Companies Act 2014, s. 137(2). The bond provides that, in the event of a failure by the company to pay the whole or part of a fine imposed in respect of an offence under the Companies Acts 1963–2005 or the Taxes Consolidation Act 1997, or a penalty under the latter legislation, an amount of money up to the value of the bond will be paid by the guarantor in discharge of the company's liability. In addition, note that the provision whereby at least one director must be a resident of an EEA State does not apply where the Registrar of Companies grants a certificate under s. 140 of the 2014 Act, which is a certificate stating that the company has a real and continuous link with one or

an EEA State to comply with this requirement.[114] A person shall not, at a particular time, be a director of more than twenty-five private companies limited by shares, or twenty-five companies, one or more of which is a private company limited by shares and one or more of which is another type of company capable of being wound up under the 2014 Act.[115] PLCs are not counted for this purpose.[116] In addition, there is a requirement that an Irish-registered company must carry on an activity in the State, but 'activity' for this purpose includes the holding or acquisition of property of any kind, thus reducing the efficacy of this legislation.[117]

60. The company must also have a company secretary. The Registrar must be informed of the first person to hold this position and of any subsequent changes (see §4, V, *infra*).

61. The memorandum of a PLC must state the name of the company,[118] and the Registrar may reject the registration if the company name is deemed to be 'undesirable'.[119] It is for the Registrar to identify what is undesirable for this purpose; the CRO website provides guidance in this regard. For example, a name might be refused if it is identical or similar to a name already on the register, if the name is offensive, or if it includes terms such as 'Ireland' that might suggest State sponsorship. Certain other terms cannot be used without the permission of relevant bodies. The words 'bank', 'banking' and 'banc' may only be used with permission from the Central Bank, and the word 'university' may not be used without permission from the Department of Education. An appeal lies to the High Court against a refusal by the Registrar to register a company name on the ground that the name is undesirable. A change in the company's name may only be effected by special resolution and with the consent of the Registrar.[120]

62. A company trading under a name other than its corporate name must register such trading name as well, but inclusion of the abbreviation 'Ltd' for 'Limited'

---

more economic activities in the State. Section 140(9) of the 2014 Act provides that such a 'real and continuous link' is established if one of the following conditions is satisfied:

(a) the affairs of the company are managed by one or more persons from a place of business established in the State and that person or those persons is or are authorised by the company to act on its behalf;
(b) the company carries on a trade in the State;
(c) the company is a subsidiary or a holding company of a company or other body corporate that satisfies either or both of the conditions specified in paragraphs (a) and (b);
(d) the company is a subsidiary of a company, another subsidiary of which satisfies either or both of the conditions specified in paragraphs (a) and (b).

114. Companies Act 2014, s. 44(8), (9) and (10).
115. Companies Act 2014, s. 142(1).
116. Companies Act 2014, s. 142(3).
117. For a PLC, see Companies Act 2014, s. 1005; and as regards a private company limited by shares, see s. 18 of the 2014 Act.
118. Companies Act 2014, s. 1006. As regards a private company, see s. 19 of the 2014 Act.
119. Companies Act 2014, s. 26(5).
120. Companies Act 2014, s. 26(4) and s. 1008(4).

or 'PLC' for 'public limited company' (or an equivalent in the Irish language) shall not of itself render such registration necessary.

63. The issuing of any prospectus is governed principally by Chapter 1 of Part 23 of the 2014 Act (see §2, IX, *infra*).

III. Publicity

64. Enforcement of company law, the effective governance of corporations and the adequate protection of various stakeholders, including in particular shareholders and creditors of all types, depend on effective corporate disclosure rules. The publication of company documents such as the Memorandum and Articles of Association (now referred to as the 'constitution' under the Companies Act 2014), various shareholder resolutions, and various other items pertaining to the financial situation of the company such as accounts and borrowing and the creation of charges on corporate property are all essential elements in an effective disclosure system and the corporate governance structures built on these elements. The Registrar of Companies is charged with maintaining a file on each registered company. The CRO website[121] provides detailed guidance on what sort of documents need to be filed, and the CRO maintains company files that can be accessed online or in person through a company search on the payment of a fee.

65. In addition to the actual disclosure and filing obligations, there is also a notification of filing and receipt procedure instituted in 1973 following the enactment of the First Company Law Directive (68/15/EEC) through the European Communities (Companies) Regulations 1973. These matters are now to be published electronically since the European Communities (Companies) Regulations 2004.[122] Under this system the filing of specified documents must be notified through *Iris Oifigiúil* (the name given in Irish to the Official Gazette). Other notices pertaining to the activities of the company must also be notified, such as resolutions that have been passed to liquidate a company; such notification must include the terms of the resolution. A further example includes the obligation to notify the names of those individuals who no longer have authority to bind the company.[123] These must be notified to the Registrar of Companies, including any changes made from time to time, and such information must also be notified to the general public through publication in *Iris Oifigiúil*.

66. The operation of this filing and notification procedure also triggers the operation of the doctrine of notice, so that individuals who are dealing with a company may be deemed to have notice of certain kinds of information that have been

121. www.cro.ie.
122. Companies (Forms No. 2) Order 2004 (S.I. 829 of 2004). These provisions are now contained in ss 39–40 of the Companies Act 2014.
123. Companies Act 2014, s. 39.

so publicized. This is not quite the same as the operation of the doctrine of constructive notice, but it can potentially have the similarly harsh effect of individuals being imputed with certain kinds of knowledge they do not actually possess.

IV. Establishing the Members and Their Contribution

A. Numbers of Members Required, Minimum Capital Requirements

67. A public company may be incorporated with only one member,[124] as may a private company limited by shares.[125] Under Irish law, as with English law, a private limited company has no minimum capital requirement. As discussed above, the minimum capital requirement for PLCs is EUR 25,000, of which one-quarter (25%) must be paid up under the provisions of the 2014 Act.[126] Within these permissive parameters, a number of terms are commonly used in Irish corporate finance law:

- nominal or authorized capital (theoretically the maximum capital), shares must be given a value and this must be stated in the objects clause.[127] The 2014 Act gives discretion to companies to increase the authorized share capital, if the articles of association provide for this;[128]
- issued or allotted capital, the amount of capital that has been sold or allotted by the company;
- called-up or paid-up capital, the amount of capital which is paid;
- reserve capital, provided for under section 79 of the 2014 Act, capital generated by issuing or allotting shares above nominal value.

68. When a company is deciding on its capital structure, it can opt for any range of variations. For example, a company may decide to have one class of shares, normally referred to as 'ordinary shares'; there can be different classes of shares, such as Ordinary 'A' and Ordinary 'B' shares, often entitled to elect 'A' and 'B' Directors respectively; or the share capital can be divided into ordinary and preference shares, with preference shares being given to promoters or original subscribers and ordinary shares being given to other investors. Other structures can be adopted and in all cases usually described in the articles of association. Redeemable shares are governed primarily by section 105 of the 2014 Act.[129] In the context of shareholders' rights and minority rights, some specific rights attaching to shareholders, including

124. Companies Act 2014, s. 1004.
125. Companies Act 2014, s. 17. Note that under s. 17 a private company limited shares shall have no more than 149 members, albeit that s. 17 provides that employees and former employees are not counted for this purpose, and it is also provided that where two or more persons hold one or more shares in a company jointly, they shall, for the purposes of s. 17, be treated as a single member.
126. Companies Act 2014, s. 1010.
127. Companies Act 2014, s. 1006.
128. Companies Act 2014, s. 83.
129. Such shares can be cancelled or held as 'treasury shares'. See *infra*, Part I, Ch. 1, s. §3, IV.

pre-emption rights, protection against the variation of shareholders' rights, voting rights[130] and notice provisions, generally, are considered in a later section.[131]

69. To raise capital, a company may issue and allot shares at the outset or issue and allot shares as the business grows. A company may start out with a particular authorized share capital but may need to increase this authorized share capital and issue and allot some of these shares with a view to raising more equity capital. The decision of the Board of Directors to issue shares will be considered under the heading of abuse of directors' powers when we consider directors' duties, where some of these actions have been challenged in the courts (the major reason being that a new issue and allotment can have a significant impact on the control structure in a company).[132] A number of legal principles will be considered both under directors' duties and under capital maintenance later in the text.

B. Consideration for Shares; Valuation; Fraudulent and Worthless Consideration

70. Various provisions of Irish company law seek to protect the capitalization value of companies by ensuring that certain standards are complied with when shares are being issued and allotted. Accordingly, the following statutory provisions have a significant role in protecting such valuations, particularly in relation to PLCs. For the most part, these provisions do not apply to private companies. The predominant piece of legislation in this context was formerly the Companies Act 1983, which enacted modern provisions on the establishment of PLCs, the capitalization of same, rules regarding the issuing and allotment of share capital, and the valuation of consideration. This Act has now been consolidated into the Companies Act 2014.[133] Sections 71, 1027, 1028 and 1034 of the 2014 Act deal with the allotment of shares to individuals at flotation point or where there may be second and third issues and allotment of shares during the course of the life of the company. These provisions seek to capture the worst sort of excesses sometimes seen in relation to the allotment or issue of shares for worthless or over-valued consideration. Section 71 of the 2014 Act prohibits an allotment of any shares in a PLC for services:

> Section 1027 of the 2014 Act prohibits the company from accepting as payment for shares any consideration that involves an undertaking to be performed outside five years from date of allotment.
> Section 1028 of the 2014 Act provides that any non-cash consideration for shares, such as property, must be independently valued.

130. The European Union has previously considered proposals introducing some mandatory provisions regarding voting rights for shareholders (such as the European Policy Forum 2006), but these have not been pursued.
131. See Part I, Ch. 1, s. §3, IV on pre-emption rights in the context of allotment and transfer of shares.
132. See generally Part I, Ch. 1, s. §4, III, D (the abuse of power doctrine under directors' duties).
133. See generally *infra* Part 1, Ch. 1, §3.

Section 1034 of the 2014 Act provides that any transaction within two years of incorporation of a PLC where the original subscriber or member sells a non-cash asset for over one tenth of the nominal value of the entire issued share capital to a company must be independently valued.

71. In private companies, even though from a creditor's point of view the issues may be even more crucial, these rules do not apply.[134]

V. Formal Incorporation Documents

A. *Incorporation Documents: An Introduction*

72. Incorporation requires the submission as described of various documents. Under the new legislation, i.e., the Companies Act 2014 'the constitution' is the term used to describe the Memorandum of Association and the Articles of Association in the case of a PLC. (For private companies the term constitution is intended to replace these documents).[135] In either case these documents form a contract between the members and the company under the provisions of the section 31 of the 2014 Act.[136]

B. *Memorandum of Association*

73. The memorandum of association of a PLC shall state: (a) its name, (b) that it is a public limited company registered under Part 17 of the 2014 Act, (c) its objects, (d) that the liability of its members is limited, and (e) its authorized share capital, being the amount of share capital with which the PLC proposes to be registered which shall not be less than the authorized minimum, and the division thereof into shares of a fixed amount.[137] The constitution of a PLC shall also state the number of shares (which shall not be less than one) taken by each subscriber to the constitution.[138] In addition, the constitution shall be in accordance with the form set out in Schedule 9 to the 2014 Act or as near thereto as circumstances permit, and the constitution shall be printed in an entire format, which is to say the memorandum and articles shall be contained in one document; and the constitution shall be signed by each subscriber in the presence of at least one witness who shall attest the signature and the constitution shall be authenticated in the manner set out in section 888 of the 2014 Act.

134. *Infra*, Part I, Ch. 2, para. 333.
135. See *infra* Part 1, Ch. 2.
136. This section has been restrictively interpreted as applying only to liabilities and obligations imposed on a member *qua* member and not in any other capacity. See *Hickman v. Kent or Romney Marsh Sheepbreeders' Association* [1915] 1 Ch. 881.
137. Companies 2014, s. 1006(2).
138. Companies Act 2014, s. 1006(3).

74. The purpose of stating the objects of a company in the memorandum was to provide an indication of the business of the company. Given the traditional application of the *ultra vires* rule, objects clauses tended to describe multiple facets of the company's businesses or potential business directions, in addition to listing various kinds of activities the company might pursue. As a result, these clauses tended to run into several pages. This is because the objects clause was taken to define the legal capacity of the company.[139] If the company went beyond its stated objects, its actions were *ultra vires* the company and therefore void.

This caused considerable problems in practical terms. A statement of the company's objects was intended theoretically to serve a double purpose: (1) to afford protection to investors in the company who may wish to know what sort of business in which they are and roughly what sort of diversification they can expect and (2) to enable outsiders who deal with the company to ascertain the extent of the company's powers.[140] However, the general consensus is that this rationale has outlived its usefulness. Furthermore, the consequent lack of capacity, in addition to the doctrine of constructive notice applicable generally to documents of public record (see publicity requirements *supra*), was interpreted so that those dealing with a company acting in an ultra vires fashion were deemed to know of the lack of capacity. This led to some extremely harsh outcomes in the past.[141]

1. Reform

75. It has been argued by a highly respected company lawyer in England that the case for abolishing the ultra vires doctrine has been 'unanswerable' for years.[142] This argument rests particularly on the many instances of mischief attributable to the manner in which the ultra vires doctrine has been argued in courts.

76. In Ireland, the former position has now been significantly altered by the Companies Act 2014. A private company limited by shares shall now have full and unlimited capacity to carry on and undertake any business or activity, to do any act or enter into any transaction and for those purposes, it shall have full rights, powers and privileges.[143] Quite understandably, the 2014 Act hastens to add that this rule does not permit a company to deviate from the general law in any way.[144] In the case of a PLC, while as noted above the memorandum of association must continue to list the objects of the company, the 2014 Act provides that the validity of an act done by a PLC shall not be called into question on the ground of lack of capacity

139. *Ashbury Railway Carriage Co. Ltd v. Riche* (1875) LR 7 HL 653.
140. *Cotman v. Brougham* (1918) AC 514 *per* Lord Parker of Waddington.
141. See, for example, *Re Jon Beauforte Ltd* [1953] Ch. 131; *Parke v. Daily News Ltd* [1962] Ch. 297; *Re Introductions Ltd* [1970] 1 Ch. 199; in Ireland, see *Northern Bank Finance Corporation v. Quinn and Achates Investment Co.* [1979] ILRM 221; *Re Frederick Inns Ltd* [1994] 1 ILRM 387 an example of mischief.
142. L.S Sealy, *Cases and Materials in Company Law* 146 (7th edn., Butterworths 2001).
143. Companies Act 2014, s. 38(1).
144. Companies Act 2014, s. 38(2).

by reason of anything contained in the PLC's objects.[145] A member of a PLC may bring proceedings to restrain the doing of an act which, but for section 1012(1) of the 2014 Act, would be beyond the PLC's capacity but no such proceedings shall lie in respect of any act to be done in fulfilment of a legal obligation arising from a previous act of the PLC. In addition, the 2014 Act provides that it remains the duty of the directors to observe any limitations on their powers flowing from the PLC's objects and action by the directors which, but for section 1012(1), would be beyond the PLC's capacity may only be ratified by the company by special resolution.[146] Furthermore, a party to a transaction with a PLC is not bound to enquire as to whether it is permitted by the PLC's objects.[147] Therefore, the doctrine of ultra vires is effectively abolished as regards private and public companies limited by shares. As regards public companies in Ireland, the approach taken in the new legislation is similar to the approach taken under the UK Companies Act 2006, whereas, the statements regarding private companies limited by shares are more clear cut where it is envisaged that generally a private company limited by shares will have no statement as to its business activities.

77. However, it is possible to form a private company limited by shares as a designated activity company (DAC's), where business activities are stated in advance.[148] Where activities are described section 966 of the Companies Act 2014 mirrors the provisions applicable to PLCs under section 1012, namely that the statement of activities serves to restrain actions of the company. Effectively, in both cases, as with the UK provisions, the statement of objects or activities serves as a rule of internal discipline and does not affect the capacity of a company.[149]

78. An issue that has sometimes arisen in tandem with the ultra vires problem is the issue of whether a particular individual had the authority to bind the company that he or she claimed to have. This issue of the authority of agents is considered *infra* (paragraphs 218–221).

C. Articles of Association: Legal Status, Content and Alteration

79. The Memorandum and the Articles of Association provide the basic constitutional documents of the PLC. As described these are now referred to as the constitution under the Companies Act 2014.

80. It has already been noted above that much of what was contained in the standard-form articles which were appended to the 1963 Act is now contained in the body of the 2014 Act and applies by default. It can now be expected that articles of association should accordingly in future be more concise, but will nevertheless

145. Companies Act 2014, s. 1012(1).
146. Companies Act 2014, s. 1012(3).
147. Companies Act 2014, s. 1012(5).
148. Companies Act 2014, Part 16.
149. See further *infra* Part 1, Ch. 2.

involve statements as to whether the provisions of the Companies Act 2014 apply in the particular case or not. Commentators are referring to the need to create 'bespoke' articles of association for PLCs (*infra* paragraph 132).

81. The articles may only be amended by special resolution, i.e., a resolution with the support of more than three-quarters (75%) of the members present in person or by proxy.[150] Any alteration or addition so made in the articles shall, subject to the provisions of this Act, be as valid as if originally contained therein and be subject in like manner to alteration by special resolution.[151] The same rule (i.e., amendment by special resolution only) applies to an alteration of a provision of the memorandum which could have been contained in the articles.[152]

82. Generally, the Articles of Association (now the constitution) describe many of the rights of shareholders, in particular the classes of shares and their rights, which include voting rights, rights to dividends, rights to elect Directors and so forth. In addition, the articles contained rules, which were again subject to the Companies Acts, on the operation of meetings. Now, under the Companies Act 2014, these rules are for the most part, contained in the legislation. For example, the articles would previously have had a significant role in describing the relative positions of the Directors and the Board. Whereas, regulation 80 of Table A had previously provided that the business of the company shall be managed by the directors, subject to any of the other articles and the provisions of the 1963 Act, and subject also to such directions being not inconsistent with the directors' power of management as may be given by the members in general meeting, this statement is now contained in section 158(1) of the 2014 Act. Section 158(2) repeats the other important provision of regulation 80, namely that no such direction given by the members in general meeting shall invalidate any prior act of the directors which would have been valid if that direction had not been given. Similarly, whereas regulation 79 of Table A, which had allowed the directors to exercise all powers of the company to borrow money, section 158(3) of the 2014 Act now contains this provision. All of the powers of directors and rules regarding the proceedings of directors which are set out in sections 158–165 of the 2014 Act are expressed to apply save where the constitution of the company provides otherwise.[153]

VI. Legal Personality and Constitutional Structures

A. *Corporate Personality: Judicial Doctrine and Judicially Defined Exceptions to the Principle*

83. The doctrine of corporate personality applies in Irish law by virtue of the English House of Lords decision in *Salomon v. Salomon & Co. Ltd.*[154] The essential

150. Companies Act 2014, s. 1015(1).
151. Companies Act 2014, s. 1015(2).
152. Companies Act 2014, s. 1016.
153. Companies Act 2014, s. 157.
154. *Salomon v. Salomon & Co. Ltd* [1897] AC 22 (reversing *Broderip v. Salomon* [1985] 2 Ch. 232).

question in the case was whether the unsecured creditors of Salomon & Co. Ltd were entitled to have recourse to the assets of Salomon, who had originally traded as a sole trader but who had taken advantage of incorporation as provided for in the relatively new legislation enacted in England at the time. In the Court of First Instance, Vaughan Williams J. held that the company, Salomon & Co. Ltd, was an agent of Salomon, the businessman who was therefore obliged to indemnify the company for all its debts. According to Vaughan Williams J., once it was clear to the court that the shareholders were all nominees of Salomon, that it was he who took all the profits, and that he intended to do so 'without running the risk of the debts and expenses' of the business, then he was liable as principal of the company. The case was appealed to the Court of Appeal where arguments were unsuccessfully made against the finding of a per se agency relationship *inter alia*. The primary focus of the judgments of the Court of Appeal was on the intention of the legislature. Lindley L.J. was clear that Salomon had made 'an attempt ... to use the machinery of the Companies Act, 1862 for a purpose for which it was never intended'. In contrast to what Salomon had done, the 'legislature contemplated the encouragement of trade by enabling a comparatively small number of persons – namely, not less than seven – to carry on business with a limited joint stock or capital. ... But the legislature never contemplated an extension of limited liability to sole traders or to a few number than seven'. Lopes L. J. stated that if Salomon's 'scheme' were to be condoned by the courts, it would be tantamount to authorizing a 'perversion of the Joint Stock Companies Acts' and giving vitality to 'a myth and a fiction'. 'It was never intended that the company to be constituted should consist of one substantial persona and six mere dummies, the nominees of that person, without any real interest in the company.' The case was finally appealed to the House of Lords, which unanimously took a very different view. Lord Halsbury reprimanded the lower court judges for not allowing in their own minds:

> the proposition that the company has a real existence. They have been struck by what they have considered the inexpediency of permitting one man to be in influence and authority over the whole company, and assuming that such a thing could not have been intended by the legislature they have sought various grounds upon which they might insert into the Act some prohibitions of such a result.

In addition, the House of Lords rejected the notion of a per se agency relationship – that is, the notion that Salomon or any other promoter, director or shareholder of a company could be liable for its debts simply because of the relationships within the company. The court also addressed the position of the creditors of the company, both secured (debenture holders in this case) and unsecured creditors. Lord MacNaghten observed that the creditors had 'only themselves to blame' as they knew they were dealing with a limited liability company and were no longer dealing with an individual, while observing that 'each creditor is entitled to get and to hold whatever security he can get'.

84. Since that time, the courts in Ireland have been careful to ensure that the doctrine of corporate personality serves its primary function – that is, to support limited liability – and will not in general support any invasion into the personal assets or even identity of anyone involved in a business run through the vehicle of a company. In other words, the veil between the company and the individuals behind the company and its business will not be removed to impose liability on those individuals in normal circumstances. 'Normal circumstances' as a rule of thumb involves everything short of fraud. There is nevertheless a relatively narrow category of exceptional circumstances in which the courts will lift the corporate veil or set aside the doctrine of corporate personality to establish circumstances surrounding certain activities or transactions. In fact, the exceptions were adumbrated by the House of Lords in *Salomon* and include fraud and avoidance of a legal duty by creating a corporate entity which is a 'sham', 'device', 'myth', or 'fiction'. Agency is a further possible exception,[155] but this was not argued successfully in *Salomon*, where it was clarified that no per se agency existed. There are also some statutory exceptions in which the courts disregard the corporate personality to identify directors and others who may then be liable for debts of the company. Primarily these exceptions arise in relation to fraudulent and reckless trading under Irish law. In Irish law (as in the law of New Zealand, but not significantly in English law), there is also a statutory exception for the imposition of liability for debts in relation to groups. See *infra*.

85. The exceptions to the doctrine of corporate personality are described very clearly in the judgment of the High Court (affirmed in the Supreme Court) in *Fyffes PLC v. DCC PLC and Ors.*[156] These are briefly outlined below.

86. The courts may lift the veil when incorporation is being used to avoid a legal duty *Gilford Motor Co. Ltd v. Horne*,[157] the defendant had agreed to a restraint of trade clause in his original contract of employment with the plaintiffs but on leaving his employment set up a company, J. M. Horne Ltd, in which his wife and son were shareholders but he had no formal involvement. Nevertheless, customers and employees identified him as being in charge of the business. The company ran a business that competed directly with the plaintiff, and it was argued that the Court should disregard the separate corporate entity to establish that the defendant had used a corporate entity to facilitate the breach of the restraint of trade covenant. The Court acceded to this request. In contrast, however, in the Irish case of *Roundabout Ltd v. Beirne*,[158] it was held that the plaintiff here had employed a legitimate legal subterfuge by incorporating and arranging to have the lease of the pub. The Roundabout transferred to the corporation with a view to avoiding the consequences of trade dispute that had been protected under the 1906 Trade Disputes Act. As Dixon J. stated, the use of the corporate form in this case was 'a subterfuge' but a legitimate one, wherein the second company is a legal entity distinct from the first company, the original owner, despite the fact that the same individuals were involved in both entities. The distinction between the two cases is clear: In the first the

155. Once an agency relationship is established, this does not in fact form a real exception to the doctrine.
156. [2005] IEHC 477. Appealed, but not on this issue to the Supreme Court, *Fyffes plc v. DCC plc and Ors.* [2007] IESC 36.
157. [1933] Ch. 935.
158. [1933] IR 425.

defendant was using the corporate entity as a myth or fiction or sham to avoid legal obligations, whereas in the latter case there is no legal obligation to continue a particular relationship with undesirable consequences.

87. Also adumbrated in the judgments in *Salomon* were the issues surrounding agency. In the House of Lords, it was held that there was no per se agency between an individual shareholder and his or her company by virtue of that relationship alone. Similarly, where there is a parent/subsidiary relationship or related company structure, there is no per se agency relationship. As in *Salomon* itself, this is particularly important regarding attempts to impose liability as between any of these parties or to identify the acts of the company as being the acts of any of the individuals. Therefore, if an agency relationship is to be established, this must be done in accordance with the ordinary rules of agency law. This question will be revisited in relation to groups of companies (see §6, *infra*).

88. In the *Fyffes* litigation[159] the court held that certain companies could be regarded as a single economic entity 'for the purpose of preventing the avoidance of the availability of an effective remedy under s. 109 (Companies Act 1990) and thus preventing an injustice to parties with a remedy under s. 109 if DCC is liable to account.' This could only occur, however, if:

(a) An evidential basis exists for finding that, as regards the holding and disposal of the shares, to borrow the terminology used by Murphy J in *Lac Minerals Ltd v. Chevron Mineral,*[160] there was a factual identification of the acts of Lotus Green and DCC.
(b) Not to so treat the companies would allow the DCC Group to evade its obligations under 'Part V. of 1990 Act' (now re-enacted in the 2014 Act).

89. There have been some very strong decisions in recent times from the courts regarding the use of corporate personality by individuals who then seek to avoid the effect of the doctrine for their own ends. In *Prest v. Petrodale,*[161] a wife sought ownership following a divorce settlement of certain properties owned by companies controlled indirectly by her husband. It must be emphasized that the husband was not a shareholder or director of these companies. It was argued that the corporate personality of this corporate group, PRL should be disregarded to establish the husband was the true owner of the properties and these should be transferred to the benefit of the wife. The decision of the House of Lords in *Prest v. Petrodale* provides a summary of the law in England regarding the strength of the doctrine of corporate personality with interesting results. The wife's claim to have the corporate veil disregarded failed. In the end the companies were held to hold part of the properties on resulting trust for the wife.

159. *Supra.*
160. [1995] 1 ILRM 161.
161. [2013] UKSC 2013.

90. Similarly, in the Irish case of *O'Donnell and Ors v. Bank of Ireland &Ors.*,[162] we find a complicated structure for the ownership of Gorse Hill, a family home occupied by the appellants in this Supreme Court case, who were the children of Brian and Dr Mary Pat O'Donnell. Gorse Hill was owned by a company called Vico Ltd. which had defaulted on a range of obligations to Bank of Ireland concerning loans made to Mr and Dr O'Donnell to the tune of EUR 14 million. Here it was claimed that the appellants were the true owners of the property with a view to evading action of the bank to enforce loans made to the company. These arguments were considered and rejected by the Supreme Court which referred to the decision of the UK Supreme Court in *Prest v. Petrodale*.

B. Attribution of Human Characteristics

91. One of the most interesting aspects of separate corporate personality doctrine is the way the law relates the corporate form to certain concepts traditionally associates only with natural persons, such as domicile and residency status, criminal intent, and human rights. This is particularly significant in relation to tax, where the concepts of domicile and residence of corporations are important. Furthermore, attempts to attribute the human characteristic of criminal intent to corporations has become of interest in recent times.

92. By analogy with a natural person, the attributes of nationality, domicile and residence can be given to a company. A company is domiciled in, and a national of, the State in which it has its registered office.[163] Under Irish law, the place of a company's registered office must at all times be within the State. Therefore, a company registered in Ireland is of Irish nationality[164] and domicile. Incorporation is, as a general rule subject to statutory exceptions, sufficient to deem a company to be resident in Ireland. In the event that a statutory exception applies, the Court, in ascertaining a company's residence, inquires as to where its 'central management and control' is located.[165] Thus, in some cases the Court will look behind the corporate personality to establish where the company 'keeps house and does business',[166] where such questions might be pertinent to identifying the actual residence of a company for tax purposes. Another tax concept, domicile, is usually determined by the corporation's place of registration. In *De Beers* it was successfully established that the company was ordinarily resident in the UK, illustrating that it is possible

162. [2014] IESC 77.

163. *Janson v. Dreifontein Mines Ltd* [1902] AC 484; *Gasque v. Commissioners of Inland Revenue* [1940] 2 KB 80.

164. *Janson v. Dreifontein Mines Ltd* [1902] AC 484, 497 ('My Lords, I assume that the corporation, which was plaintiff in the action and is now respondent here, was to all intents and purposes in the position of a natural-born subject of the late South African Republic. I do not think it can be entitled to any exceptional favour or to any peculiar indulgence by reason of the fact, if it be a fact, that the bulk of its shareholders were of European nationality. If all its members had been subjects of the British Crown, the corporation itself would have been none the less a foreign corporation and none the less in regard to this country an alien.' *Per* Lord Macnaghten).

165. This test derives from the old case of *De Beers Consolidated Mines Ltd v. Howe* [1906] AC 455.

166. *De Beers Consolidated Mines Ltd v. Howe* [1906] AC 455, 458 per Lord Loreburn LC.

for a company to be ordinarily resident in a jurisdiction distinct from its place of registration, in this case South Africa. While acknowledging that a company could not eat or sleep, *De Beers* held that the question of where a company 'keeps house and does business' was 'a pure question of fact to be determined, not according to the construction of this or that regulation or by-law, but upon a scrutiny of the course of business and trading'.[167] In the more recent case of *Re Little Olympian Each Ways Ltd (No. 2)*,[168] Lindsay J. analysed the prior case law and summarized the factors that the Court will take into account as follows: (i) the congruence between the facts of management and the articles' requirements as to location of management; (ii) the company's objects; (iii) the place of incorporation; (iv) where the real trade and business of the company is carried on; (v) where the company's administrative work is carried out; (vi) where directors' meetings are held; and (vii) where the chief office of the company is physically located.

93. It is clear that companies in Ireland are subject to the criminal law. This is so at common law,[169] and recently the Oireachtas has mandated that, as a matter of statutory interpretation, the word 'person' is to be read as including bodies corporate and unincorporated associations.[170]

94. A necessary pre-condition of criminal liability is a mental element, whether that be intentional, reckless or grossly negligent conduct. With the exception of what are described as strict liability offences, *mens rea* must coincide with *actus reus*. A good starting point is the English case of *Tesco Supermarkets Ltd v. Nattrass*,[171] which arose from the prosecution of a supermarket chain for the offence of selling goods above the advertised retail price, a statutory offence requiring intent. It was held that, apart from the recklessness of the branch manager, all other individuals within the company had been blameless regarding compliance with the Act and had ensured a system of supervision that would avoid such offences in most cases. Lord Reid cited the following passage from an earlier judgment of Denning L.J.:

> A company may in many ways be likened to a human body. It has a brain and nerve centre which controls what it does. It also has hands which hold the tools and act in accordance with directions from the centre. Some of the people in the company are mere servants and agents who are nothing more than hands to

167. *De Beers Consolidated Mines Ltd v. Howe* [1906] AC 455, 458 per Lord Loreburn LC; see also *Unit Construction Co. Ltd v. Bullock* [1959] 3 All ER 831, 835–836.
168. *Re Little Olympian Each Ways Ltd* (No. 2) [1995] 1 BCLC 48; see in particular 56–57.
169. *D.P.P. v. Mutual Enterprises Ltd* (unreported, High Court, 29 Nov. 1985); *D.P.P. v. Trident Homes Ltd* (*The Irish Times*, 19 Jul. 1997); *People (D.P.P.) v. Roseberry Construction Ltd* (Court of Criminal Appeal, Hardiman J.; 6 Feb. 2003); *D.P.P. v. Kent and Sussex Contractors Ltd* [1944] KB 146; *Moore v. Bressler* [1944] 2 All ER 515; *Tesco Supermarkets Ltd v. Nattrass* [1972] AC 153; *Meridian Global Funds Management Asia* [1995] 2 AC 500; *R v. Rozeik* [1996] 1 BCLC 380; *Attorney General's Reference 2/1999 under Section 36 of the Criminal Justice Act 1972* [2000] QB 796.
170. Interpretation Act 2005, s. 18(c).
171. *Tesco Supermarkets Ltd v. Nattrass* [1972] AC 153.

> do the work and cannot be said to represent the mind or will. Others are directors and managers who represent the directing mind and will of the company, and control what it does. The state of mind of these managers is the state of mind of the company and is treated by the law as such.[172]

Lord Reid held that this was a correct statement of the law, and added that: 'Normally the Board of Directors, the managing director and perhaps other superior officers of a company carry out functions of management and speak and act as the company. Their subordinates do not.'[173] Lord Reid went on to say, however, that a Board of Directors may delegate management functions and empower delegates to act independently of instructions from them, so that 'within the scope of the delegation he can act as the company'.[174]

95. The case of *R v. P and O Ferries (Dover) Ltd*[175] illustrates the difficulties inherent in this approach. Following the capsizing of The Herald of Free Enterprise, attempts to prosecute the corporation that ran the ferry collapsed because of a failure to identify someone representing the company who had the necessary criminal intent. Following an official inquiry into the tragedy, from which a report had issued, the apportionment of blame was equivocal although the report noted that the corporation was 'infected with the disease of sloppiness' and that the underlying fault for these actions lay 'higher up in the company'. At the subsequent criminal trial for corporate manslaughter, the evidence indicated that the assistant bosun and chief officer had been careless in the execution of their duties, but Turner J. held that there was 'no direct evidence that a reasonably prudent person occupying the positions of any of the five senior defendants would have perceived the risk was obvious or serious'. The risk entailed setting sail with the ferry doors open, which in turn caused the ferry to capsize and resulted in the deaths of 192 people. Similar failures of prosecution followed the Hillsborough football stadium disaster, and more recently, more than fifteen years afterward, similar issues arose in relation to the Hatfield train crash. In that case although Network Rail was convicted of safety breaches (as the successor organization to Railtrack, which had been responsible for the railway infrastructure at the time of the crash in October 2000), five executives were cleared of responsibility. These executives had originally been charged with manslaughter but the Court dismissed these charges during the trial. Similar charges against the company had not been brought to trial. These issues have been the focus of a Law Reform Commission Report in Ireland,[176] but as yet we have no statute on corporate manslaughter, unlike the UK, which has recently passed legislation in this area.[177]

---

172. *Ibid.*, 171 (quoting *H. L. Bolton Engineering Co. Ltd v. T. J. Graham & Sons Ltd* [1957] 1 QB 159, 172). This 'directing mind and will' test was accepted by the Irish Supreme Court in the context of an allegation of insurance fraud in *Superwood Holdings PLC v. Sun Alliance & London Alliance PLC* [1995] 3 IR 30. See also the discussion of J. McCarthy as regards the tort of conspiracy in *Taylor v. Smith* [1991] 1 IR 142, 166.
173. *Ibid.*, 171.
174. *Ibid.*
175. *R v. P and O Ferries (Dover) Ltd* (1990) 93 Cr. App. Rep. 72.
176. Law Reform Commission, Report on Corporate Killing (LRC 77-2005) (October 2005).
177. Cf. Corporate Manslaughter and Corporate Homicide Act 2007 (UK).

96. The fact that a company suffered loss as a result of the crime is not a bar to it being convicted of that offence.[178] Persons in positions of control within the company may be convicted of conspiring with the company[179] or of aiding and abetting it to commit a crime.[180]

97. Ireland has a written Constitution, unlike the UK jurisdictions, and so a further important question arises in relation to whether corporations are entitled to the protection of constitutionally guaranteed rights protected under the Irish Constitution or rights that may be protected by human rights treaties or conventions, such as the European Convention of Human Rights, which has been incorporated into Irish law.[181]

98. In the United States, where constitutional jurisprudence has been developed for over a century, corporations early on sought protection from the Fourteenth Amendment, which had been enacted following the Civil War to provide equal protection of the law for African Americans and now other minorities. However, corporations were not slow to assert the same protection, and this has been successfully obtained from the United States Supreme Court. In contrast, the Irish courts have been much more conservative on this question. In *Quinn's Supermarket v. Attorney General*[182] the Supreme Court considered a challenge to the provisions of a Ministerial Order that exempted the proprietors of Kosher shops from a ban on evening opening. Kenny J. offered the following interpretation of the human personality phrase as a justification for his rejection of the plaintiff's claim:

> This guarantee, however, is one of equality before the law in so far as the characteristics inherent in the idea of human personality are involved: it does not relate to trading activities or to the hours during which persons may carry on business for neither of these is connected with the essentials of the concept of human personality.[183]

Walsh J. likewise held that the Article 40.1 'refers to human persons for what they are in themselves rather than to any lawful activities, trades or pursuits which they may engage in or follow'.[184] Thus, the guarantee applies only to discrimination relating to some inherent aspect of the 'human person', such as ethnic, racial, social or religious background[185] – that is, persons' 'essential attributes as persons, those features which make them human beings'.[186]

---

178. *Moore v. Bressler* [1944] 2 All ER 515.
179. *Taylor v. Smith* [1991] 1 IR 142 (involving the tort of conspiracy, not a criminal charge).
180. *McMahon v. Murtagh Properties* [1982] ILRM 342.
181. This question has received thorough and comprehensive treatment by Dr Ailbhe O'Neill in her work *The Constitutional Rights of Companies* (Thomson Round Hall 2007).
182. *Quinn's Supermarket v. Attorney General* [1972] IR 1.
183. *Ibid*., 31.
184. *Ibid*., 13–14.
185. *Ibid*.
186. *Murtagh Properties v. Cleary* [1972] IR 1, 335. O'Neill, *Constitutional Rights*, n. 147, 259–260, expresses the view that although it has not done so explicitly, the Supreme Court appears to have

99. In the EU context, Article 43 of the EC Treaty, which prohibits discrimination on the basis of nationality in the context of freedom of establishment, applies to legal persons as well as to natural persons.[187] It also bears noting that the European Court of Human Rights has accepted that Article 14 of the European Convention on Human Rights may be invoked by companies.[188]

100. Similarly, the Irish courts have held that property rights guaranteed under Articles 40.3 and 43.1 of the Constitution of Ireland 'cannot be construed as conferring a constitutional right on a corporate body'.[189] Thus, for example, in *Chestvale Properties Ltd v. Glackin*,[190] in which sections of Part II of the 1990 Companies Act were challenged on constitutional grounds relating to property rights, Murphy J. held that 'the absence of an individual Irish citizen asserting his own constitutional rights is fatal to the argument based on the constitutionality of the 1990 legislation'. A discordant note was struck in *Iarnrod Éireann v. Ireland*, where Keane J. expressed the view that, notwithstanding the language of Articles 40.3 and 43.1, 'artificial legal entities must also be protected by the laws of the State against unjust attacks on their property rights'.[191] There is a lack of clarity around two distinct questions that have not been fully teased out in case law, namely: Is it open to an individual member or shareholder to assert a threat to (or violation of) his or her constitutionally protected rights arising from damage to the corporation? And if so, can a further distinction be maintained between the individual's property rights as a shareholder and the corporation's property rights? The second question, in effect, asks whether, if the corporation does not enjoy the constitutional protection of property rights, would the joining of an individual member or shareholder to the potential corporate claim regarding its constitutional rights resolve the issue? This concept is questionable for reasons springing from the fundamental concept of corporate personality and, in particular, the consequences of what would effectively be the identification of an individual shareholder's interests with those of the company.[192]

101. In Ireland Article 40.6(1)(i) of the Constitution, provides that the State 'guarantees liberty for the exercise, subject to public order and morality, of … The right of the citizens to freely express their convictions and opinions'. It goes on to say:

---

edged somewhat away from this approach, while the High Court appears not to have always strictly applied the above quotations to their logical conclusion.

187. Case C-140/03, *Commission v. Hellenic Republic*, Opinion of Advocate-General Ruiz-Jarabo Colomer delivered on 7 Dec. 2004 at para. 5.

188. *Pine Valley Developments Ltd v. Ireland* (1992) 14 EHRR 319; *National & Provincial Building Society v. UK* (1997) 25 EHRR 127.

189. *Private Motorists' Provident Society v. Attorney General* [1983] IR 339, 349.

190. *Chestvale Properties Ltd v. Glackin* [1993] 3 IR 35, 45.

191. *Iarnród Éireann v. Ireland* [1996] 3 IR 321, 345–346.

192. See *Kerry Co-operative Creameries Ltd v. An Bord Bainne* [1990] ILRM 664; *O'Neill v. Ryan* [1993] ILRM 664; O'Neill, *The Constitutional Rights of Companies* 135 (Thomson Round Hall 2007).

> The education of public opinion being, however, a matter of such grave import to the common good, the State shall endeavour to ensure that the organs of public opinion, … while preserving their rightful liberty of expression, including criticism of Government policy, shall not be used to undermine public order or morality or the authority of the State.

In *Attorney General for England and Wales v. Brandon Books Publishers Ltd*,[193] Carroll J. held that the company had a constitutionally protected right of free expression under Article 40.6(1)(i) to publish information. Recently, the European Court of Human Rights has held in relation to a competition matter that a company is entitled to certain rights under the European Convention on Human Rights.[194] On this issue, the US approach[195] is the most conceptually clear, but whether it is the most doctrinally desirable is another matter.

C. *Corporate Personality: Statutory Exceptions*

102. In addition to the judicially developed exceptions to the doctrine of corporate personality, some statutory provisions allow the fact of incorporation to be ignored with a view to identifying directors and others who may, because of their actions, incur liability for the debts of the company. The provisions are both an exception to the doctrine of corporate personality and a removal of limited liability.

1. Fraudulent and Reckless Trading

103. Under the fraudulent and reckless trading provisions in the Irish Companies Acts 1963–2006, the courts have discretion to impose personal liability in certain circumstances. This imposing liability for fraudulent or reckless trading has been re-enacted in section 610 of the Companies Act 2014. The criminal offence of fraudulent trading, that is, where 'any person was knowingly part to the carrying on of any business of the company with intent to defraud creditors of the company, or creditors of any other person or for any fraudulent purpose' has also been re-enacted in section 722 of the Companies Act 2014 The section applies to directors and others, including shadow directors, and even to outside parties – in effect, anyone who is party to carrying on the business of the company as described above.

104. Judicial interpretation of the 1963 Act, the later enactment of this provision in the 1990 Companies Act, and the similar English provisions provide guidance on what amounts to fraudulent trading. It is clear that there must be an intention to

193. *Attorney General for England and Wales v. Brandon Books Publishers Ltd* [1986] IR 597.
194. See, for example, *Societas Colas Est SA v. France* 2002-III 421; (2004) 39 EHRR 17 (holding that the right to respect for one's home under Art. 8 extended to protection of a company's head office against a search conducted without a warrant). See further A. Grear, *Challenging Corporate 'Humanity': Legal Disembodiment, Embodiment and Human Rights*', 7 Hum. Rights L. Rev. 511–543 (2007).
195. See, for example, the discussion of *Nike v. Kasky* 539 US 654.

defraud; the respondent must be knowingly a party to the conduct. As stated by Maugham J. in *Re Patrick and Lyon Ltd,*[196] the provisions require evidence of 'actual dishonesty involving, according to current notions of fair trading among commercial men, real moral blame'.[197] The court can impose personal liability on the respondents for all or any of the debts of the company. In *Re Aluminium Fabricators Ltd,*[198] O'Hanlon J. imposed personal liability following evidence of diversion of company funds for personal use by the directors. In *Re Kelly's Carpetdrome Ltd,*[199] Costello J. imposed personal liability on individuals who were not described as directors of the company. In fact, no formalities whatsoever had been complied with, and there was evidence of destruction of records and other evidence of irregular behaviour. In *Re Hunting Lodges Ltd,*[200] the respondents were respectively a director, a nominal director (spouse) and outsider who transacted with the company and assisted in non-disclosure of full value of assets. All of them were found personally liable to varying degrees by the Court, which exercised its discretion in accordance with its view of the culpability of the individual.[201]

105. Where a criminal charge of fraudulent trading, is prosecuted section 722 of the Companies Act 2014 provides that this is a Category 1 offence. Such offences carry the following penalties under the provisions of the Companies Act 2014, section 871:

(a) on summary conviction, … a class A fine or imprisonment for a term not exceeding 12 months or both, or
(b) on conviction on indictment, … a fine not exceeding €500,000 or imprisonment for a term not exceeding 10 years or both. Despite the fact that this provision for criminal liability has been on the statute books since 1963, there have been very few criminal convictions on charges of fraudulent trading. In the first case,[202] the defendant sought investors for an investment scheme, promising annual returns of up to 20%. The money received was never invested; instead it was put into a bank account. The defendant was imprisoned for four years and disqualified from acting as a director. In the second case,[203] on a plea of guilty a director of a company in liquidation was convicted of fraudulent trading for failing to keep proper books

196. *Re Patrick and Lyon Ltd* [1933] Ch. 786.
197. This statement is considered to be closer to what is required than the behaviour described in earlier statements by the same judge in *Re William C. Leitch* [1932] All ER 71, [1932] All ER 892.
198. *Re Aluminium Fabricators Ltd* [1984] ILRM 399. O'Hanlon J. imposed personal liability following evidence of diversion of company funds for personal use by the directors.
199. *Re Kelly's Carpetdrome Ltd* (unreported, High Court, Costello J., 1 Jul. 1983). See also *Monck Properties Ltd v. Gaynor and Tuffy* (unreported, High Court, O'Hanlon J., 13 Jul. 1984).
200. *Re Hunting Lodges Ltd* [1985] ILRM 75. In contrast see Re PSK Construction Ltd [2009] IEHC 538 where the partner of the main director was treated quite leniently in comparison.
201. See *infra*, Part I, Ch. 1 s. §4 on liability of nominal directors etc., §3.II.
202. *D.P.P. v. Synott* (unreported, Circuit Court, 7 May 1996).
203. *Director of Corporate Enforcement v. Gannon* (Naas District Court, 18 Mar. 2004); see *The Irish Times*, 19 Mar. 2004.

of account and failing to file annual returns; the director received two concurrent sentences of six months, suspended for twelve months, in respect of the charges of fraudulent trading and failing to keep proper books.

106. The reckless trading provisions were introduced in Irish law under section 137 of the 1990 Companies Act inserting a redrafted section 297 into the 1963 Act. This is now repeated in section 610(1)(a) of the Companies Act 2014. The provision was introduced following the UK Cork Committee Report on insolvency, which *inter alia* recommended such a reform in light of the inadequacy of the fraudulent trading provisions. In the UK Insolvency Act of 1986, this is reflected in the imposition of a somewhat similar liability for 'wrongful trading'.[204] Section 610 (1)(a) provides for civil liability only; there is no provision for criminal liability in respect of reckless trading in Irish law. Section 610(3) provides that an officer of a company shall be deemed to have been knowingly a party to the carrying on of any business of the company in a reckless manner if:

(a) he was a party to the carrying on of such business and, having regard to the general knowledge, skill and experience that may reasonably be expected of a person in his position, he ought to have known that his actions or those of the company would cause loss to the creditors of the company, or any of them; or
(b) he was a party to the contracting of a debt by the company and did not honestly believe on reasonable grounds that the company would be able to pay the debt when it fell due for payment as well as all its other debts (taking into account the contingent and prospective liabilities).[205]

107. Section 610(8) provides a defence to reckless trading '[w]here it appears to the Court that the person in respect of whom a declaration has been sought … has acted honestly and responsibly in relation to the conduct of the affairs of the company … the Court may, having regard to all the circumstances of the case … relieve him either wholly or in part, from personal liability on such terms as it may think fit'. This defence, based on subjective notions of honesty, seems to displace the original purpose of the legislation, which was to introduce an objective standard of directorial behaviour.

108. In *Re Hefferon Kearns Ltd.*[206] Lynch J. held the respondents were not liable and observed that a defendant must be shown to have had 'knowledge or imputed knowledge that the defendant's actions or those of the company would cause loss to creditors: it is not sufficient that there might be some worry or uncertainty as to the ability to pay all creditors'. Lynch J. held that he was not satisfied that the defendants did not honestly believe on reasonable grounds that the company would be

204. Insolvency Act 1986, s. 214 (UK).
205. Companies Act 1963, s. 297A(1), as inserted by Companies Act 1990, s. 137.
206. *Re Hefferon Kearns Ltd* [1992] IRLM 51; [1993] 3 IR 191. See generally, I. Lynch Fannon & G. Murphy, *Corporate Insolvency and Rescue* (Bloomsbury Professional 2012) Ch. 10.

able to pay the debt as it fell due. Subsequent decisions have given rise to liability for reckless trading.[207]

2. Other Insolvency-Related Provisions

109. Sections 281–282 of the 2014 Act impose an obligation to keep adequate accounting records. Adequate accounting records are those that are sufficient to: (a) correctly record and explain the transactions of the company, (b) enable, at any time, the assets, liabilities, financial position and profit or loss of the company to be determined with reasonable accuracy, (c) enable the directors to ensure that any financial statements of the company and directors' report which are required under the Act are compliant with the Act and, where applicable, Article 4 of the IAS Regulation and (d) enable those financial statements of the company so prepared to be audited. Section 282 of the 2014 Act addresses in further detail what shall constitute adequate accounting records.

The Court may impose personal liability on officers of the company where there has been a failure to keep proper books and accounts and such failure has '(i) contributed to the company's inability to pay all of its debts, or (ii) resulted in substantial uncertainty as to the assets and liabilities of the company, or (iii) has substantially impeded the orderly winding up of the company'.[208] The Court shall not make such a declaration in respect of a person who it considers took 'all reasonable steps to secure compliance by the company' with the requirement to keep adequate accounting records, or who had reasonable grounds for believing that a competent and reliable person acting under the supervision of a director had been formally allocated responsibility for compliance and was in a position to discharge that duty.[209] It is important to note in this regard that directors have a right to inspect the company's books and records, and this may be enforced by injunction.[210] The courts, in the case of *Re Mantruck Services Ltd, Mehigan v. Duignan*[211] and subsequent decisions, have identified the following elements as essential to an application under to have officers of the company fixed with personal liability for the company's debts:

(1) The company is being wound up.
(2) The company is unable to pay debts.
(3) There is a contravention of the requirement to keep proper books and records (or 'adequate accounting records' under the 2014 Act).
(4) Such contravention has contributed to the company's inability to pay all of its debts or has resulted in substantial uncertainty as to the assets and liabilities of

207. *Re PSK Construction Ltd* [2009] IEHC 538. And for a final twist in relation to the position of spouses as directors the decision of Barrett J in *Re Mint Restaurant Ltd* [2014] IEHC 370. See generally, Thomas B. Courtney, (gen. ed.), N. Cahill, et al., *The Professional's Guide to the Companies Act 2014* (Bloomsbury 2015).
208. Companies Act 2014, s. 609(1).
209. Companies Act 2014, s. 609(8).
210. *Healy v. Healy Homes Ltd* [1973] IR 309.
211. *Re Mantruck Services Ltd; Mehigan v. Duignan* [1997] 1 IR 341.

the company or has substantially impeded the orderly winding up of the company.

(5) The officer (or former officer) of the company knowingly and wilfully authorized or permitted the contravention by the company, or, the 'officer' is a person convicted in relation to a statement concerning the keeping of proper books of account (or adequate accounting records).

(6) The discretion to apportion personal liability to officers must be exercised in a responsible and constitutional manner. Save in exceptional circumstances, liability should not be imposed for contraventions not resulting in loss or for losses reasonably foreseeable as a consequence of the contravention.[212]

110. The final insolvency-type provision that can be described as an exception to the corporate personality doctrine is found under section 612 of 2014 Act, which provides for misfeasance proceedings. The provision applies to promoters, officers, a liquidator, receiver and an examiner. (For an explanation of these terms, see *infra).* Potential applicants include a liquidator, creditor or contributory of a company. The Court can order restoration or contribution of funds as it thinks just. Costello J. held in the *Mount Clare Hotel* case that liability for misfeasance requires a showing of 'something more than mere carelessness', rising instead to 'gross negligence'.[213]

111. Section 567 of the 2014 Act provides that a number of provisions of the 2014 Act, including sections 281, 282, 286, 599, 609, 610, 611 and 612, may be invoked where the company is insolvent but not wound up. However, it must be shown that the reason or the principal reason for its not being wound up is the insufficiency of its assets.

D. *Corporate Personality: Groups*

1. Introduction

112. In relation to groups of companies the doctrine of corporate personality usually underlines the separate and distinct nature of each company within a corporate group. However, in Ireland, as in England a line of jurisprudence has been developed that has recognized some judicially created exceptions to this doctrine. This line of case law, together with the statutory provisions referred to *infra* will be considered further in the section on Holding Companies and Subsidiaries (see Part I, Chapter 1, §7).

---

212. *Ibid.*, 356–357. The sixth proposition listed is taken from the judgment of the Supreme Court in *Re Ashclad Ltd (in liquidation)* (unreported, Supreme Court, Keane C.J., *ex tempore*, 21 Jan. 2004). At first instance in that case –*Re Ashclad Ltd* [2000] IEHC 174 (unreported, High Court, Geoghegan J.; 5 Apr. 2000) – Geoghegan J. said he 'broadly accept[ed] the approach – adopted and the principles – applied' by Shanley J. in *Re Mantruck Services Ltd.*

213. *Re Mount Clare Hotel; Jackson v. Mortell* (unreported, High Court, Costello J., 2 Dec. 1986).

2. Pooling and Contribution Orders

113. The final important statutory exception to the doctrine of corporate personality applies under sections 599 and 600 of the 2014 Act to the group situation. This legislation does not have an equivalent under English company law and is in fact similar to legislation in force in New Zealand.[214] These provisions are discussed further in relation to groups (see *infra*, Part I, Chapter 1, §7).

3. Conclusion

114. In conclusion of this part, two observations are apt. First, as we consider these cases, it is important to bear in mind that they are representative of a class of exceptional cases; some arise in common law and some arise because of particular provisions of statutes, but all are exceptions to the general position in company law as enunciated in *Salomon*. As Davies observes, the list of these cases and instances is now 'impressively long', but he also notes that even though company lawyers (and students) have expended much effort and thought on these exceptions, no general explanation can be found nor indeed is there any clear unifying rule.[215] It is well to remember the orthodox starting point of *Salomon* as we get lost in this particular maze. Secondly, as far as principle is to be maintained, a statement of Richmond P. in the New Zealand case of *Re Securitibank Ltd (No. 2)*[216] is instructive: 'any suggested departure from the doctrine laid down in *Salomon v. A. Salomon and Co. Ltd* should be watched very carefully'.

VII. Pre-incorporation Contracts

115. Because of the artificial nature of a body corporate, a conceptual difficulty arises as to whether a company can be bound by a contract that was entered into on behalf of the company or in relation to the business of that company before the company was formed. It is impossible for a company to enter into a contract before it is formed. The question raised is whether it is possible for a company to subsequently ratify such a contract – that is, a contract entered into on its behalf – once it is incorporated. At common law this was considered to be impossible,[217] but legislation has altered that position. Thus, under the 1963 Act, any contract or transaction 'purporting to be entered into by a company prior to its formation or by any person on behalf of the company prior to its formation may be ratified by the company after its formation … ', and, where such ratification takes place, the company is bound by the contract or transaction as if the company had been in existence on

214. See *Lewis Holdings Limited & Others v. Steel and Tube Holdings Limited* [2014] NZHC 3311.

215. P.L. Davies, *Introduction to Company Law: Clarendon Law Series* (Oxford University Press 2002), ch. 3.

216. *Re Securitibank Ltd* (No. 2) [1978] 2 NZLR 136, 159.

217. *Natal Land Co. v. Pauline Syndicate* [1904] AC 120 (P.C.) (holding that instead a new contract had to be entered into on the terms of the old one, after the company is incorporated).

the date of the contract or transaction.[218] Absent such ratification, however, 'the person or persons who purported to act in the name or on behalf of the company shall in the absence of express agreement to the contrary be personally bound by the contract or other transaction and entitled to the benefit thereof'.[219] Thus, where contracts are being concluded between a company that has yet to be formed and, for example, a promoter of that company or indeed conversely by the promoter on behalf of the company with other parties, it is important to address this question of potential personal liability or the possibility of excluding such liability.

VIII. Promoters

116. In Irish company law, the term 'promoter' refers to an individual who forms and establishes a company and its business. In the PLC context, a promoter may well be someone who has been involved with the business of the company while it operated as a private company or may become involved in re-forming the company as a PLC with a view to bringing the company to the market. A promoter may also be the person who establishes a company in to which he or she transfers a business hitherto conducted on a sole trader basis. In common law a promoter was defined as 'one who undertakes to form a company with reference to a given project and to set it going and who takes the necessary steps to accomplish that purpose'.[220]

117. As a promoter an individual owes a range of duties that can be divided into two broad categories: first, the duty which he or she owes to the company as fiduciary and, second, the duties which he or she may owe to investors on foot of prospectuses, where this arises. However, as we shall see, such obligations in relation to prospectuses are obviously not confined to promoters alone. In relation to the first category of duties, the promoter is identified as occupying a position of trust not dissimilar to that occupied by company directors. In this capacity the promoter is fixed with a similar range of fiduciary obligations which the law attaches to directors and others who occupy similar positions of trust. These duties will be considered in considerable detail in the sections on directors,[221] but in essence fiduciaries are prohibited from placing themselves in a position where their interests conflict with those of the company. They are prohibited from making undisclosed profits at the expense of their companies and must disclose any profits they make by virtue of their positions of trust. As Sealy and Worthington note, 'The principles of fiduciary obligations are rules applied by the courts of equity to impose high standards of selfless conduct upon trustees and others, such as agents and solicitors, who undertake responsibility to look after their interests or handle the property of others. Company promoters and company directors are subject to these rules.'[222]

---

218. Companies Act 2014, s. 45(1)-(2) This provision only applies to companies incorporated in Ireland after 1 Apr. 1964: cf. s. 37(3).
219. Companies Act 2014, s. 45(3).
220. *Twycross v. Grant* (1877) 2 CPD 469.
221. See *infra*, paras 223–241.
222. L.S. Sealy & S. Worthington, *Cases and Materials on Company Law* 82 (10th edn., Oxford University Press 2014).

118. Older cases involving a promoter who seeks to sell an asset, whether worthless or not, to a newly formed company, with the money for the transaction being raised from a public flotation of the company's shares include *Re Darby*,[223] a case of outright fraud, and *Gluckstein v. Barnes*,[224] where the full benefit of a transaction accruing to the promoters was not disclosed. In both cases, the promoters were held to have breached their fiduciary duties to the company. Nowadays, cases of a two-stage transaction, in which an asset is sold to the company and the money to pay for it is raised from an unsuspecting investing public (as occurred in *Gluckstein* and *Re Darby*), are less likely to occur as the second stage of the transaction, the raising of money from the investing public through the issue of a prospectus, is now heavily regulated. Nevertheless, the first stage of the transaction, the selling of an asset either at an overvalue or without full disclosure of the promoter's interest is still governed by fiduciary principles. These cases are rare, but an Irish case illustrating the operation of these principles is the decision of the High Court in *Hopkins v. Shannon Transport Systems Ltd.*[225] Thus, although aspects of the older cases that involve making offers of shares to the public are rendered obsolete by modern-day regulation of the securities market, these principles remain relevant in relation to the obligations imposed on promoters regarding the acquisition and sale of property to their companies, whether these companies are public or private. It bears emphasizing though that, as with the breach of directors' duties, disclosure and ratification by the shareholders may save the promoter from liability. As Phillimore J. stated in *Re Darby*, 'if disclosure had taken place the transaction might have stood'. Some discussion of what amounts to adequate disclosure has arisen in older cases such as *Erlanger v. New Sombrero Co.*[226] and *Lagunas Nitrate Co. v. Lagunas Syndicate*,[227] but perhaps decisions of the courts in relation to disclosure by directors might be more apt as they are generally more recent.

119. In cases regarding transactions between promoters and their companies, there are some modern statutory provisions that regulate these kinds of transactions. (See *infra*, Part I, Chapter 1, §3 regarding the transfer and allotment of shares for a detailed discussion of these provisions.) These provisions – sections 71, 1027, 1028 and 1035 of the 2014 Act – do not specifically relate to the duties of promoters alone, but regulate the kind of transaction often entered into by a promoter when he or she seeks to transfer property into his or her newly formed company. The provisions only apply to PLCs and so would arise on the transfer of property to a newly floated PLC in return for consideration that involves shares or in return for other kinds of consideration. (These provisions would apply to the factual scenarios in the *Gluckstein* and *Darby* cases outlined *supra*.) Nowadays a more difficult problem is presented by the activities of a promoter that might involve the sale of shares in a company to the public, activities of a kind that were central to the frauds perpetrated in the *Darby* and *Gluckstein* cases.

223. *Re Darby* [1911] 1 KB 95.
224. *Gluckstein v. Barnes* [1900] AC 240.
225. *Hopkins v. Shannon Transport Systems Ltd* (unreported, High Court, 10 Jul. 1972).
226. *Erlanger v. New Sombrero Co.* (1878) 3 App Cas. 1218.
227. *Lagunas Nitrate Co. v. Lagunas Syndicate* [1899] 2 Ch. 392.

IX. Prospectuses

120. A prospectus is defined in section 2 of the 2914 Act as:

> a document or documents in such form and containing such information as may be required by or under Irish prospectus law or EU prospectus law (within the meaning of Chapter 1 of Part 23 [of the 2014 Act]), howsoever the document or documents are constituted, but does not include any advertisements in newspapers or journals derived from the foregoing.

A prospectus will be used by a company in an issue of new shares when the company is already quoted on the stock market. A prospectus will also be used in a 'flotation', sometimes now referred to as initial public offerings (IPOs), in which the company is being floated on the market for the first time, having been a private company. A third instance is when a company is 'privatized'– that is, when the shares were largely or entirely state-owned but are now being offered to the public through the stock market. Once a company issues a prospectus involving an offer of shares to the public, there are certain obligations attaching to disclosure of information about the company's affairs to the public. These obligations, described initially in the Companies Act 1963 and later overhauled by Investment Funds, Companies and Miscellaneous Provisions Act 2005 (the '2005 Act'), Part 5 (as amended in further by an Act of the same name in 2006) and the Prospectus Directive (2003/71/EC) Regulations 2005 (S.I. 324 of 2005),[228] are now to be found in Part 23 of the 2014 Act.[229]

121. Section 1349 of the 2014 Act provides that certain persons shall be liable 'to pay compensation to all persons who acquire any securities on the faith of a prospectus for the loss or damage they may have sustained by reason of – (a) any untrue statement included therein; or (b) any omission of information required by EU prospectus law to be contained in the prospectus'. The persons liable for any such misstatements or omissions are:

(i) the issuer who has issued the prospectus or on whose behalf the prospectus has been issued;
(ii) the offeror of securities to which the prospectus relates;
(iii) every person who has sought the admission of the securities to which the prospectus relates to trading on a regulated market;
(iv) the guarantor of the issue of securities to which the prospectus relates;
(v) every person who is a director of the issuer at the time of the issue of the prospectus;

228. Also of note are the Prospectus Rules made by the Central Bank and Financial Services Regulatory Authority of Ireland, www.ifsra.ie. This overhaul was in response to, and necessitated by, developments at the European level: Directive 2003/71/EC of the European Parliament and of the Council; and Commission Regulation (EC) No. 809/2004 (29 Apr. 2004).

229. Also of note are the Prospectus Rules, issued by the Irish Financial Services Regulatory Authority (IFSRA), as it was then known, under s. 51 of the 2005 Act – see now s. 1363 of the 2014 Act.

(vi) every person who has authorized himself or herself to be named and is named in the prospectus as a director of the issuer or as having agreed to become such a director either immediately or after an interval of time;
(vii) every person who is a promoter of the issuer;
(viii) every person who has authorized the issue of the prospectus (not being the competent authority designated under Irish prospectus law).[230]

Section 1348(6) of the 2014 Act excludes professional advisers (and underwriters and professional advisers to underwriters) from the definition of a 'promoter,' or person authorizing the issue of a prospectus.

122. Defences available focus primarily on a defendant's state of knowledge or position in relation to the information provided in the prospectus. So a defence is available when there is a reasonable belief in the truth of statements in a prospectus under section 1350 of the 2014 Act. A defence is available for a director where consent to be a director is withdrawn. Similarly, a defence is available to any individual who withdraws consent to a prospectus or when a prospectus was issued without a person's knowledge or consent; or without a person's knowledge or consent, a prospectus contained a false statement or omitted required material; or where untrue statements or omissions are based on expert advice and believed to be properly included or omitted.[231] Section 1353 of the 2014 Act requires consent from any expert to statements made in a prospectus purporting to be made by such an expert.[232] Special exceptions apply to a prospectus issued solely in respect of non-equity securities. In all cases, consent must be in writing and not withdrawn before the issue of the prospectus, and a statement to this effect must be in the prospectus.

123. Section 1357 of the 2014 Act provides for criminal liability and sanctions for persons authorizing the issue of a prospectus that includes any untrue statement or omits any information required by EU prospectus law, unless he or she proves (i) as regards an untrue statement, that it was immaterial or he or she honestly believed it to be true, or (ii) as regards any information omitted, that it was immaterial or he or she did not know it, or (iii) that the making of the statement or omission ought reasonably be excused.

§3. Capital and Shares

I. Concepts of Share Capital, Raising of Capital, Flotation of a PLC and Capital Maintenance

A. Introduction

124. Parts 3 and 4 of the consolidated Companies Act 2014 governs matters pertaining to share capital. The structure of the capital provisions in the new Act is the

230. Companies Act 2014, s. 1349.
231. Companies Act 2014, s. 1350.
232. *Ibid.*, s. 43.

same as for other matters, namely that Parts 3 and 4 describe provisions which are applicable to private companies limited by shares and then the Act disapplies certain provisions in relation to each different type of company. Of particular relevance in this part of this work is the Table provided for in section 1002 of the Companies act 2014 which disapplies some of the private company limited by shares provisions to PLCs. The following provisions are disapplied to PLCs:

- section 68 which limits offerings of securities to the public;
- section 69 and section 70 relation to the authorization for allotment of shares;
- the enabling provision relating to reduction of capital in section 84(2)(a);
- the enabling provision regarding variation of capital in section 88 is disapplied;
- the enabling provision regarding capital in reorganizations in section 91(4)(a) is disapplied.

The structure of share capital in most Irish companies continues as described in the following paragraphs. There are some additional exemptions referred to above which do not apply to PLCs. These will be considered in more detail in Part 1, Chapter 11.

B. Ordinary Shares

125. Ordinary shares are the most common kind of share adopted by companies of all different sizes and types. The ordinary share will generally carry the right to a vote, without any particular weighting attached to that vote. In addition, an ordinary shareholder will typically be entitled to participate in any surplus funds on a pro-rated basis, which may be left after all the creditors have been paid. They are thus described as being the residual claimants in a company. Although generally not carrying weighted voting rights, it is common to see ordinary shares in more sophisticated share structures being delineated into different classes of ordinary shares; for example, they may be denominated as Ordinary Shares Class A, Ordinary Shares Class B with rights to vote on the election of B directors or A directors or some such structure.

C. Preference Shares

126. Preference shares carry preferential rights, which generally are financial rights and relate to rights to dividend or capital. Preference shareholders' entitlements to dividends are generally expressed as a right to a percentage per annum of the nominal amount of the share. Such shares may be described as cumulative preference shares so that when the dividend is declared, the shareholder is entitled to a cumulative dividend and may have a preferential entitlement to the payment of this dividend in full before other shareholders are paid dividends. A share that is preferred as to capital entitles the member to have his or her capital investment in the company repaid in full before the ordinary shareholders are returned their capital in a winding up. These rights are largely undetermined by any statutory provisions and are generally described as a matter of contract law.

D. *Redeemable Shares*

127. Redeemable shares are shares the company is entitled to redeem from its members. When shares are redeemed, the company generally cancels them. However, a treasury share is retained on redemption by the company and can subsequently be re-issued.

E. *Bonus Shares*

128. Bonus shares are issued to the shareholders in proportion to their existing shareholdings. They are issued as having been fully paid up – that is, the shareholders are not required to pay for them. They are usually paid from accumulated profits that have been transferred to capital that is capitalized.

II. Capital Movements: Increase, Acquisition and Redemption of Shares, Reduction of Share Capital

A. *Introduction*

129. The following sections II and III on Capital Movements concern the rules relating to both the increase of share capital and the reduction of share capital, including redemption of shares. These provisions also concern obligations imposed on companies concerning the maintenance of capital (generally considered to be for the benefit of creditors in particular). In the new structure provided for in the Companies Act 2014 private companies limited by shares may opt to state the amount of authorized share capital from the outset or may opt not to state that amount, but to state that the share capital of the company shall be divided into shares of a fixed amount as stated in the Constitution section 19(1)(d) (*infra*). Where a company does have a capital structure which will be the case in all PLCs, company capital is now defined in section 64(1) (which is the definition section for this part) to include the following:

(a) the aggregate value, expressed in currency, of the consideration received by a company in respect of the allotment of shares and
(b) that part of the company's 'undenominated' capital constituted by transfer of sums referred to in ss 106 (4) and 108(3).

The definition continues in what has to be the most awkward of drafting approaches, 'subsection (2) supplements this definition'.

This supplemental provision definition includes the following sums:

(i) amounts standing in the share premium account where premiums on previous share sales have been lodged;
(ii) capital redemptions reserve funds; and
(iii) capital conversion reserve funds pre-existing the legislation.

130. The capital maintenance rules discussed below now explicitly refer to the concept of company capital rather than to share capital as in the previous legislation. Thus for example the new provisions regarding reduction of capital contained in section 84 refer to 'company capital' and not share capital as before. The new legislation attempts to clarify the application of these rules to various kinds of capital received as a result of equity sales.

131. Shareholders' rights are exercisable usually when the shareholder is a registered shareholder. This will be considered further in section IV *infra*. As described in paragraph 25 (above) the new Companies Act 2014 creates a different framework from that which had existed hitherto, particularly for private companies. There is no model set of internal regulations (i.e., no Table A) available in the Act. Instead many of the rights and provisions which were contained in Table A are now presented as statutory 'default' provisions which may be disapplied by the company's constitution. Parts 1–14 of the Act concern the governance of the private company limited by shares and Part 17 of the Act deals with the PLC by way of modification or adaptation of these standard provisions. Section 1002 of the Act sets out the table of provisions which are disapplied or modified in relation to the PLC. Section 1006 of the Act provides that the Constitution of a PLC will comprise a Memorandum and Articles of Association (as before); that the Memorandum will contain an objects clause (again as before) and, of relevance here, a statement of the authorized share capital of the company 'which shall not be less than the authorized minimum capital' for PLCs registered in Ireland. Currently, the value of the allotted share capital must not be less than EUR 25,000 but this can be varied by the relevant Minister.[233]

132. The bundle of shareholders' rights will be contained in this Constitution. It is expected that as with current practice whereby a PLC's articles exclude Table A, the new format will involve an exclusion of all the statutory default provisions and that the PLC Constitution will be created on a bespoke basis.[234] That is not to say that the statutory default provisions will not be included in the Constitution of the PLC but that these will be included as a matter of choice. The bundle of shareholders' rights therefore will normally include voting rights, but not necessarily. It should be noted that normally the share indicates that the shareholder has a vote per

233. Companies Act 2014, s. 1000(2).
234. T.B Courtney, *Changes in the Basics, Constitutions, Share Capital and Governance* (Bloomsbury Professional Seminar Series) See also Bloomsbury's Professional Guide to the Companies Act 2014. (Bloomsbury, 2015) Ch. 2.

share, but again shares may have weighted voting rights exercisable in some circumstances or on all occasions. In addition, the shareholder is entitled to dividends[235] once these are declared by the Board of Directors and not vetoed by the shareholders in the general meeting. However, there is no obligation on the directors to declare dividends out of distributable profits if there is a decision that such profits ought to be retained by the company. The entitlement to dividend (created once the dividend is declared) is also determined by the kind of share, whether this is an ordinary share, preference share, cumulative preference share and so on. As previously mentioned, the shareholder is also considered to have residual rights to a pro rata distribution of surplus funds on dissolution if surplus assets are available once the creditors have been paid. However, where a dividend has been declared the shareholders' rights to payment of that dividend is a contractual right whilst the company is solvent, but these claims become deferred claims in insolvency. The shareholders' rights are described in the company's Constitution and are also described in contracts referred to as 'shareholders' agreements', which are entered into in addition to the framework rules provided for in the 'constitution' of the company. All rights so described are subject to the overriding principles of common law and in particular to the principles enshrined in the Companies Acts 2014. These rights can be altered through an alteration of the company's Constitution.[236] In addition, section 1013 allows for the alteration of the provisions of the memorandum of association of a PLC. This section provides that any alteration of the objects which is made in accordance with this section 'shall be as valid as if originally contained therein, and be subject to alteration in like manner.'

B. *Variation in Capital*

133. The starting point regarding the variation of share capital is section 83 of the 2014 Act. The provides that a company may, except to the extent that its constitution provides otherwise, do a number of things regarding its capital structure including consolidation or division of shares, subdividing shares, reducing or increasing nominal value and increasing or cancelling shares. This provision is not disapplied in by Part 17 and so also applies to PLCs. These matters can be effected by ordinary resolution.

---

235. Dividends are declared subject to rules contained in the Companies Act 2014, Part 3, Ch. 7.
236. The Articles of Association of a PLC can be altered in the manner described in the Companies Act 2014 s. 1015:

> –(1) *Subject to the provisions of this Act and to the conditions contained in its memorandum, a PLC may by special resolution alter or add to its articles.*
> (2) *Any alteration or addition so made in the articles shall, subject to the provisions of this Act, be as valid as if originally contained therein, and be subject in like manner to alteration by special resolution.*

C. Increase in Share Capital

134. Section 83(1)(f) provides that a company may increase its share capital by 'new shares of such amount as it thinks expedient'. This can be done by ordinary resolution.[237]

135. Irish PLCs may offer equity securities and debt securities for sale to the public. Under the Companies Act 2014, a new distinction is now made between private companies limited by shares on the one hand (these companies are prohibited from offering any type of security on a public market) and on the other hand, designated activity companies (DACs) – these are private companies limited by shares with designated activities specified in their Constitution. DACs are permitted to list debt securities on a public market. This facility is also available to companies limited by guarantee (CLGs), private unlimited companies (PUCs) and public unlimited companies (PULCs). There is a significant volume of trading on the Irish Stock Exchange of debt securities.[238]

136. In relation to the allotment of existing authorized share capital, the statutory provisions relating to a private company are found in section 69 of the 2014 Act. This provision, however, is disapplied to PLCs under the table in section 1002 and accordingly section 1021 of the Act applies to allotment of shares in a PLC. Section 1021 provides that the allotment of securities must be pursuant to a general authority granted by ordinary resolution or the constitution of the company and further provides that this authority will provide for a maximum number of securities which can be allotted and that the authority must be specified for a time not exceeding five years. Initially, the allotment can only be within the authorized share capital provisions.[239] The decision to allot shares will be made by the Board of Directors on the basis of a general authority as described. The authority to allot may be limited to a period which is renewable under section 1021(4)(3).

137. Where allotments of authorized share capital are made, statutory pre-emption rights will apply. This is the right which shareholders have to be offered new shares on a pro rata basis, relative to their existing holding when the company engages in a new issue and allotment of shares. Pre-emption rights are now enshrined in legislation as a default rule in section 1022 for PLCs and in section 69(6) for private limited companies subject to certain instances in which they do not apply in PLCs. This will include the normal rule allowing directors who have a general power to allot shares following a special resolution under section 1021 of the Act to disregard pre-emption rights as provided for in section 1023(3).

---

237. Section 83(1).
238. The Irish Stock Exchange describes itself as the 'leading European debt listing venue'.
239. Companies Act 2014, s. 1021(2).

138. Litigation on this issue regarding the abolition or abrogation of pre-emption rights is still relevant. In the second hearing in *Greenhalgh*,[240] the plaintiff sought to set aside a special resolution rejecting the pre-emption rights of the shareholders prior to the sale of a controlling interest to an outsider. The plaintiff's argument was that the shareholders, in voting for the removal of preemption rights, had not acted 'bona fide for the benefit of the company as a whole'. The Court held that on any particular vote, a shareholder must proceed on the basis of what he honestly believes is for the benefit of the company as a whole and that the latter phrase ordinarily does not mean the company as a commercial entity as distinct from its corporators, but rather the corporators as a general body. The Court was satisfied that the resolution in this case had been passed bona fide. This reasoning would apply to the abrogation of pre-emption rights on a sale or allotment.

139. When different classes of shares are created and offered, further rules apply in relation to the protection of those existing shareholders. Shareholders must consent *by class* to the alteration of the Articles of Association, now the constitution of the company. Established case law provides a narrower interpretation of when shareholders' rights are altered than one might first imagine. Thus, in the English case of *Greenhalgh v. Arderne Cinemas*,[241] (a second hearing in the case is referred to in the preceding paragraph) the plaintiff held 40% of the pre-existing class of two shilling shares and argued that the proposed split by the company of each ten shilling share (hitherto in a separate class) into five two shilling (2s) shares was an alteration of his rights, thus requiring consent of the class of two shilling shares (which he would have been in a position to withhold, given his percentage). The court held that despite the effective swamping of the plaintiff's existing holding of 40% of the two shilling shares, there was no variation of his rights per se. The plaintiff's rights had not been varied, only the context in which they were exercised.

III. Capital Movements: Capital Maintenance

140. Irish company law contains a number of rules regarding the maintenance of capital. The sources of these rules are varied: some derive from principles originally set out in case law, some of which have been codified in statute, while others derive from more modern statutory provisions (including in particular, the enactment of EU Directives). In all cases, the statutory provisions are subject to judicial interpretation. The theoretical rationale for capital maintenance rules is primarily to protect creditors from dilution of the capital fund and to secure the integrity of the capital value of the company for all. This is particularly important in the context of creditors' remedies. The minimum capital requirement for a PLC in Ireland is currently set at EUR 25,000.[242] of which a quarter must be paid up before the

240. *Greenhalgh v. Arderne Cinemas Ltd.* [1951] Ch. 286. Note that the series of actions pre-date the introduction of the equivalent of a right of a shareholder to sue for oppression which is now part of English company law. Section 459 Companies Act 1985 and its re-enactment in s. 994 of the Companies Act 2006).

241. *Greenhalgh v. Arderne Cinemas* (No. 1) [1946] 1 All ER 512.

242. Section 1000(2).

company commences business, and this must be stated in the memorandum as part of the constitution of the company but in Ireland, as with the UK, there is no minimum capital requirement for private companies or indeed no requirement at all for a private limited company to state an authorized share capital under section 19 of the 2014 Act. Generally, these rules are driven by provisions of EC Directives.[243] Nevertheless, statutory provisions will apply even in this case or even where there are few creditors or shareholders.[244] Thus, in private companies the rules are relevant even in companies with little or no issued capital. (See further, Part I Chapter 2) The capital maintenance rules generally have the following aims:

- Ensuring value is maintained in the company by ensuring that the company receives value for its shares. This objective is served by provisions such as those prohibiting the issuing of shares at a discount, provisions regarding the maintenance of the share premium account and provisions regarding the valuation of consideration paid for shares, in particular non-cash consideration.
- Ensuring that a stated capital structure is not changed without the consent or authorization of shareholders and without the knowledge of creditors. Such provisions include provisions regarding redemption or purchase by a company of its own shares and provisions regarding the alteration or reduction of share capital.
- Protecting the company's working capital, which includes provisions regarding the payment of dividends by a company or other kinds of distribution of a company's profits.[245]
- Section 84 of the Companies Act 2014 states that the capital maintenance rules apply to the reduction of 'company capital' (defined above) and not 'share capital' as stated by the provisions of the 1963 Act.

A. *Ensuring Value Is Maintained in the Company by Ensuring That the Company Receives Value for Its Shares*

141. Under the 1983 Act, and now under the Companies Act 2014 considerable improvements were made to the maintenance of the capital fund provisions; in particular, significant clarity was provided in relation to the operation of these provisions. As a rule the relevant provisions in the Companies Act 2014 apply primarily to public companies with exemptions provided for private companies.

1. Issuing of Shares at a Discount

142. The common law rule regarding the prohibition on issuing shares at a discount provided for in the House of Lords decision in *Ooregum Gold Mining*

243. See Ch. 2 on the Private Company and new provisions which provide more flexibility in this context for private limited companies.
244. See generally Keane, *Company Law* (4th edn., Tottel 2007), Ch. 15. See Courtney: The Law of Companies Courtney: Paras [10.001]–[10.010].
245. Part 3, Ch. 7 ss 117ff Companies Act 2014. Courtney: The Law of Companies (Bloomsbury Professional, 2012) paras [8.073]–[8.078] pp. 450–453 and [10.089]–[10.096]. pp. 601–604, 606.

Company of India v. Roper[246] is now provided for in section 71 of the 2014 Act. An exempting provision[247] allows for the payment of a commission of not more than 10% to facilitate the underwriting of an issue of shares, but indications are that this would be strictly interpreted, following English case law. This rule will not prevent the issuing of bonus shares within the terms of Part 3 of the 2014 Act.[248]

2. The Share Premium Account

143. Where shares are issued at a price above the nominal value of the shares, the difference between the nominal or par and the market value is referred to as the 'share premium'. Section 71(5) seeks to protect capital by providing that where a company issues shares at a price in excess of the shares nominal value, whether for cash or otherwise, a sum equal to the value of the excess capital will be included in the definition of the 'company capital' as described above. This is now described as being part of the 'undenominated capital'[249] As stated in the introductory paragraph the 'company capital' will also include amounts standing in the share premium account where premiums on previous share sales have been lodged, and will also include capital redemptions reserve funds and capital conversion reserve funds.[250] This rule regarding the share premium account is subject to some specific provisions contained in sections 72, 73 and 75 regarding mergers, group restructurings and share swaps. So, for example, section 72(2) provides that 'if the equity shares in the issuing company allotted ... in consideration for the acquisition or cancellation of shares in the other company ... (ie a share swap or exchange) ... are issued at a premium s. 71(5) does not apply ... ' to those premiums. section 106(4) and section 108(3) provide for the different treatment of premiums raised during the acquisition or redemption of its own shares by a company.

3. Payment for Shares in Non-cash Consideration

144. As stated most of the Irish provisions on capital maintenance are now derived from EU Directives. Under the 1983 Act the following provisions were enacted pursuant to the Second EC Company Law Directive regarding the issuing

246. [1982] AC 125.
247. Previously contained in the Companies Act 1963, s. 59, this provision is now to be found in the European Communities (Transferable Securities) Stock Exchange Regulations 1992 (S.I. 202 of 1992), with s. 59 having since been repealed by the Investment Funds, Companies and Miscellaneous Provisions Act 2005, s. 40. Parts 3, 4, 5 and 6 of this Act have been repealed by the Companies Act 2014. See Schedule 2, Part 1 which contains a list of statutes which have been repealed. Schedule 2 Part 2 contains a list of statutory instruments which have been repealed but the Stock Exchange Regulations have not been repealed.
248. Section 71(4) Companies Act 2014.
249. Section 71(5) Companies Act 2014 which states that such sums will continue to be paid into a 'share premium account'. Section 64 Companies Act 2014 which provides definitions for Part 3 of the Act dealing with 'Share Capital, Shares and Certain Other Instruments' provides a definition of undenominated capital which does not specifically refer to the share premium account.
250. Companies Act 2014 ss 106(4), 108(3) and s. 64.

or distribution of shares for consideration, in particular for non-cash consideration. The 1983 Act has now been repealed and these provisions have been re-enacted in the Part 3 of the Companies Act 2014. In providing that a share allotment may be paid for in non-cash consideration, section 71(1) recognizes a common law principle of long standing.[251]

145. However, additional prohibitions apply to public limited companies (PLCs) as before, although these are now contained in separate provisions in Part 17 of the Act. Thus, section 1025(1) provides that:

> A PLC shall not accept at any time, in payment up of its shares or any premium on them, an undertaking given by any person that he or she or another should do work or perform services for the company or any other person.

146. Regard should also be had to section 1027 of the 2014 Act, which provides as follows: – (1) A PLC shall not allot shares as fully or partly paid up (as to their nominal value or any premium payable on them) otherwise than in cash if the consideration for the allotment is or includes an undertaking which is to be or may be performed more than five years after the date of the allotment.

147. Sections 1028 and 1029 and sections 1031 and 1033 of the 2014 Act provide certain controls regarding the independent valuation of non-cash consideration in all other cases and these are discussed in the section on Promoters. Effectively these sections are a re-enactment of the 1983 Act which in turn was derived from provisions of EU Directives. Accordingly, the provisions are enacted to take account of any developments since that time. In particular provisions of the Investment Funds, Companies and Miscellaneous Provisions Acts 2005 and 2006.[252]

B. *Ensuring That a Stated Capital Structure Is Not Changed without the Consent or Authorization of Shareholders and without the Knowledge of Creditors Do We Need This?*

1. Acquisition by a Company of Its Own Shares

148. The prohibitions regarding a company acquiring its own shares are now contained in Chapter 6 of Part 3 of the Companies Act 2014. A company cannot acquire its own shares unless the transaction is one of the transactions described therein. The original provision in Irish law (provided for in the 1963 Act) enacted the general prohibition provided for at common law in the House of Lords decision

251. *Re Leinster Contract Corporation* [1902] 1 IR 349; *McCoy v. Greene* (unreported, High Court, Costello J, 19 Jan. 1984).

252. Note that Schedule 2, Part 1 of the 2014 Companies Act states that Parts 3,4,5 and 6 of the Investment Funds, Companies and Miscellaneous Provisions Act of 2005 have been repealed, along with Parts 2 and 3 of the Act of 2006 of the same title.

in *Trevor v. Whitworth,*[253] which held that the acquisition of its own shares by a company was ultra vires and therefore void. The decision also held that this was the case regardless of whether, as in this case, it was authorized by the objects. The authorization was invalid. As Lord Watson observed, creditors and others who deal with a company 'rely upon the fact that the company is dealing with a certain amount of capital already paid up, as well as the responsibility of its members for capital remaining at call; and they are entitled to assume that no part of the capital which has been paid into the coffers of the company has been subsequently paid out, except in the legitimate course of its business'.[254]

149. The development of the legislative rules in this context has now tended towards a liberalization of the rule as traditionally set out in the case law. The liberalization of the general prohibition outlined in *Trevor v. Whitworth* began with the recognition that a limited company could reduce its capital by special resolution, if so authorized by its articles. (Reduction of capital specifically is discussed below). Accordingly, section 102[255] of the 2014 Act states somewhat more positively that: (1) 'Subject to the provisions of this Chapter a company may acquire its own fully paid shares' and goes on to list when this can occur. These include:

(i) transfer or surrender otherwise than for valuable consideration;
(ii) cancellation following reduction of capital;
(iii) as a remedy for oppression under s. 212;
(iv) redemption of shares;
(v) permissible purchase under s. 105;
(vi) redemption of preference shares under s.108 or
(vii) pursuant to a merger or division under Chapters 3 and 4 of Part 9.

The provision goes on to state in subsection (2) that '… a company may not acquire any of its own shares otherwise than as described in the preceding subsection…'. Very importantly this provision also states (although already included above) that 'nothing in that subsection or any other provision of this section affects the lawfulness of a merger effected in accordance with Chapter 3 of Part 9 or a scheme of arrangement sanctioned under that Part.'[256]

150. The shift away from the stringency of the common law approach began in earnest in 1983 where following the Second EU Company Law Directive the range of exemptions from the general rule against a company acquiring its shares expanded to the exemptions which are now included in section 102 of the Companies Act 2014 as described above.

---

253. (1887) 12 App. Cas. 409.
254. *Ibid.*, 423–424.
255. Section 1039 Adaptation of s. 102(1) and (2) in relation to a PLC. 'Section 102(1) and (2) shall apply in relation to a PLC as if references in them to Chapter 3 or 4 of Part 9 were references to *Chapter 16,* or as the case may be, *Chapter 17* of this part.' These Chapters of Part 17 relate to divisions and mergers.
256. See below s. 6 on Reconstructions.

151. Under Irish law further facilitating provisions were enacted in Part XI of the Companies Act 1990 and these facilitating provisions are re-enacted in the Companies Act 2014. Section 102 provides the list of situations where this is permissible. The provisions relevant to capital concern the cancellation of shares following reduction of capital; redemption of shares and the purchase of shares under section 105.

152. Section 105 of the Act provides a power to a company to acquire its shares by purchase. A company may also redeem or purchase its shares which were issued as redeemable shares. The provisions of section 105 relating to funds available to purchase such shares must be complied with. There is also provision for the cancellation of these shares, or alternatively, there is provision for the holding of such shares as 'treasury shares' under section 106 of the Act. In addition to these provisions, supplemental provisions regarding PLCs are provided for in Part 17 Chapter 5. Section 1071 provides 'Additional (general) provisions relating to acquisition by PLCs of own shares.' Section 1072 makes a distinction between 'market' and 'off-market' purchase of shares and the provisions reflect that distinction. Section 1074 provides for the market purchase of its shares by a company, once authorized by the company by ordinary resolution in general meeting. Section 1074(4) outlines the terms of the authorization from the members, which can be quite general in nature, but which must specify the number of shares that can be acquired, the maximum and minimum price to be paid, and the period of the authorization which shall not be longer than five years.[257]

153. Section 1075 mirrors the provisions of section 105 regarding the authorization of 'off-market' purchases of shares, which will obviously be more pertinent to private companies. This requires authorization by the shareholders in a general meeting through a special resolution. A significant feature of these provisions is the notification provisions toward the end of the relevant part of the legislation. Section 112 provides for copies of the contracts regarding either kind of purchase (market or off-market) to be kept at the registered office of the company for a period of ten years and provides that these must be available for inspection by any member or, in the case of a public company, by any member of the public. In the same vein, section 116 provides for returns of such purchases to be made to the Registrar of Companies.

154. These obligations are amplified for PLCs under sections 1079, 1080 and 1081 where the latter section imposes obligations regarding the notification of the 'authorised market operator'. Non-compliance with the provisions attracts criminal liability as specified in the legislation. Failure to notify the Registrar is a Category 3 offence under section 116(3) and failure to notify the market operator is similarly a Category 3 offence under section 1081(4).

---

257. See s. 1074(4)(c). Readers are advised to consult Part 17 Ch. 5, generally, where specific detailed provisions are contained relating to PLC actions in this context.

2. Reduction of Share Capital

155. Although obviously involving a change in the capital structure of the company, provisions regarding the reduction of share capital are usually considered with the body of rules regarding capital maintenance and are discussed below. These matters are addressed in Part 3, Chapter 4 of the 2014 Act. Certain provisions are disapplied in relation to PLCs, as described above in the Introduction to this Section.

156. Section 84 of the 2014 Act deals with the reduction of share capital arising from a simple alteration of capital structure. Section 84(2) provides that such reduction can be effected either by the company:

(a) employing the Summary Approval Procedure; or
(b) passing a special resolution that is confirmed by the court.

157. However, the Summary Approval Procedure (SAP) is disapplied for PLCs. Where PLCs wish to reduce their capital they must use the more formal procedure provided for in section 84(2)(b). Where shareholders in different classes are treated differently, the consent of each class is required, in addition to the approval of the general meeting.[258] As stated in the section above such resolutions must then be confirmed by the Court. In considering an application to approve the reduction of share capital, the Court will consider: whether the reduction is fair and equitable and whether shareholders in the same class are treated similarly. The creditor protection element is strong here, and so the legislation provides that creditors must be notified and may object at the relevant court hearing where the proposed reduction of share capital involves either diminution of liability in respect of unpaid share capital or the payment to any shareholder of any paid-up share capital.[259] In other cases where no payments are being made to shareholders – that is, where the capital structure is being altered to reflect reality – the Court may direct that the provisions just noted as to creditors' entitlements to notification and to object shall not apply as regards any class or classes of creditors.[260]

158. If no such authorization is to be found in the company's articles, a general meeting must pass separate special resolutions providing authorization and approving the specific proposed purchase. Before the Court confirms a reduction of share capital, it must be satisfied that the resolution was passed bona fide and that the reduction is fair, equitable and reasonable as between the shareholders generally and as between any different classes of shareholders. A reduction will be regarded as fair and reasonable when the same order of priorities is followed as would obtain in a winding up. Furthermore, following the order of priorities as would apply on a

258. *Re John Power and Sons Ltd* [1934] IR 412.
259. Companies Act 2014, s. 84. See also Companies Act 2014, s. 83.
260. *Ibid.*

winding up means that the reduction does not constitute a variation of class rights, such as would have to be approved by different classes of shareholders.[261]

C. The Provision of Financial Assistance for the Purchase of Its Own Shares

159. Such transactions are generally prohibited under section 82 of the Companies Act 2014. Again, there is a blanket prohibition for PLCs, but an exemption is provided for private companies where the conditions as set out in the legislation are followed. These provisions have been included in the Summary Approval Procedure (SAP). (See *infra*, Part I, Chapter 2). The blanket prohibition provides that a company cannot give financial assistance for the purchase of its own shares. Prohibited financial assistance includes loans, guarantees from the company to potential purchasers and security from its assets to secure loans entered into between a bank and the purchaser, for example, and any other securitized transactions. These provisions apply to any transaction that displays these characteristics.[262] For a PLC there are some limited exceptions that address specific situations, covering such matters as payment of dividends, discharge of lawfully incurred debts and lending by financial institutions in the ordinary course of business, but generally these transactions are prohibited.[263]

160. The consequences of the section being contravened are severe as the transaction is 'voidable', and thus unenforceable, 'at the instance of the company against any person (whether a party to the transaction or not) who had notice of the facts which constitute [the] breach'.[264] There has been considerable case law in relation to whether the party has notice of the transaction or not, the required notice must be actual and not constructive in any way. However, in more recent case law, such as the decision in *CH (Ireland) Inc. v. Credit Suisse Canada*,[265] the courts have been less sympathetic to parties who failed to appreciate the significance of various pieces of information available in the course of the transaction. As observed by McCracken J. in that case, there was a clear statement of a particular fact that directly informed CSC of the nature of the transaction, namely that the transaction amounted to a breach of company law. In these circumstances, the Court cannot protect parties who may not have appreciated the legal significance of the facts disclosed. (See *infra*, Part I, Chapter 2 for more detail on the 'private company exception' to this prohibition.) In addition, where a company gives financial assistance in breach of section 82, there is a provision for criminal liability whereby 'every officer of the company who is in default' shall be liable to conviction of an offence.

---

261. Companies Act 2014, s. 85(4).
262. *Wallersteiner v. Moir* [1974] 3 All ER 217.
263. Companies Act 2014 s. 82.
264. Companies Act 2014, s. 82.
265. *CH (Ireland) Inc. v. Credit Suisse Canada* [1999] 4 IR 542. See *Quinn and Ors v. Irish Bank Resolution Corporation Ltd. And Anor.* [2012] IEHC 36. Re Cognotec Ltd. [2010] IEHC 309 and *Eccles Hall Ltd. v. Bank of Nova Scotia* (Unreported, High Court, February, 1995, Murphy J.).

161. The difficulty with this provision is that in certain circumstances transactions that might be beneficial to the company will be prohibited, such as management buy-outs where some part of the finance is raised through a securitization of the company's assets, changes in share structure using corporate assets, or corporate restructuring where corporate assets are used by way of security or direct finance to fund the transaction. It is not universally agreed that all of these kinds of transactions will be detrimental to the company over time, and so some argue that a blanket prohibition does not necessarily serve the company or its stakeholders. This argument has been recognized in English law,[266] but there has been no move to make a similar change in Irish law as yet.

D. *Provisions regarding the Protection of the Company's Working Capital*

162. The declaration and payment of dividends is governed by provisions to be found in Chapter 7 of Part 3 of the Companies Act 2014. The legislation provides strict rules for the calculation of distributable profits. Once distributable profits are calculated, the Board of Directors has the discretion to declare a dividend or not. The dividend can then be approved or rejected by the shareholders in GM as per the Articles of Association. The declaration of a dividend is at the discretion of the Directors, who cannot be compelled by the shareholders to do so except in extreme cases, such as in the case of *Re Sam Weller & Sons Ltd.*[267]

IV. Shares and Share Transfer

A. *Transfer of Shares*

163. The free transferability of shares is one of the elements of what has been described as 'the genius of company law', which supports the creation of one of the most flexible forms of business vehicles used today – namely, the limited liability company. In PLCs, the free transferability of shares is axiomatic to the working of capital markets. Chapter 5 of Part 3 of the Companies Act 2014 sets out the law in relation to the transfer of shares for all companies. These provisions codify as statutory defaults, provisions which hitherto would have appeared in the company's Articles of Association. As stated previously, the structure of the Act is such that the main provisions are stated and then disapplied in relation to particular types of companies, in this case PLCs. However, none of the provisions of Chapter 5 of Part 3 are automatically disapplied for PLCS. Therefore, the restrictions on transfers of shares must be expressly disapplied by the particular PLC. In particular, the right of the Board of Directors to refuse to register certain transfers is now provided for in section 95(1)(a) for all companies *including* PLCs and so the Articles of Association will have to disapply this provision. See *infra*, Part I, Chapter 2 for more detail on this for private companies.

266. Companies Act 2006 (UK), ss 677–683.
267. *Re Sam Weller & Sons Ltd* [1990] Ch. 682, [1990] BCLC 80.

164. Pre- emption rights are provided for in section 1022 of the 2014 Companies Act in relation to the *allotment* of shares in PLCs and in section 69(6) of the 2014 Companies Act for private companies. Section 1022(1) provides that when a company issues equity securities a pro rata offer of these securities must be made to the holders of 'relevant shares' or 'relevant employee shares'. Supplemental provisions are found in section 1023 which includes the statutory definition of 'equity securities' which excludes subscriber shares and bonus shares. The operation of the statutory provision does not apply to allotments of shares that are wholly or partly paid up, otherwise than in cash[268] or to allotments of shares that would be normally held under employees' share schemes.[269] The relevant period of the offer is stipulated at fourteen days under section 1022(9). During this time the offer to existing shareholders must stand until it is refused.

B. *Form of Transfer of Shares*

165. Chapter 5 of Part 3 of the Companies Act 2014 governs the transfer of shares. Section 94(4) of the Companies Act 2014, provides that a transfer of shares cannot be registered unless a proper instrument of transfer has been delivered to the company. Under the Stock Transfer Act 1963, section 2, registered securities to which the Act and its provisions apply may be transferred 'by means of an instrument under hand in the form set out in the First Schedule to this Act (in this Act referred to as a stock transfer)'. Section 94(8) of the Companies Act 2014 states that section 94 is without prejudice to Stock Transfer Act 1963 'save to the extent that a company's constitution regulates the execution of instruments by any particular company or other body corporate.'

166. Once a transfer has occurred, the registration of a shareholder is significant as the shareholder cannot exercise rights without being registered. Section 66(6) of the Companies Acts 2014 provides that 'except as required by law, no person shall be recognized by a company as holding any share upon any trust and the company shall not be bound by or compelled in any way to recognize, (even when having notice of it) (a) any equitable, contingent, future or partial interest in any share or any interest in any fractual part of a share or (b) save only as this Act or other law otherwise provides, any other rights in respect of any share, except an absolute right to the entirety of it in the registered holder. The practical implication of this provision is that the company is only bound to serve notice on and to be subject to the exercise of rights solely by those registered as shareholders.[270] Accordingly, in relation to the transfer of shares, there are essentially two stages in the process of

268. Companies Act 2014 s. 1022(5).
269. Companies Act 2014 s. 1022(6).
270. This has become significant in relation to the creation of modern trust and shareholding arrangements. See further I. Lynch Fannon, *A Transatlantic Case: The Derivative Action as a Corporate Governance Tool*, 27 Dublin U. L. J., 1 (2005) and R. Nolan, *Indirect Investors: A Greater Say*, 3 Co. J. Corp. L. Stud., 73 (2003).

acquiring rights exercisable by the shareholder, namely the completion of the transfer, at which point the shareholder will acquire an equitable interest in the shares,[271] and registration of the shareholder, without which the shareholder cannot exercise any of the rights normally attaching to the share. Therefore registration is of the utmost importance.

C. Directors' Decision to Accept or Refuse Registration

167. The absolute discretion to refuse to register a transfer of shares which had hitherto been given to directors of private companies in the standard-form Articles of Association is now enshrined in statute, in section 95 of the Companies Act 2014 which applies this discretion, 'save where the constitution of the company provides otherwise'. This is not disapplied automatically in section 1002 to public companies so that the Articles of Association of a PLC will have to disapply this provision. The principles governing the exercise of this discretion are described in Part I Chapter 2, *infra.*

D. Transmission of Shares

168. When a shareholder dies, his or her shares, as with all other items of property, vest in a personal representative. Section 94(5) provides that nothing in subsection (4) of the section described above 'shall prejudice any power of the company to register a shareholder or debenture holder, any person to whom the right to any shares in or debentures of the company, has been transmitted by operation of law'. The personal representative (i.e., as a person to whom the rights to any shares or debentures have been transmitted by operation of law) can be registered as a member under section 96(4)(a) of the Companies Act 2014 Act), or may elect under section 96(4)(b) to have a nominee registered as the transferee, thus enabling the exercise of rights attaching to the shares. For many reasons the personal representative may not wish to be registered as a member and can proceed to transferring the shares without such registration. This is facilitated by the operation of sections 94(6) which provides that: 'A transfer of the share or other interest of a deceased member of a company made by his personal representative shall, although the personal representative is not himself a member of the company, be as valid as if he had been such a member at the time of the execution of the instrument of transfer.' Where shares are partly paid, the personal representative will become liable for any calls on the shares if he or she is registered under the decision in *Buchan's Case*,[272] whereas the liability ensures to the shareholder's estate if the personal representative is not registered.

---

271. *Wood Preservation Limited v. Prior* [1969] 1 WLR 1977; *Musselwhite v. Musselwhite* [1962] 1 Ch. 964.
272. *Buchan's Case* (1879) LR 4 App. Cas. 549.

E. Mortgages

169. Shares can form a significant part of an individual's asset base. Because of the effect of section 66(6) of the Companies Act 2014, legal mortgages of shares are not common, because the mortgagee rather than the mortgagor will be liable for calls[273] and other obligations relating to share ownership. In view of the impracticalities of this situation, equitable mortgages are more common; these are achieved by the deposit of the share certificate or indeed such an equitable charge can be created by agreement, which is more relevant where share certificates are no longer issued.[274]

F. Trusts

170. Shares can be held under a trust agreement, where usually the trustee will be registered as the shareholder to facilitate the exercise of the rights attaching to the share, which will be exercised in accordance with the terms of the trust deed. In modern times the use of trust deeds has facilitated the quotation of shares of companies on non-domestic stock exchanges, such as the NASDAQ and New York Stock Exchange in the case of Irish and British companies. The holding instruments are referred to as ADR or ADS, American Depository Receipts or American Depository Securities. Again, because of the operation of section 66(6) of the Companies Act 2014 and its equivalent in English company law, such arrangements are not without their difficulties for those holding securities under such trust instruments.[275]

G. Liens

171. A lien is an equitable charge, and it is possible for shares to become the subject matter of a lien, to provide security regarding non-payment of certain kinds of debts. Usually a lien is created by an individual asserting rights of possession over the asset until whatever liability which is due to him or her is met. Section 80 of the Companies Act 2014, governs the creation of liens over shares and provides a set of default provisions which a company may disapply by virtue of its constitution. Section 80(2) states that a company shall have a 'first and paramount lien on every share (not being a fully paid share) for all moneys (whether immediately payable or not) called, or payable at a fixed time, in respect of that share' Section 80(2) provides that the directors may exempt some shares from this provision and section 80(3) states that the lien will extend to 'all dividends payable on it'. Additional provisions apply,[276] (See further, *infra*, Part I, Chapter 2.)

273. *Re Land Credit Company of Ireland; Weikersheim's Case* (1873) LR 8 Ch. App. 831.
274. *Swiss Bank Corporation v. Lloyds Bank* [1981] 1 WLR 893.
275. See I. Lynch Fannon, *A Transatlantic Case: The Derivative Action as a Corporate Governance Tool*, 27 Dublin U. L. J., 1 (2005) and R. Nolan, *Indirect Investors: A Greater Say*, 3 Co. J. Corp. L. Stud. 73 (2003): n. 76.
276. See further Companies Act 2014, s. 80.

V. Loan Capital and Debentures

A. *Introduction: Equity and Loan Capital*

172. Even though the issue of debentures can be considered under the general heading of raising capital, the nature of loan capital as distinct from equity capital, the latter having been discussed in sections I–IV, is very different. Whereas the provision of equity capital in the form of shares for cash is essentially a 'control for capital' transaction, the provision of loan capital is not understood in this way. It is not the primary motive of the lender to achieve control of decision making in the company but rather to lend capital with view to making a profit through the charging of interest. In a generalized sense, the lender does not seek control over the company's activities. (On the other hand, the lender will usually seek control over some assets, as we will see later. See *infra*, Part I, Chapter 1, §5 on Liquidations.) In providing capital in this way the lender is much more risk averse than the provider of equity capital whose investment may return substantial profits over time, but is at risk of returning no profit at all. The lender's investment, in contrast, will usually not involve the risk of a fluctuating return. Leaving aside issues of control and risk, equity capital is cheaper to obtain where possible from the company's point of view, whereas loan capital must be paid for through the payment of interest. Capital raised through lending is not considered 'capital' for most company law purposes and is not subject to the rules on capital maintenance, statements of capital and so forth described in previous paragraphs.

B. *Issuing Debentures*

173. A debenture document is the term used to describe the loan document issued by a company to the lender. The issuing of debentures is governed primarily by the Constitution of the company, which will give the directors the power to borrow and to secure borrowing on assets over which securities can be created. The loan document will typically describe a payment date, or dates where instalments are concerned, and will also describe the assets charged to secure repayment. The debenture document can be one document issued in relation to one loan, or it can be one of a series of documents or instruments issued to a number of lenders. The company can issue debentures to the public in identical terms but for different amounts, but it is more common now to see this as an issue of debenture stock to the public, much like a Government bond. The company will thus issue debenture stock to individuals or other entities, and this stock indicates their particular share in the loan fund. The holder of debenture stock is thus able to avail of free transferability of the debenture stock. Underlying the issue of debenture stock in this manner will be a trust deed executed between the company and trustees, who are appointed to look after the interests of the debenture stock holders. The company agrees under the trust agreement to repay the capital sum secured at a fixed date or in some other manner. Section 422 of the Companies Act 2014 provides that any provision in a trust agreement that exonerates or relieves trustees of liability for breach of their trust to debenture holders where there is a failure to show 'care and diligence' required of them will be void.

C. Charging the Assets

174. Any charges created to secure the lending described in the debenture document, which will also describe the terms and conditions of the lending, must be registered under section 409 of the Companies Act 2014. The registration process has been changed considerably under the 2014 Act by introducing a built in option of registering the charge in a 'one stage procedure' – section 409(3) or in a 'two stage procedure' – section 409(4). Failure to register the charge in one or other of these ways will lead to the charge being void 'against the liquidator and any creditor of the company'. This provision and the issues that have been raised regarding the creation of charges will be discussed in Part I, Chapter 1, §5 on Liquidations.

D. Transferring Debentures

175. As with shares, debentures or debenture stock can be transferred. As described above under section 94(4) of the Companies Act 2014, a transfer of shares cannot be effected without a valid instrument of transfer that must be delivered to the company. Similarly, the same section provides that a company cannot register the transfer of a debenture, where this is applicable unless a proper instrument of transfer is delivered to the company, the same principle that applies to share transfers discussed *supra*. The company usually will keep a register of debenture holders, and if this is done, it must be done in the prescribed form. However, it is possible to issue bearer debentures, the transfer of which is effected in much the same way as share transfers. Bearer debentures are regarded in law as negotiable instruments.

E. Convertible Debentures

176. It is also possible for a company to issue debentures that can later be converted into shares, depending on the terms of the loan agreement of document. Such debentures are usually referred to as 'convertible debentures' and are designed to capture a certain degree of flexibility between the predictability of a loan investment and the less risk-averse advantages of an equity investment. The conversion rates and terms will be specified in the debenture document.

F. Remedies of a Debenture Holder

177. The debenture document is essentially a loan document, and so the document will describe remedies available to the debenture holder in the event of the company defaulting on the loan or on any of its repayment terms. The remedies included will usually include the right to appoint a receiver, which is a significant feature of Irish insolvency law discussed in Part I Chapter 1, §5. Alternative remedies are to commence a winding up and in certain circumstances, where it might seem advantageous to the lender to do so, to appoint an examiner. These processes and remedies are described *infra* in §5. The realization of any charges securing the loan will be an integral part of the debenture holder's remedies. If a debenture stock trust deed has been created underlying, as has been described, the issuing of debenture stock, the trustee normally exercises the rights relating to the remedies.

§4. Shareholders, Management and Control

I. Introduction

178. The following is a description of the powers and responsibilities within the corporate structure of most companies. In recent times the study of corporate governance has become a lively area of enquiry. Corporate governance is particularly concerned with issues of accountability of management to shareholders in the first instance and to what are called 'other stakeholders' in the second instance. In addition, corporate governance is significant beyond corporate law because of the impact the governance movement has had on institutions generally.

179. Under the organic theory of company law, the organs of the company are those bodies that can act on behalf of the company. These include the shareholders in a general meeting, the Board of Directors, the Managing Director, the Company Secretary in relation to specific functions, and similarly the Auditor in relation to other functions. The theory recognizes the shareholders in a general meeting as residual owners of the company who delegate their authority to the Board, which in turn delegates to the Managing Director, the Company Secretary and the Auditor. Prior to the enactment of the Companies Act 2014, these particular relationships were recognized and governed by the standard-form Articles of Association, the companies legislation and judicial interpretations of both decided in case law. The Articles of Association have now been displaced by provisions of the new Companies Act 2014. Accordingly, PLCs will have specific 'bespoke' Articles of Association drafted with reference to, and subject to these provisions and it is expected that private limited companies will largely be governed by the provisions of the Companies Act 2014 without reliance on Articles of Association. There are, of course, other possibilities for specific delegation of duties, such as from the Board to a particular individual or employee, but these delegations will be conducted primarily through contract law and are not regulated under company law in a general way. Section II of this section concerns shareholders' meetings. Section III deals with shareholders' rights. Section IV discusses the authority and duties of directors and officers. Sections V and VI deal with the roles of auditors and company secretaries, respectively.

II. Shareholder Meetings

A. *Introduction*

180. The law relating to shareholders' meetings is now codified, in the Companies Act 2014. Generally the rules relating to shareholders' meetings are contained in sections 177–195 of the 2014 Act. The principal source of law and regulation relating to the conduct of meetings is the 2014 Act. Much of what was previously contained in the standard-form articles of association has now been adopted into the 2014 Act which replaces the former 'Table A' as the default regulation of company meetings. The shareholders in general meeting are considered to be capable of acting on behalf of the company and making decisions on behalf of the company. The theory is that as residual owners, the shareholders' meeting is often described as the repository of all residual un-delegated powers.

B. *Types of Meetings*

1. Annual General Meeting (AGM)

181. Four types of meetings are described in the Companies Act 2014. First there is the AGM, which normally must be held on an annual basis. Despite its nomenclature, however, the requirement to hold an AGM does not correspond exactly to a calendar year. The AGM must be held within each calendar year, but does not necessarily have to be held within twelve months of the preceding AGM. There is a limit on the intervening period of fifteen months. On first formation this period of time between formation and the holding of the AGM can be up to eighteen months. However, the obligation to hold an AGM can be dispensed with for LTDs under section 175 of the Companies Act 2014. This exemption had applied to single member private companies since 1994 but the new Act extends this to LTDs. Section 175(3) states that AGMs can be dispensed with where all the members sign a written resolution acknowledging receipt of the financial statements which are usually presented at the AGM and the resolution also resolves all matters which would have been resolved at the AGM. The same exemption is not extended to multi-member DACS[277] or to PLCs.[278] A member of the company can apply to the Director of Corporate Enforcement to call or direct the convening of an AGM when one is overdue.[279]

182. The business of the AGM shall include certain items which are set out in statute,[280] namely:

277. Companies Act 2014, s. 988.
278. Companies Act 2014, s. 1089.
279. Companies Act 2014, s. 175(5).
280. Companies Act 2014, s. 186.

(a) the consideration of the company's statutory financial statements and the report of the directors and, the report of the statutory auditors on those statements and that report;
(b) the review by the members of the company's affairs;
(c) save where the company's constitution provides otherwise – (i) the declaration of a dividend (if any) of an amount not exceeding the amount recommended by the directors; and (ii) the authorisation of the directors to approve the remuneration of the statutory auditors (if any);
(d) where the company's constitution so provides, the election and re-election of directors;
(e) the appointment or re-appointment of statutory auditors; and
(f) where the company's constitution so provides, the remuneration of the directors.

2. Extraordinary General Meeting (EGM)

183. An EGM will be held where extraordinary matters of business arise. Effectively an EGM is conducted as an AGM would be, except that the function of the meeting is to consider matters of business beyond the normal items of business conducted at the AGM. The Companies Act 2014 states that 'all general meetings of a company, other than annual general meetings, shall be known, and in this Act are referred to, as "extraordinary general meetings"'.[281]

184. EGMs as described are called normally by directors where an item of business out of the ordinary must be considered, such as a certain transaction for which the approval of the members is required for a certain transaction under the Companies Acts 2014. The directors of a company may, whenever they think fit, convene an extraordinary general meeting.[282] If, at any time, there are not sufficient directors capable of acting to form a quorum, any director of the company or any member of it may convene an extraordinary general meeting in the same manner as nearly as possible as that in which meetings may be convened by the directors.[283] Reduction of capital and removal of pre-emption rights are just two examples of transactions that cannot be accomplished without the approval of the shareholders in a general meeting. The directors are also obliged to convene an EGM in certain circumstances specified under the Companies Acts, for example where the company's net assets (i.e., total assets less total liabilities) have fallen to 50% or less of its called-up share capital.

3. Shareholders' Power to Requisition a Meeting

185. A meeting of the shareholders may be requisitioned in a number of ways:

(i) One or more members of a company holding, or together holding, at any time not less than 50% (or such other percentage as may be specified in the

281. Companies Act 2014, s. 177(1).
282. Companies act 2014, s. 177(2).
283. Companies Act 2014, s. 177(3).

constitution) of the paid up share capital of the company as carries voting rights may convene an EGM.[284] This rule is subject to amendment by the constitution of the company.[285]

(ii) The directors of a company must convene an EGM on the requisition of one or more members holding, or together holding, not less than 10% of the paid up share capital as carries voting rights.[286]

(iii) If the directors do not, within twenty-one days of the requisition, call an EGM for a date within two months, the requisitionists (or 50% or more of them) may convene an EGM themselves.[287]

4. Meetings of Particular Classes of Shareholders

186. Where there are different classes of shares, such shareholders may have separate meetings of the particular class, depending on the authority and decision-making capacity reserved for them in the articles. There are also particular times when the Acts require a separate meeting of different classes of shareholders, such as in relation to a proposed scheme of arrangement that would affect different classes differently.

5. Court-Conducted Meetings

187. Finally, and exceptionally, the 2014 Act provides for the convening of meetings of the shareholders by the High Court where it otherwise proves impossible for a meeting to be convened in any other way. The Court may order an EGM to be held on the application to it of a director, a member or the personal representative or assignee in bankruptcy of a member, or the Court may call a meeting of its own motion.[288]

The Court shall not require a meeting to be held, unless it is satisfied that for any reason it is impracticable or otherwise undesirable – (a) for any person to call a general meeting of the company in any manner in which meetings of that company may be called; or (b) to conduct a general meeting of the company in any manner provided by this Act or the company's constitution.[289]

The Court may attach any conditions or give directions as to the conduct of the meeting as it thinks fit.[290] These sort of situations typically involve some kind of deadlock either due to the deterioration in relationships within the company or because technical difficulties have arisen regarding procedural aspects of holding the meeting such as providing a quorum. The Court may direct that one member of the company, or the personal representative of a deceased member of the company

284. Companies Act 2014, s. 178(2).
285. Companies Act 2014, s. 178(2).
286. Companies Act 2014, s. 178(3).
287. Companies Act 2014, s. 178(5).
288. Companies Act 2014, s. 179(1) and 179(3).
289. Companies Act 2014, s. 179(2).
290. Companies Act 2014, s. 179(4).

or the assignee in bankruptcy of a bankrupt member of it, present in person or by proxy, is a quorum.[291]

C. Types of Resolution

188. In relation to shareholders' meetings, there are five types of resolutions by which the shareholders in general meetings make their decisions:

(i) The first type of resolution is an ordinary resolution, which requires a majority of 50% plus one vote, or a simple majority, on a show of hands. A meeting at which an ordinary resolution is passed must be preceded by seven days' notice to shareholders.[292]

(ii) The second type of resolution is a special resolution, which requires a 75% majority or three-quarters of the votes on a show of hands. These resolutions require a twenty-one day notice period for the holding of the meeting. The terms of any proposed special resolution must also be provided in the notice.

(iii) Third is a hybrid resolution, which in effect is a simple resolution to which particular notice requirements attach because of the nature of the subject matter. In effect, these resolutions require the same simple majority as a normal ordinary resolution but require a longer notice period of twenty-eight days for the meeting at which the resolution will be considered. The Companies Act specifies what kind of resolution is required; thus, in the case of these hybrid resolutions, section 146 of the 2014 Act refers to the ability of shareholders to remove directors from the Board. This requires a vote by ordinary resolution, but requires the longer notice period of twenty-eight days. Where it is proposed to pass a resolution to do so, this can be done by an ordinary resolution of the shareholders, but the longer notice period of twenty-eight days must be provided. Similarly, section 396 of the 2014 Act states that a resolution to replace an auditor or a resolution to remove an auditor before the expiration of his or her term of office can be passed but requires longer notice.

(iv) **Unanimous written resolutions** are now provided for in section 193 of the Companies Act 2014. These kinds of resolutions were originally permitted in common law. In *Buchanan v. McVey,*[293] it was held that evidence of unanimous informal agreement can bind any company in the absence of dishonesty or some provision in the Memo or Arts to the contrary. This case is considered *in Re Greendale Developments Ltd.*[294] [in the context of ultra vires. The principle in *Buchanan v. McVey* was originally given statutory effect in section 141(8) of the Companies Act 1963. The 2014 Act provides that, notwithstanding anything else contained in the Act, a written resolution of all of the members who would be entitled to attend and vote at a general meeting shall be as

291. Companies Act 2014, s. 179(5).
292. Companies Act 2014, s. 1919(1).
293. [1954] IR 89.
294. [1998] IR 8.

valid and effective for all purposes as if the resolution had been passed at a general meeting of the company duly convened and held. Such a resolution shall be deemed to have been passed at a meeting held on the date on which it was signed by the last member to sign.

(v) The Companies Act 2014 also provides for **majority written resolutions** which will be considered to be valid where the requisite majority signs the relevant resolution. This is provided for under section 194 and applies to both ordinary resolutions under section 194(1) and special resolutions under section 194(2). It will not apply where there is a resolution to remove a director under section 195 of the Companies Act 2014.

D. Procedure: Quorum

189. No business shall be transacted at any general meeting of a company unless a quorum of members is present at the time when the meeting proceeds to business.[295] Save to the extent that the constitution provides otherwise, two members shall constitute a quorum.[296] Obviously, this will not apply to single member companies.

In the case of a single-member company, one member of the company present in person or by proxy at a general meeting of it shall be a quorum.[297]

The general rules under the 2014 Act regarding the absence of a quorum (subject to amendment by the constitution of the company) are that if, within fifteen minutes after the time appointed for the holding of a general meeting, a quorum is not present: (a) where the meeting has been convened upon the requisition of members, the meeting shall be dissolved; or (b) in any other case: (i) the meeting shall stand adjourned to the same day in the next week, at the same time and place or to such other day and at such other time and place as the directors may determine; and (ii) if at the adjourned meeting a quorum is not present within half an hour after the time appointed for the meeting, the members present shall be a quorum.[298]

E. Procedure: Notice of Meetings

190. Save where the constitution of the company makes provision for the giving of greater notice, a meeting of a company, other than an adjourned meeting, shall be called – (a) in the case of the annual general meeting or an extraordinary general meeting for the passing of a special resolution, by not less than twenty-one days' notice; (b) in the case of any other extraordinary general meeting, by not less than seven days' notice.[299] A meeting of a company shall, notwithstanding that it is called by shorter notice than that just outlined, be deemed to have been duly called if it is

295. Companies Act 2014, s. 182(1).
296. Companies Act 2014, s. 182(2).
297. Companies Act 2014, s. 182(3).
298. Companies Act 2014, s. 182(5).
299. Companies Act 2014, s. 181(1).

so agreed by – (a) all the members entitled to attend and vote at the meeting; and (b) unless no statutory auditors of the company stand appointed in consequence of the company availing itself of the audit exemption under the 2014 Act, the statutory auditors of the company.[300] In the case of a PLC which is classified as a 'trading PLC,' the possibility of a seven-day notice period for the holding of an EGM and the possibility that the members and statutory auditors may agree to waive the necessary notice period (whether twenty-one days or seven days) does not apply, save to the extent that the constitution of the company shall provide otherwise.[301] However, the 2014 Act further provides that a general meeting of a traded PLC (other than an AGM or an EGM for the passing of a special resolution) may be called with not less than fourteen days' notice, if: (a) the members are provided with a facility to vote by electronic means; and (b) a special resolution reducing the necessary notice period to fourteen days was passed at the immediately preceding AGM or at a general meeting held since that meeting.[302]

Where notice of a meeting is delivered by post, it shall be deemed to have been effected on the expiration of twenty-four hours following posting[303] and in determining whether the correct period of notice has been given by a notice of a meeting, neither the day on which the notice is served nor the day of the meeting for which it is given shall be counted.[304]

The company shall be given twenty-eight days' notice of intention to move a resolution to remove a director or appoint someone else in place of a director so removed at the meeting at which he is removed except when the directors of the company have resolved to submit it; and on receiving such notice, the company shall give the members not less than twenty-one days' notice of the holding of the meeting.[305] Any resolution which does not comply with foregoing provisions shall not be effective, except that if, after notice of the intention to move such a resolution has been given to the company, a meeting is called for a date twenty-eight days or less after the notice has been given, the notice, though not given within the time required (i.e., twenty-one days), shall be deemed to have been properly given.[306] It has been commented that the intention behind the latter rule was to prevent a company from frustrating a member's resolution for the removal of a director by deliberating calling a meeting at insufficient notice, in order to have the meeting rendered ineffective.[307]

Extended notice of twenty-eight days shall also be given for certain types of resolutions regarding a company's statutory auditors, namely the following: (a) a resolution at an annual general meeting of a company appointing as statutory auditors any persons other than the incumbent statutory auditors or providing expressly that

300. Companies Act 2014, s. 181(2).
301. Companies Act 2014, s. 1102(1).
302. Companies Act 2014, s. 1102(2).
303. Companies Act 2014, s. 181(3).
304. Companies Act 2014, s. 181(4).
305. Companies Act 2014, s. 146(3).
306. Companies Act 2014, s. 146(4)-(5).
307. L. MacCann & T. Courtney, *The Companies Acts 1963-2009* 143 (Bloomsbury Professional 2010).

the incumbent statutory auditors shall not be re-appointed; (b) a resolution at a general meeting of a company removing statutory auditors from office; and (c) a resolution at a general meeting of a company filling a casual vacancy in the office of statutory auditor.[308]

F. Procedure: Voting and Proxy Voting

1. Polls

191. Save to the extent that the company's constitution provides otherwise, the following rules apply to proceedings at general meetings of the company. Every resolution shall be decided by a show of hands unless a poll is demanded.[309] Unless a poll is demanded, a declaration by the Chairman that a resolution has been carried or lost on a show of hands will be conclusive evidence of the proceedings.[310] Where there is an equality of votes, whether on a show of hands or on a poll, the chairperson of the meeting at which the show of hands takes place or at which the poll is demanded, shall be entitled to a second or casting vote.[311]

A poll (vote) may be demanded as follows: by the Chairman of the meeting; by at least three members voting in person or by proxy; by any member or members present in person or by proxy and representing not less than one-tenth of the total voting rights of all the members having a right to vote at the meeting; or by a member or members holding shares conferring voting rights, being shares on which an aggregate sum has been paid up equal to at least 10% of the total amount paid up on all voting shares.[312] The right to demand a poll is a statutory right.

2. Proxies

192. Any member of the company who is entitled to vote at a general meeting of the company can appoint a 'proxy'.[313] A proxy is a person nominated by the member to attend the meeting and to exercise the member's vote on his or her behalf. A proxy is also entitled to speak at the meeting on behalf of the member. Unless the company's constitution otherwise provides, a member of a company shall not be entitled to appoint more than one proxy to attend on the same occasion.[314]

The instrument appointing a proxy (the 'instrument of proxy') shall be in writing (a) under the hand of the appointer or of his or her attorney duly authorized in

308. Companies Act 2014, s. 396.
309. Companies Act 2014, s. 187(7).
310. Companies Act 2014, s. 187(7).
311. Companies Act 2014, s. 187(8).
312. Companies Act 2014, s. 189(2).
313. Companies Act 2014, s. 181(1).
314. Companies Act 2014, s. 183(3).

writing; or (b) if the appointer is a body corporate, either under seal of the body corporate or under the hand of an officer or attorney of it duly authorized in writing.[315]

The instrument of proxy shall be deposited at the registered office of the company not later than forty-eight hours (or such lesser period as the company's constitution may provide) before the time for holding the meeting or adjourned meeting at which the person named in the instrument proposes to vote.[316]

A vote given in accordance with the terms of an instrument of proxy shall be valid notwithstanding the previous death or insanity of the appointer or revocation of the proxy or of the authority under which the proxy was executed or the transfer of the share in respect of which the proxy is given, except if notice in writing of such death, insanity, revocation or transfer is received by the company concerned at its registered office before the commencement of the meeting or adjourned meeting at which the proxy is used.[317]

G. Procedure: Business at Meetings

193. The business of the AGM has been described above (paragraph 182).[318]

Irish company law distinguishes between the *ordinary* and *special* business of a general meeting.

The AGM may also deal with any other business, which could include, for example, the amendment of the company's memorandum or Articles of Association. It must be noted, however, that this business can only be conducted by vote through a special resolution; thus, this kind of business is indicated as being special business. Special business must be set out in at least general terms in the notice convening the meeting; otherwise the notice will be invalid.

III. Shareholder Rights

A. Introduction

194. The rights of shareholders were hitherto described in the Articles of Association of the company. In PLCs these rights will now be described in the constitution of the company which will consist of 'bespoke' Articles of Association and a Memorandum of Association and the provisions of the Companies Act 2014. Such rights typically include a description of the voting rights attaching to the share, the dividend percentage attaching to the share and any other specific rights that might attach. In the normal case, particularly regarding smaller private companies, there will be only one type of issued share, usually referred to as an 'ordinary share'. However, it is open to the company to have different classes of shares, and even ordinary shares may be divided into different classes of ordinary shares and given

315. Companies Act 2014, s. 183(4).
316. Companies Act 2014, s. 183(6).
317. Companies Act, s. 183(9)-(10).
318. Companies Act 2014, s. 186.

different voting rights, for example. Furthermore, a company may further divide its capital into preference shares of different classes or cumulative preference shares, redeemable shares and so on. Again, the flexibility afforded to any company regarding its corporate finance structure is subject to the provisions of the constitution and the Companies Act 2014. Some constraints may also occur through the conclusion of shareholders' agreements.[319]

B. Alteration of Rights

195. Section 31 of the 2014 Act provides that, subject to the provisions of the 2014 Act, the constitution of the company shall form the basis of a contract as between the company and the members that is binding on all parties. In particular, these provisions are binding on individual members 'as if they respectively had been signed and sealed by each member, and contained covenants by each member to observe all the provisions of the memorandum and of the articles'.

The 2014 Act provides that, subject to the provisions of the Act, a company may amend its constitution by special resolution and such amendment shall be as valid as if it were originally contained in the constitution.[320] Thus, the shareholders' rights, such as voting rights and any other rights that might be specifically described, can be altered if the majority of the shareholders agree to such alteration by special resolution.

As a general rule, no member of the company shall be bound by an amendment made to the constitution after the date on which he or she became a member, if and so far as the amendment – (a) requires him or her to take or subscribe for more shares than the number held by him or her at the date on which the amendment is made, or (b) in any way increases his or her liability as at the date referred to in paragraph (a) to – (i) contribute to the share capital of the company, or (ii) otherwise pay money to the company.[321] Such an amendment can only apply to a member where the member agrees in writing, either before or after the amendment is made, to be bound by the amendment.[322]

In the case of a PLC, subject to the conditions contained in the 2014 Act and in its memorandum, a PLC may, by special resolution, alter or add to its articles.[323] Again, the amendment shall be valid as if it had originally been contained in the articles.[324] Also as regards a PLC, the company may alter the provisions of its memorandum of association by abandoning, restricting or amending any existing object or by adopting a new object.[325] If an application is made to the court in accordance with this section for the alteration to be cancelled, it shall not have effect except in so far as it is confirmed by the court.[326] Within twenty-one days after the

319. See *infra*, Part I, Ch. 2, §4, II.
320. Companies Act 2014, s. 32(1)-(2).
321. Companies Act 2014, s. 32(4).
322. Companies Act 2014, s. 32(5).
323. Companies Act 2014, s. 1015(1).
324. Companies Act 2014, s. 1015(2).
325. Companies Act 2014, s. 1013(1).
326. Companies Act 2014, s.1013(2).

passing of the resolution altering the company's objects, an application requesting the Court to cancel the alteration may be made by the following persons: (a) by the holders of not less, in the aggregate, than 15% in nominal value of the PLC's issued share capital or any class thereof, or (b) by the holders of not less than 15% of the PLC's debentures, entitling the holders to object to alterations of its objects.[327] An application for cancellation may not be made by any person who has consented to or voted in favour of the alteration.[328]

C. *Voting Rights*

196. As stated *supra*, the rights attaching to shares may vary according to the different types and classes of share. Some shares may have no votes, double votes, casting votes, or particular votes. It is possible, for example, for two different classes of ordinary shareholders to have voting rights in relation to the election of certain denominated directors and not others, so that A ordinary shares vote to elect A directors and B ordinary shares vote to elect B directors. Typically, where shares are described as preference shares, they will have fewer voting rights but better rights to dividends. Cumulative preference shares usually have a denominated percentage entitlement to a dividend once it is declared and such rights accumulate over years. A 'One Share, One Vote' project was initiated by the European Commission in 2003 with a view to harmonizing practice across the EU regarding the creation of voting rights of shareholders. Following an initial consultation document[329] and an external study of the subject commissioned and published by the Commission across the EU Member States,[330] this project was abandoned by the Commission in 2007.

D. *Dividends*

197. In general under Irish company law, the shareholders have no entitlement or right to a dividend.

The rules set out below apply, save to the extent that the company's constitution provides otherwise.[331] A company may, by ordinary resolution, declare dividends but no dividend shall exceed the amount recommended by the directors of the company.[332]

327. Companies Act 2014, s. 1013(5) and (3).
328. Companies Act 2014, s. 1013(4).
329. Commission Action Plan, *Modernisation of Company Law and Corporate Governance*, COM (2003) 284 (21 May 2003).
330. Institutional Shareholder Services (ISS) Europe, European Corporate Governance Institute (ECGI), Shearman & Sterling LLP, 'Report on the proportionality principle in the European Union: Proportionality between Ownership and Control in EU Listed Companies' (18 May 2007).
331. Companies Act 2014, s. 124(1).
332. Companies Act 2014, s. 124(2).

The directors of a company may from time to time – (a) pay to the members such interim dividends as appear to the directors to be justified by the profits of the company, subject to section 117; (b) before recommending any dividend, set aside out of the profits of the company such sums as they think proper as a reserve or reserves which shall, at the discretion of the directors, be applicable for any purpose to which the profits of the company may be properly applied, and pending such application may, at the like discretion either be employed in the business of the company or be invested in such investments as the directors may lawfully determine; (c) without placing the profits of the company to reserve, carry forward any profits which they may think prudent not to distribute.[333]

The principal rule is that dividends can only be declared where the company has realized a profit net of all losses and liabilities. These are now calculated in accordance with rules derived from EU Directives enacted in the Companies Act 2014. As observed by Clarke J in *Re Irish Life and Permanent PLC*[334] '... profits for the purposes of considering whether distribution under s. 45 can take place, must mean profits calculated in accordance with the relevant applicable accountancy standards. It follows, therefore, that it is movements in the assets of the company by reference to such standards that need to be considered in the context of determining whether profits within the meaning of the Act, can be said to have occurred.' However, even where such a profit is realized in any given year, there is no obligation on the directors to declare a dividend. Doing so is entirely a matter for the discretion of the board. Once the dividend is declared, this must be presented to the shareholders to approve. The shareholders retain what is essentially a right to veto the declaration of the dividend, but they are not entitled to recommend a particular amount or take the initiative in declaring the dividend. It may be that in extreme situations the shareholders may force the payment of a dividend where there has been persistent non-declaration of a dividend over a number of profitable years. This occurred in the famous US case of *Dodge v. Ford Motor Company*, but a perhaps more relevant and compelling authority in Irish law is the English case of *Re Sam Weller & Sons Ltd*.[335] Finally, it should be noted that where a company is solvent upon liquidation, the shareholders are entitled to a pro rata distribution of surplus funds as residual owners of the company's assets.

IV. Classes of Shareholders: Classes of Shares

198. As described *supra*, the company may divide its shares into different classes of shares depending on its corporate finance requirements. Irish and English company law provide a great deal of flexibility to companies in this respect. As with a company that has only has one class of ordinary shares in a typical situation, the rights of different classes of shareholders in a more sophisticated structure are usually contained in the Articles of Association; the capital clause of the memorandum

333. Companies Act 2014, s. 124(3).

334. *Re Irish Life and Permanent plc* [2009] IEHC 567.

335. *Re Sam Weller & Sons Ltd* [1990] Ch. 682, [1990] BCLC 80; *Dodge v. Ford Motor Company* 170 N.W. 668 (1919).

of association may refer to such classes. In both cases these rights are subject to the provisions of the Companies Act 2014.

199. Where the share capital is divided into shares of different classes, Where the rights are attached to a class of shares in the company otherwise than by the constitution, and the constitution does not contain provisions with respect to the variation of the rights, those rights may be varied if, but only if – (a) the holders of 75%, in nominal value, of the issued shares of that class, consent in writing to the variation; or (b) a special resolution, passed at a separate general meeting of the holders of that class, sanctions the variation.[336]

Where such a variation is consented to by the requisite majority, a minority protection device is provided in section 789 of the 2014 Act, which allows for the 'holders of not less in the aggregate than 10% of the issued shares of that class, being persons who did not consent to or vote in favour of the resolution for the variation' to apply to the court for that variation to be cancelled and further provides that where any such application is made that 'the variation shall not have effect unless and until it is confirmed by the court'.

These provisions depend, however, on whether the particular proposal made by the board of directors is considered to amount in law to a variation of the shareholders' rights. In *Greenhalgh v. Arderne Cinemas Ltd*,[337] a company had at least two classes of shares, 10s shares and 2s shares. The plaintiff held 40% of the 2s shares. It was proposed to split each 10s share into five 2s shares each, thus swamping plaintiff's existing holding. The question for the Court was whether this proposal amounted to a variation of the rights of the existing class of 2s shares, so as to require a vote from each class of shares – a vote which the plaintiff could clearly block in his class. The Court held on a strict interpretation of the meaning of the concept of variation that the plaintiff's rights had not been varied, only the context in which those rights were exercised. Thus, the class was not entitled to a separate vote and so the split was successful. In a second unsuccessful action, the same plaintiff sought to set aside a special resolution setting aside the pre-emption rights of the shareholders prior to the sale of a controlling interest to an outsider. The Court held that a shareholder voting on such a resolution may proceed on the basis of what he honestly believes is for the benefit of the company as a whole.[338]

A. The Balance of Power

200. In governance terms, shareholders in any company are considered to be the residual owners of the company with residual ownership of the company's power to act. Previously the standard-form Articles of Association provided for a general delegation of these powers to the Board and from the Board on to the Managing Director. However, the Companies Act 2014 now provides for this delegation by statute.

336. Companies Act 2014, s. 88.

337. *Greenhalgh v. Arderne Cinemas Ltd* (No. 1) [1946] 1 All ER 512.

338. *Greenhalgh v. Arderne Cinemas Ltd* (No. 2) [1951] Ch. 286. See also *White v. Bristol Aeroplane* [1953] Ch. 65 and *Re Holders Investment Trust Ltd* [1971] 1 WLR 583.

Accordingly, the provisions of what was Article 80 of the standard form Articles of Association in Table A of the 1963 Act are now included as provisions of the Companies Act, 2014. Section 158 states that:

> (1) The business of the company shall be managed by its directors … who may exercise all such powers of the company as are not, by this Act or by the constitution, required to be exercised by the company in general meeting, but subject to- any regulations contained in the constitution; the provisions of this Act; and such directions, not being inconsistent with the foregoing regulations or provisions, as the company in general meeting may (by special resolution) give … .

201. Similarly, the authority of the Managing Director which used to be provided for in standard form Articles of Association (Articles 110–112 inclusive described the position of the Managing Director) is now described in Section 159 of the Companies Act 2014 which states that:

> The directors of a company may from time to time appoint one or more of themselves to the office of managing director (by whatever name called) for such period and on such terms as to remuneration and otherwise as they see fit, and, subject to the terms of any agreement entered into in any particular case, may revoke such appointment … .

There are a number of other provisions in the section regarding remuneration, removal and so on.[339]

202. Section 160(8) of the Companies Act now replaces the old Article 104 of the Articles of Association. It provides that:

> The directors may elect a chairperson of their meetings and determine the period for which he or she is to hold office, but if no such chairperson is elected, or, if at any meeting the chairperson is not present within 15 minutes after the time appointed for holding it, the directors present may choose one of their number to be chairperson of the meeting.

203. Board Meetings: As with shareholders' meetings the rules regarding the conduct of Board meetings are now statutory default rules and must be specifically excluded by the company's constitution if they are not to apply. Section 161(1) provides that a resolution in writing signed by all the directors of a company … shall be valid as if it has been passed at a meeting of the directors. But note that section 166 concerning minutes cannot be excluded.

---

339. *Holdsworth and Co Ltd v. Caddies* [1955] 1 WLR- held that the usual authority of a Managing Director is not described in company law and these must be described in the articles (now the Constitution). This has not changed in s. 159 of the Companies Act 2014. s. 159 simply states in subs. (4) 'Without prejudice to section 40, the directors may confer upon a managing director any of the powers exercisable by them upon such terms and conditions and with such restrictions as they may think fit.'

204. The delegation of the power of shareholders to a Board and from the Board to the Managing Director will always be subject to the Companies Act 2014, The Companies Act will therefore explicitly reserve to the shareholders in general meeting a number of important powers. For example, section 146(1) of the 2014 Act provides that the shareholders 'may by ordinary resolution remove a director before the expiration of his period of office notwithstanding anything in its constitution or in any agreement between it and him or her.'[340] This shall not, in the case of a private company, authorize the removal of a director holding office for life.[341] Irish company law does still allows for directors to be appointed for life in private companies, but this is not permissible in public companies where directors must retire from office after a period of years.[342] Further areas where the shareholders retain residual powers concern the alteration of the constitution which can only be done with the consent of the shareholders. Other matters that explicitly require the consent of the shareholders include a reduction or increase in capital. (Section on Capital). In addition, as noted, the shareholders must be given the opportunity to consider the accounts of the company at an AGM at intervals described *supra*.

V. Shareholders' Remedies

205. In relation to the rights described in the preceding paragraphs, shareholders have remedies in relation to the specific enforcement of each of the rights described. It is common in the provisions of the Companies Act 2014, which describe such rights to provide for a method by which specific rights can be enforced. It is also common that particular enabling sections are provide for a minority shareholder remedy. For example, section 1013 of the 2014 Act which provides for the alteration by special resolution of the objects clause of the memorandum of association of a PLC, permits a minority of 15% to petition the court to object to the changes proposed. In addition to specific remedies regarding each enabling provision, the shareholder has a specific remedy provided for under section 212 of the 2014 Act, which is somewhat equivalent to the 'unfair prejudice' remedy under English company law.

206. Section 212 of the 2014 Act provides that a member of a company who complains that 'the affairs of the company are being conducted or that the powers of the directors of the company are being exercised in a manner oppressive to him or any of the members (including himself), or in disregard of his or their interests as members' may petition the High Court for relief. Members of the company, as well as personal representatives of deceased members, may apply for relief under section what is now section 212 but which was section 205 under the Companies

340. Companies Act 2014, s. 146(1).
341. Companies Act 2014, s. 146(2). This latter provision does not apply to a PLC – see s. 1002(4) of the 2014 Act.
342. See *infra*, Part I, Ch. 2, para. 352 (cf. s. 1090 of the 2014 Act, which requires, subject to variation by the constitution of the company, that all directors of a PLC shall retire at the first AGM and thereafter one-third retire at each subsequent AGM).

Act 1963.[343] Persons whose names remain on the register despite having disposed of their shares do not have standing, however.[344] 'Member' has the meaning given to it by section 168 of the 2014 Act.[345] Under section 168(2), a person to whom shares have been transferred but whose name has not been entered on the register is not a member of the company,[346] and cannot petition under section 212. English cases holding that ex-shareholders[347] and employees[348] also lack standing to petition must also represent the law in this country. Perhaps more controversially, the High Court (Gannon J.) has held that the definition of 'member' in section 168 (as it is now) is exhaustive for the purposes of section 212 (as it is now), and that accordingly where shares are held on trust the beneficial owners do not have standing.[349]

207. Must a petitioning member be a *minority* shareholder? There is no doubt that a 50% shareholder may apply, at least in the case of a company made up of equal 50–50 shareholders.[350] In *Re Westwinds Holding Company Ltd*, Kenny J. said '[t]he word "minority" does not appear in any part of the section and the heading is merely a convenient way of describing the majority of cases in which the section will apply'. Thus it appears that, in theory at least, a majority member could apply for relief under section 212. The point has not been conclusively decided, although in one English case a motion to strike out a petition, on the ground that the petitioner was a majority shareholder, failed.[351]

208. A final point to note regarding standing is that the second limb of section 212 refers to conduct 'in disregard of his or their interests *as members*', a qualification that is absent from the preceding 'oppression' limb. The courts have accordingly held that a shareholder who is also a director, employee or creditor of the company may apply to the court on foot of conduct alleged to be *oppressive* of him or her in one of those other capacities, rather than strictly *qua* shareholder. For

343. Companies Act 1963, ss 205(1) and 205(6). So, too, may the Minister for Enterprise, Trade and Employment, after inspectors appointed under the Companies Act 1990 present their report to the Court. See Companies Act 1963, ss 205(2) and 170.
344. See *Re Via Net Works* [2002] IESC 24 (unreported, Supreme Court, 23 Apr. 2002) (shareholder-petitioner held not to have standing, even though he retained his shares, because he had contractually bound himself to divest himself of all shares in the company).
345. Section 168 of the 2014 Act provides: '(1) The subscribers to the constitution of a company shall be deemed to have agreed to become members of the company, and, on its registration, shall be entered as members in its register of members. (2) Every other person who agrees to become a member of a company, and whose name is entered in its register of members, shall be a member of the company.'
346. As noted by Carroll J. in *Ramathan Arulchelvan v. Wright* (unreported, High Court, Carroll J, 7 Feb. 1996).
347. *Re Baltic Real Estate Ltd* (No. 1) [1993] BCLC 498.
348. *Jaber v. Science and Information Technology Ltd* [1992] BCLC 764.
349. *Re Allied Metropole Hotel Ltd; O'Tuama v. Allied Metropole Hotel Ltd* (unreported, High Court, Gannon J, *ex tempore*, 19 Dec. 1988). See Lyndon MacCann, *Locus Standi and Section 205 of the Companies Act 1963*, 7 Irish L. Times 195 (1989). See also I. Lynch Fannon, *A Transatlantic Case* Dublin U. L. J. CHECK.
350. *Irish Press PLC v. Ingersoll Irish Publications* (unreported, High Court, 16 Dec. 1993).
351. *Re Baltic Real Estate Ltd* (No. 1) [1993] BCLC 498.

example, an injunction may be granted under section 212 restraining the company in general meeting from exercising its power under section 146 to remove a director, pending the hearing of a section 212 petition.[352] Likewise, in *Re Murph's Restaurants Ltd*,[353] McWilliam J. at interlocutory stage was of the view that section 205 applied 'only to members of a company as members'. But in the later full hearing, Gannon J. (though ultimately ordering that the company be wound up) did not doubt that the Court would have had jurisdiction to make an order under section 205 on foot of complaints by the petitioner that he was excluded as a director.[354]

209. The concept of oppression has been held to refer to conduct of the company's affairs (or exercise of directors' powers) 'in a manner burdensome, harsh and wrongful'.[355] In *Re Irish Visiting Motorists' Bureau Ltd*,[356] Kenny J. held that the affairs of a company may be conducted oppressively, even though those in charge are acting honestly and in good faith. It is not an answer that those conducting the company's affairs or exercising the powers of directors *believe* they are within their rights. The question rather is whether conduct, 'judged by objective standards', is oppressive.[357] Nothing in the statute requires a deliberate scheme or intent.

210. The phrase 'disregard of his or their interests as members' in the second limb of section 212 encompasses more than a petitioner's strictly defined legal rights. A petitioner must point to an identifiable interest related to, and prejudiced by, thc conduct of the affairs of the company or exercise of the directors' powers.[358] A single act or transaction, if sufficiently prejudicial, may be sufficient for the court to invoke the jurisdiction of section 212,[359] and the contrary view (that there is some rule or presumption that an isolated act cannot amount to oppression) cannot be regarded as correct, being an unnecessary gloss on the wording of the statute.[360]

211. The court has wide discretion to make 'such order as it thinks fit', and in doing so, section 212 permits it to cancel or vary any transaction, order the purchase of shares of any member's shares by other members or by the company (with the consequent capital reduction), or make an order regulating the company's future affairs. The section provides that the remedy ordered by the court must be made

---

352. *Gilligan v. O'Grady* [1999] 1 IR 46, [1999] 1 ILRM 303 (disapproving of *Feighery v. Feighery* [1999] 1 IR 321).
353. *Re Murph's Restaurants Ltd* [1979] ILRM 141.
354. *Ibid*. J. Gannon said 'the purported exclusion of [the petitioner] by the [respondents] in an irregular and arrogant manner is undoubtedly oppressive'. (*Re Murph's Restaurants Ltd* [1979] ILRM 141, 152).
355. *Re Greenore Trading Company Ltd* [1980] ILRM 94, 100–101 (citing *Scottish Co-operative Wholesale Society Ltd v. Meyer* [1959] AC 324, 342 per Viscount Simonds).
356. *Re Irish Visiting Motorists' Bureau Ltd* (unreported, High Court, 7 Feb. 1972).
357. *Ibid*., 33.
358. *Re Leeds United Holding PLC* [1996] 2 BCLC 545 (sale of a member's shares cannot amount to conduct of the 'affairs of the company').
359. *Re Westwinds Holding Company Ltd* (unreported, High Court, 21 May 1974), 17 (sale of lands was 'fraudulent and oppressive to the petitioner and was in total disregard of his interest as a member of the company'); *Re Williams Group Tullamore Ltd* [1985] IR 613.
360. *Re Greenore Trading Company Ltd* [1980] ILRM 94.

'with a view to bringing to an end the matters complained of'. Prior to the coming into operation of the 2014 Act, the Supreme Court had held that this remedial discretion does not extend to awarding compensatory damages,[361] where such an award adds nothing to the ending of the matters complained of, but that when an order is made that a petitioner's shares be purchased, determination of a fair price might validly include 'an incidental element of compensation'.[362] Section 212(3) of the 2014 Act now provides that among the types of order which the Court may make on a section 212 petition is an order 'for the payment of compensation'.

212. All of these elements in this remedy point to a great deal of flexibility. The section 212 remedy has proved popular with shareholder litigants and is particularly useful in addressing particular issues that arise in private companies. See further *infra*, Part I, Chapter 2.

VI. Directors and Other Executive Officers

A. *Introduction*

213. As described in the previous section, what were hitherto the Articles of Association have been largely codified into statutory form under the Companies Act 2014. As described earlier on in the text, the Articles of Association of a private company limited by shares have been replaced with a constitution, a much shorter document. To this end, it is expected that for private companies limited by shares the statute will replace provisions which would have been in the Articles of Association. For PLCs, the constitution of the company is a term used to collectively describe the Memorandum and Articles of Association. The statute provides the default provisions in the case of PLCs also and it will be a matter of opting out of these default provisions for a PLC. This can be done in what has been referred to by one commentator as 'bespoke' Articles of Association.[363]

B. *Board of Directors*

214. Section 158 of the Companies Act 2014 and the following provisions create the structure for the operation of the Board of Directors in Irish company law. Under sections 146 and 147 of the 2014 Act, the shareholders in general meeting may remove any director on foot of an ordinary resolution. This right on the part of the shareholders is an important element in the balance of power between the shareholders in a general meeting and the Board of Directors. This power to remove

---

361. *Irish Press PLC v. Ingersoll Irish Publications Ltd* (No. 4) [1995] 2 IR 175.
362. *Ibid.*, 190. See also *Horgan v. Murray* [1997] 3 IR 23.
363. See Courtney in Courtney et al., *Bloomsbury Professional's Guide to the Companies Act 2014* (Bloomsbury 2015).

directors is without prejudice to any rights under contract the directors might have. In addition, some authority in Ireland indicates that the directors may have constitutional rights in relation to procedure.[364]

215. Before the enactment of the Companies Act 2014 the standard form Articles of Association envisaged a general delegation of management functions to the board of directors, which in turn delegates to a managing director. Section 158 of the Companies Act 2014 repeats this delegation in statutory form as described above. The courts have repeatedly held that the effect of a provision (hitherto contained in the Articles of Association) is to render void and inoperative a shareholder resolution passed in general meeting purporting to instruct the board to carry out its management functions in a particular manner. Under English law, this approach has been held to apply to the decision to initiate litigation. The Companies Act 2014 also specifically refers to borrowing powers to be exercised by the directors on behalf of the company. Thus, section 158(3) refers to the power to borrow. Any limitations on the authority of a director to act on behalf of the company are now dealt with under section 40 of the Companies Act 2014. Any outsider is entitled to rely on the authority of an individual registered with the authority to bind the company. The following changes will arise pursuant to the new Companies Act 2014:

(i) The registration of particular individuals with the authority to bind the company is much more important under Irish law.
(ii) Where representations are made or transactions entered into by an individual without authority, any such representations made by an unregistered person present the third party with a slightly different proposition from before as now there is a formal system of registration.
(iii) Following on from this section 40 of the Companies Act 2014 now provides that the constitution of a company cannot be relied upon to build up authority. (This is slightly different from the position under previous case law).
(iv) Finally, section 40 states that the rule in Turquand's case[365] still applies. In *Re Motor Racing Circuits Ltd*[366] Blayney J. stated: ' … Turquand's case says that where a matter appears to be regular then the party dealing with the company is not affected if in fact by reason of some error in the internal management of the company there is an irregularity.'

However, this applies only to internal errors, and not where the irregularity is of public record. It would seem therefore that a third party could not as readily rely on the ostensible authority of an individual purporting to act when that individual is not registered (*infra* paragraph 221).

364. See *Glover v. BLN Ltd* [1973] IR 388.
365. The Rule in Turquand's Case: *Royal British Bank v. Turquand* [1856].
366. (SC, 31 Jan. 1997).

C. *The Managing Director*

216. Section 159 goes on to elaborate the powers of a Managing Director as described above and section 159 simply states in sub-section (4) 'Without prejudice to section 40, the directors may confer upon a managing director any of the powers exercisable by them upon such terms and conditions and with such restrictions as they may think fit.

D. *The Chairman of the Board*

217. In accordance with the statutory scheme described above section 160 places the old Article 104 of the standard form Articles of Association and now describes the role of the Chairman of the Board.

E. *Authority to Act*

218. Section 40 of the Companies Act 2014 provides that '(a) the board of directors of the company; and b) any registered persons' shall be deemed to have authority to exercise any power of the company and to authorize others to do so. Any person who is authorized by the Board to bind the company must be registered. When all is done appropriately this statement is not problematic. However, where individuals act without actual authority, these provisions must be considered in the light of the existing case law.

219. Several cases[367] form the basic framework for resolving issues surrounding the authority of a company's agents. Specifically, this problem normally arises in relation to either a director or a managing director purporting to act on behalf of the company where he or she lacks authority. Authority is usually described as being actual or implied. Where there is actual authority, there is usually no difficulty as the acts of the director or other are agreed to by the company. However, where a company seeks to deny the actions of the director, difficulties arise. Where the director or other officer has actual authority, the company is bound:

> Actual authority can be expressly conferred on a company's board of directors or it can be expressly conferred by the board of directors on an agent or it can impliedly be conferred by them on an agent. Thus, when a board of directors appoints a 'managing director' or a 'secretary' it impliedly confers on the person so appointed the powers usually associated with holders of such offices.[368]

---

367. *Holdsworth and Co. Ltd v. Caddies* [1955] 1 WLR 352; *Freeman and Lockyear v. Buckhurst Park Properties Ltd* [1964] 2 QB 480; *Hely-Hutchinson v. Brayhead Ltd* [1968] 1 QB 549; *Allied Irish Banks v. Ardmore Studios International Ltd* (No. 2) (unreported, High Court, Finlay J., 30 May 1973); *Ulster Investment Bank v. Euro Estates Ltd* [1982] ILRM 57.

368. *Thomas Williamson Ltd v. Bailieborough Co-Operative Agricultural Society Ltd* (unreported, High Court, Costello J., 31 Jul. 1986).

220. Where there is no actual authority, the authority may be implied or ostensible. The different kinds of authority are described by Henchy J. for the Supreme Court in *Kett v. Shannon and English*[369] (following the analysis of English case law in the decision of Diplock L.J. in *Freeman and Lockyear v. Buckhurst Park Properties Ltd*):[370]

> Actual authority exists when it is based on an actual agreement between the principal and the agent. ... Ostensible authority, on the other hand, derives not from any consensual arrangement between the principal and the agent, but is founded on a representation made by the principal to the third party which is intended to convey, and does convey, to the third party that the arrangement entered into under the apparent authority of the agent will be binding on the principal.

These principles have been applied consistently over time in both the English and Irish courts. In *Ulster Factors Ltd v. Entonglen Ltd and Maloney*,[371] the court held that the plaintiffs were entitled to rely on the ostensible authority of the agent in question as the company had made a tacit representation of his authority upon which the plaintiff had relied, and the authority had not been explicitly rebutted by any action of the company.

221. In this context it is important to note that the doctrine of constructive notice is important in terms of imputing knowledge to the third party of the authority or otherwise of the alleged agent.[372] Although the common law assumes persons dealing with ostensible agents to have read the company's publicly available constitutional documents (i.e., the Memorandum and Articles of Association which form the constitution of the company), the rule in *Royal British Bank v. Turquand*,[373] also known as the 'indoor management rule', ameliorates the position by allowing any third party or outsider dealing with the company to proceed on the basis that any matter that is properly regarded as an internal management matter has been properly effected with no irregularities. This reflects the fact that such matters are not matters of public record and cannot be verified by an outsider dealing with the company.[374] Thus, for example, when an ordinary resolution or board resolution is required to effect a particular transaction, the outsider is entitled to rely on representations that such resolutions have been passed. However, the new rule provided for in section 40(9) that where a question of ostensible authority arises, no 'reference shall be made to the company's constitution' may disadvantage an outsider in certain circumstances. Section 40(11) states that the entire section is 'in addition to,

369. *Kett v. Shannon & English* [1987] ILRM 364. See also *EES-Food ES v. Crown Shipping (Ireland) Ltd* [1991] ILRM 97.
370. *Freeman and Lockyer v. Buckhurst Park Properties (Mangal) Ltd* [1964] 2 QB 480.
371. *Ulster Factors Ltd v. Entonglen Ltd and Maloney* (unreported, High Court, Laffoy J., 21 Feb. 1997).
372. See *supra* Part I, Ch. I, s. 2.1.4.
373. *Royal British Bank v. Turquand* (1856) 6 E & B 327; [1843–60] All ER 435.
374. *Ulster Investment Bank Ltd v. Euro Estates Ltd* [1982] ILRM 57; *Cox v. Dublin Distillery Co.* (No. 2) [1915] IR 345; *Montreal and St Laurence Light and Power Co. v. Robert* [1906] AC 196.

and not in substitution for, the Rule in *Royal British Bank v. Turquand'* otherwise known as the 'indoor management rule.' This changes the position of the outsider when they are dealing with unregistered persons as an individual's authority is more directly linked to provisions in the Companies Act 2014 as they pertain to the office of director or managing director, coupled with the question of whether the individual is registered or not. If an individual is not registered, it would seem the ability of the third party to reply on their authority is curtailed.

VII. Obligations of Directors

222. The duties that directors owe are both fiduciary in character and inclusive of a duty to exercise powers in good faith and for the benefit of the company. The duty of skill and care is generally not considered to be of the same fiduciary provenance but is nevertheless significant and becomes increasingly so with the advent of new legislative standards discussed *infra*. These duties are now codified for the first time in sections 227ff of the Companies Act 2014.

A. To Whom Are the Duties Owed?

223. Section 227(1) of the Companies Act 2014 states that 'Without prejudice to the provisions of any enactment (including this Act), a director of a company shall owe the duties set out in section 228 (the "relevant duties") to the company (and the company alone).' This reiterates the position under the existing case law- directors' duties are owed to the company itself as a separate entity and are not, as a matter of course, enforceable by individual shareholders.[375] In certain narrow circumstances that rule does not hold. It is sometimes possible that a director may owe a duty to particular shareholders enforceable by them, such as by virtue of a representation or undertaking made by a director.[376] As to when directors' duties to the company may be enforced by shareholders on behalf of the company, see paragraphs 245 ff., *infra*. As a company nears or enters insolvency, it appears that directors owe duties (albeit of uncertain scope) to creditors but this duty has not been codified.[377] In regard to other 'corporate stakeholders,' section 228(1)(h) of the Companies Act 2014 states that directors owe a duty to take into account the interests of members of the company in addition to the statement in section 224 that directors must have regard to the interests of employees. These provisions reflect the statement previously contained in the 1990 Act which stated that '[t]he matters to which the directors of a company are to have regard in the performance of their functions shall include the interests of the company's employees in general, as well

375. *Percival v. Wright* [1902] 2 Ch. 421.

376. *Crindle Investments v. Wymes* [1998] 2 ILRM 275; *Coleman v. Myers* [1977] 2 NZLR 225; *Re Chez Nico (Restaurants) Ltd* [1992] BCLC 192; *Peskin v. Anderson* [2000] 2 BCLC 1.

377. *Re Frederick Inns Ltd* [1994] 1 ILRM 387; *Jones v. Gunn* [1997] 2 ILRM 245; *Parkes v. Hong Kong & Shanghai Bank Corp.* [1990] ILRM 341.

as the interests of members'.[378] The relevant section goes on to provide that 'the duty imposed by this section on the directors shall be owed by them to the company (and the company alone) and shall be enforceable in the same way as any other fiduciary duty owed to a company by its directors'.[379] Section 227 of the Companies Act 2014 clarifies the position regarding the first codification of these duties as follows: 'The relevant duties (other than those set out in section 228 (1)(b) and (h)) are based on certain common law rules and equitable principles as they apply in relation to the directors of companies and shall have effect in place of those rules and principles as regards the duties owed to a company by a director' and s. 228 (5) states that:

> The relevant duties (other than those set out in section 228 (1)(b) and (h)) shall be interpreted, and the provisions concerned of section 228 shall be applied, in the same way as common law rules or equitable principles; regard shall be had to the corresponding common law rules and equitable principles in interpreting those duties and applying those provisions.[380]

B. *Fiduciary Duties*

224. Directors owe fiduciary duties to the companies of which they are officers, by analogy with the duties of trustees.[381] Such duties derive historically from principles developed by the Courts of Equity and have in modern times been affirmed by the courts and supplemented by statute. In the UK, this area of law has been codified since 2006[382] and has now been codified in Ireland under the Companies Act 2014 following recommendations from the Company Law Review Group.[383] It is open to doubt, however, whether such approach is preferable to broad principles outlined by the courts and applied case-by-case.

C. *No Secret Profits*

225. Duties that are fiduciary in character include a no-conflict principle, which prohibits a director from placing himself or herself in a position of conflict of interest. A fiduciary may not 'enter into engagements in which he has, or can have, a personal interest conflicting, or which may possibly conflict, with the interests of those whom he is bound to protect'.[384] A subset of this is the rule that a director cannot use his or her position to make a secret profit. If this occurs, the director will

378. Companies Act 1990, s. 52(1).
379. Companies Act 2014, s. 224(2).
380. The duties set out in s. 228(1)(b) and s. 228(1)(h) are the duties to act honestly and responsibly and the duty to members, respectively.
381. *Boardman v. Phipps* [1967] AC 46, 124.
382. Companies Act 2006 (UK), s. 39.
383. Company Law Review Group, First Report (31 Dec. 2001) (available at www.clrg.org).
384. *Aberdeen Railway Co. v. Blaikie* (1854) 1 Macq HL 461, 471 *per* Lord Cranworth LC.

be liable to account for the monies so made. In *Regal (Hastings) v. Gulliver*,[385] the directors made a somewhat incidental profit in relation to the transfer of the shares in Regal Hastings, which was part of a restructuring plan. The directors had originally invested in shares of Regal to assist in financing the company. Despite the fact that this agreement was entered into in good faith and partly for the benefit of the company, this matter was held to be irrelevant. The House of Lords held that:

> The rule of equity which insists on those who by use of a fiduciary position make a profit, being liable to account for that profit, in no way depends on fraud, or absence of bona fides; or upon questions or considerations as whether the property would or should otherwise have gone to the plaintiff, or whether he took a risk or acted as he did for the benefit of the plaintiff, or whether the plaintiff has in fact been damaged or benefited by his action.[386]

The House indicated that if the profit had been disclosed and ratified by the shareholders, the directors would have been exonerated from liability. Essentially disclosure is key to absolution of directors. Certain kinds of transactions are not capable of ratification though, and the dividing line in that regard is uncertain. See *infra*, paragraphs 242–246. Finally, in *Regal*, this liability to account only applied to the investors who were directors. The company's solicitor, Garton, was not liable as he was not in a fiduciary position to the company. Nor, indeed, was Gulliver, who, although a director, had not invested himself but had simply sought investment from the directors.

D. Corporate Opportunity Doctrine

226. A second aspect commonly played out in the case law on directors' fiduciary duties is the rule against directors taking corporate opportunities. This rule prohibits a director from taking for themselves or 'direct[ing] to another person or company with whom or which he is associated'[387] a business opportunity properly belonging to the company. In *IDC Ltd v. Cooley*,[388] the defendant undertook to secure contracts for the plaintiff with the Eastern Gas Board in England, but in the course of negotiations he was given an indication that the Gas Board would be interested in contracting with him personally rather than with the plaintiff company. The defendant resigned and took up this opportunity. Subsequently, the company successfully sued the defendant to account for all profits made under this contract. These duties are regarded as almost similar to strict liability claims, in that once a breach is found, the director is liable to account for all profits, regardless of the loss his or her actions actually caused and regardless of the probability for the company receiving the benefit, as is aptly illustrated by *IDC Ltd v. Cooley*. Furthermore, the

385. *Regal (Hastings) v. Gulliver* [1942] All ER 378; cf. see also *Aberdeen Railway Co. v. Blaikie* (1854) 1 Macq HL 461 and *Bray v. Ford* [1896] AC 44.
386. *Ibid.*, 386 *per* Lord Russell of Killowen.
387. *Canaero v. O'Malley and Ors.* [1974] S.C.R. 592, 606–607.
388. *IDC Ltd v. Cooley* [1972] 2 All ER 162.

issue of good faith or bad faith is not centrally relevant to liability being imposed. In *Canaero Ltd v. O'Malley*,[389] Laskin J. found against the defendants and imposed on them the liability to account for all profits to the company. The resignation of the defendants was held to be immaterial as the opportunity had come to their attention prior to their resignation while they were still directors.

227. These lines of authority are now encapsulated in the following provisions of the Companies Act 2014:

> '228. (1) A director of a company shall – … .
>
> (d) not use the company's property, information or opportunities for his or her own or anyone else's benefit unless –
> (i) this is expressly permitted by the company's constitution; or
> (ii) the use has been approved by a resolution of the company in general meeting;'
>
> And
>
> '228. (1) A director of a company shall – … .
>
> (f) avoid any conflict between the director's duties to the company and the director's other (including personal) interests unless the director is released from his or her duty to the company in relation to the matter concerned, whether in accordance with provisions of the company's constitution in that behalf or by a resolution of it in general meeting.'

228. There are some possible defences to be made out on the facts. For example, it is possible for the defendant director to argue that the opportunity which the plaintiff company seeks to reclaim is not a corporate opportunity, either because the company had already rejected the particular opportunity, as occurred in *Peso Silver Mines Ltd v. Cropper*,[390] or because the particular contract can be separated from the pattern of trading in which the company was engaged and regarded as a separate opportunity. In *Peso*, apart from the fact that the company had rejected the opportunity offered to it, it was also considered to be significant that the defendant had come across the information regarding the license agreement separately and outside of this position on the Board. In *Island Export Finance Ltd v. Ummuna*,[391] the information at issue related, it was argued, to a separate, albeit similar, contract. The defendant argued that even where previous contracts he had negotiated with the third party on behalf of the plaintiff were subject to the full range of fiduciary duties, the contracts at issue were not. The Court found as a fact that the defendant had resigned out of dissatisfaction with the plaintiff company rather than out of a desire to appropriate its business and that at that time the plaintiff was not actively seeking repeat or further orders of that type. In effect, the defendant had left the company

389. *Canaero v. O'Malley and Ors* [1974] S.C.R. 592.
390. *Peso Silver Mines Ltd v. Cropper* [1966] S.C.R. 673.
391. *Island Export Finance Ltd v. Ummuna* [1986] BCLC 460.

and pursued similar opportunities but not the same opportunities that had been pursued when he was a director of the plaintiff. The court accepted this argument.

229. Bhullar v. Bhullar[392] involved a family company owned and run by two brothers and their families. Relations between the two families broke down, and it was agreed in principle that the company should not acquire any further properties. Two member-directors, who together with their father held 50% of the shares and a 3:2 board majority, purchased a property adjacent to an investment property owned by the company in the name of a separate company controlled by them. The other 50% shareholders – in effect, the other family – issued a petition under section 459 of the Companies Act 1985 (UK),[393] seeking that the respondents be ordered to sell their shares and/or an order that the purchase was a breach of fiduciary duty. The Court granted the latter relief, and that ruling was upheld by the Court of Appeal. It was sufficient for liability that the respondents did not disclose an opportunity that would have been advantageous to the company. 'Whether the company could or would have taken the opportunity, had it been made aware of it,' said Jonathan Parker L.J., was 'not the point'. The appellants' query to their solicitor as to whether there may be a conflict of interest was 'eloquent of the existence of a possible conflict of duty and interest'.[394] It is arguable that, if the petitioners in *Bhullar* wished to allege breaches of fiduciary duties, the correct course would have been to proceed by way of derivative action. That latter remedy is considered further *infra* (see paragraphs 243 ff.).

E. Involvement with a Competitor

230. A further subset of this area of law is whether a director is permitted to be involved in a competing company while a director of the first company. In *Bell v. Lever Bros Ltd*,[395] the Courts held that there is no absolute bar to this kind of activity, but nevertheless the courts are wary of such arrangements. For example, in the older Irish case of *Moore v. McGlynn*,[396] the Court advised a trustee of a trust who was involved in an arrangement that potentially placed him in a conflict situation with the trust that he ought to resign as trustee as a precautionary measure. However, in the commercial world such a recommendation is not always practicable, and so the courts have provided some leeway. Nevertheless, in *Spring Grove Services Ltd*,[397] the court expressed the view, albeit on a motion for discovery, that a director's fiduciary duties 'include a duty not to compete with the company', in the context of an allegation that a director had used confidential information obtained as director otherwise than for the benefit of the company.

392. *Bhullar v. Bhullar* [2003] 2 BCLC 241.
393. For discussion of the Irish equivalent cause of action under Companies Act 2014, s. 212, see *infra*, Part I, Ch. 1, §4, II, F and Part I, Ch. 2, §4, B.
394. *Bhullar v. Bhullar* [2003] 2 BCLC 241, 256.
395. *Bell v. Lever Bros* [1932] AC 161.
396. *Moore v. McGlynn* [1894] 1 IR 74.
397. *Spring Grove Services (Ireland) Ltd v. O'Callaghan* (unreported, High Court, 31 Jul. 2000).

231. Section 231(1) of the Companies Act 2014 states that:

> It shall be the duty of a director of a company who is in any way, whether directly or indirectly, interested in a contract or proposed contract with the company, to declare the nature of his or her interest at a meeting of the directors of the company.
> (2) Subsection (1) does not apply in relation to an interest that cannot reasonably be regarded as likely to give rise to a conflict of interest … .

F. Abuse of Power Doctrine

232. The abuse of power doctrine imposes an obligation on directors to exercise powers delegated to them by the shareholders in a general meeting for proper purpose, in good faith and for the benefit of company. In surveying the litigation, the sorts of powers that are usually at issue are the powers to issue shares, the power to borrow and the power of giving guarantees and making payments or donations. In other jurisdictions, most notably the US (in particular, the state of Delaware), where the incidence of corporate litigation is higher, the cases have also focused on decisions directors and boards have made regarding takeover bids and executive remuneration. *Smith (Howard) Ltd v. Ampol Petroleum Ltd*[398] is illustrative of this category of case. In this case, the actions of the directors in issuing shares to a 'white knight' takeover bidder in defending a takeover bid from a competing and hostile shareholder interest were challenged. It was held that, in considering the purpose for which a particular power has been exercised, courts should consider motivations for which there is evidence. The dominant or primary purpose must be identified. If there is evidence of a predominantly proper purpose, the courts should not be concerned with other incidental motivations or desired results. In that case, a share issue for the purpose of diluting a majority shareholding block, so as to prevent that majority rejecting a takeover bid favoured by the board, was held to be an exercise of a power for an improper purpose, irrespective of whether the directors genuinely considered it to be in the best interests of the company. In *Re Jermyn Street Turkish Baths Ltd*,[399] an issue of shares, made to confer a predominant position on a 50% shareholder, was considered to be an exercise of power for a proper purpose, even though its purpose was not directly linked to the raising of capital, but rather to the securing of an equity for cash deal that involved the allocation of control of the company to the investing shareholder.

233. In *Smith (Howard) Ltd v. Ampol Petroleum Ltd*, the court also articulated a rule equivalent to that described in US jurisprudence as the 'business judgment rule': The Court, in examining proper purpose in relation to the exercise of a power, must 'give credit to the *bona fide* opinion of the directors, if such is found to exist, and will respect their judgment as to matters of management'.[400] Further decided

398. *Howard Smith Ltd v. Ampol Petroleum Ltd* [1974] AC 821.
399. *Re Jermyn Street Turkish Baths Ltd* [1971] 1 WLR 1042.
400. *Howard Smith Ltd v. Ampol Petroleum Ltd* [1974] AC 821, 835.

English cases have re-iterated this rule or approach. In *Regentcrest PLC v. Cohen*[401] the court referred to Lord Green in *Re Smith and Fawcett Ltd.*[402] where it was stated that 'The principles to be applied are for present purposes free from doubt. They must exercise their discretion bona fide in what they consider – not what the court may consider – is in the interests of the company and not for any collateral purpose.'

234. The duty of a director to act in good faith regarding the exercise of a power delegated to him or her is now codified in section 228(1)(a) of the Companies Act 2014 which states:

> A director of a company shall –
> act in good faith in what the director considers to be the interests of the company.

There is no statement of what is called the 'business judgment rule in the statute. However, section 228 goes on to provide a number of specific rules which reflect existing case law. Section 228 (2) states that:

> If a director of a company considers in good faith that it is in the interests of the company for a transaction … to be entered into … a director may restrict the director's power to exercise an independent judgment in the future by agreeing to act in a particular way to achieve this.

Furthermore, section 228 (3) states that:

> Without prejudice to the director's duty under subsection (1)(a) to act in good faith in what the director considers to be the interests of the company, a director of a company may have regard to the interests of a particular member of the company in the following circumstances.
> (4) Those circumstances are where the director has been appointed or nominated for appointment by that member, being a member who has an entitlement to so appoint or nominate under the company's constitution or a shareholders' agreement.

These provisions recognize that it is possible for a director to 'fetter his discretion' as the older cases described it in certain circumstances.

235. In Irish law, there is some confusion between the principles set out in relation to this area of law and the enquiry under the ultra vires doctrine as to whether a power purportedly delegated to a board or a director is ultra vires the power of the company. The latter test involved exploring whether the exercise of a particular power, such as the power to borrow, is reasonably incidental to the business of the company. If this test is not met, then the power is regarded as being ultra vires and

401. *Regentcrest plc v. Cohen* [2001] 2 BCLC 80.
402. *Re Smith and Fawcett Ltd* [1942] Ch.

void. This test has been applied in numerous cases. For example, in *Parke v. Daily News Ltd*,[403] the making of *ex gratia* payments to the dependants of former employees, in circumstances where the company faced insolvency, was held by the court to have failed the ultra vires test as not being reasonably incidental to the business of the company. The court was unable to perceive a benefit for the company in the making of such payments.[404] However, the test for whether a particular director or board has exercised a power in breach of their obligations *to the company* is whether the power is exercised in good faith and for the benefit of the company. If the particular exercise of the power fails this test, the director will be found to be in breach of his or her duties, but this does not affect the validity of the transaction per se. This distinction will no longer be so clear cut following the abolition of the ultra vires rule under the Companies Act 2014. In *Nash v. Lancegaye (Ireland) Ltd*,[405] the board of directors sanctioned the issue of shares to secure a controlling interest for a particular director. In an action brought by a minority shareholder, the defendants argued that this issue of shares was in recognition of the individual's particular contribution to the company but primarily to raise much-needed capital. Dixon J. expressed himself to be unconvinced by the need for more capital and unconvinced therefore that the power was exercised in good faith and for the benefit of the company.

G. The Duty of Skill and Care

236. A final area of obligation owed by directors to their companies is the common law obligation to exercise skill and care in the exercise of their duties. The duty of skill and care has been articulated in English and Irish company law in early cases such as *Re City Equitable Fire Insurance Co.*[406] The following principles are ascertainable from this decision. First, the duty of skill and care owed by each director relates to circumstances of the individual appointee and the company.[407] Second, a director is not liable for mere errors of business judgment. As stated in the nineteenth century decision of *Lagunas Nitrate Co. v. Lagunas Syndicate*:

> If directors act within their powers, if they act with such care as is reasonably to be expected of them, having regard to their knowledge and experience, and if they act honestly for the benefit of the company they represent, they discharge both their equitable as well as their legal duty to the company.[408]

---

403. *Parke v. The Daily News Ltd* [1962] Ch. 927.
404. Note that s. 52 of the 1990 Act includes an 'other stakeholder' provision permitting the directors to take into account the interests of employees in the exercise of their powers. These kinds of legislative provisions are therefore generally considered to be permissive, serving to broaden the scope of the directors' discretion, but s. 52 appears difficult if not impossible to enforce.
405. *Nash v. Lancegaye (Ireland) Ltd* (1958) 92 ILTR 11.
406. *Re City Equitable Fire Insurance Company Limited* [1925] 1 Ch. 407.
407. For an extreme example of variation, textbooks often refer to *Re Cardiff Savings Bank Ltd; Marquis of Bute's Case* [1892] 2 Ch. 100.
408. *Lagunas Nitrate Co. v. Lagunas Syndicate* [1899] 2 Ch. 392, 435.

Third, a director is not obliged to give continuous attention to board matters and finally in the same context, in the absence of grounds for suspicion or enquiry, the director is entitled to rely on the actions and expertise of others.[409]

237. In this area the focus is less on the bona fides or honesty of a director than on the concept that there must be some minimum standard of competence below which a director should not fall. This idea or standard proved difficult to apply in company law as the courts and legislature were mindful of the fact that the term 'company director' is applicable to a broad range of individuals in companies varying both in terms of size and sectoral activities. However, in the more modern context the courts and legislature have sought to establish some objective criteria. Accordingly the traditional view is that negligence in and of itself will be insufficient to attract liability. Romer J. in the *City Equitable* case said that although a director must act honestly, he or she also must exercise some degree of skill and care. The question was what degree of care: 'For myself, I confess to feeling some difficulty in understanding the difference between negligence and gross negligence.'[410]

In the Irish decision of *PMPA Insurance Co. Ltd v. New Ireland Assurance Co. Ltd*, Kenny J. stated that 'the management of a company will not be interfered with unless it was in breach of Articles of Association, dishonest or grossly negligent'.[411]

These principle of regarding the duty of skill and care of directors has been influenced in modern company law by judicial consideration of the actions of directors under the directors' restriction and disqualification provisions introduced by the 1990 Companies Act, as amended by the 2001 Company Law Enforcement Act, and now re-enacted in Part 14 of the Companies Act 2014.[412] The extent to which there is cross-fertilization between that area of law, primarily dealing with insolvency matters, and the standards discussed here, which arise because of shareholders' actions against directors in a solvent, ongoing situation, will continue to be clarified over time.

One area that is particularly difficult for directors, particularly those holding what are termed non-executive directorships (although this term is not a legal term) is the question of the extent to which they are entitled to delegate to others in the company and the extent to which, when they delegate, as they must in larger companies, they must continue to supervise or monitor the activities of those to whom work is delegated. This issue arose in the older Irish case of *Jackson v. Munster Bank Ltd, ex parte Dease*,[413] in which a director who was primarily responsible for activities of the bank confined to one city was held responsible for failing to act to prevent abuses occurring in a branch in a different city. The fact that the defendant director had been notified of possible grounds for suspicion was held to be critical in that case. In *Dorchester Finance Co. Ltd v. Stebbing*,[414] the defendant directors who had carelessly signed blank cheques and who had not exercised any oversight

409. *Jackson v. Munster Bank Ltd*, ex parte Dease (1885) 15 LR IR 356.
410. *Re City Equitable Fire Insurance Company Limited* [1925] 1 Ch. 407, 427.
411. *PMPA Insurance Co. Ltd v. New Ireland Assurance Co. Ltd* [1975] IR.
412. See *infra*, paras 251 forward.
413. *Jackson v. Munster Bank Ltd*, ex parte Dease (1885) 15 LR IR 356.
414. *Dorchester Finance Co. Ltd v. Stebbing* [1989] BCLC.

function were held to be liable for losses caused to the plaintiff on foot of unenforceable loans. In *Barings Bank PLC (No. 5)*,[415] directors were disqualified for exhibiting serious failures of management and oversight regarding the rogue trading of Nick Leeson, which effectively brought the bank to insolvency. These directors ignored audit recommendations to split the dealing and settlement offices in Singapore. They oversaw the granting of requests for huge funding from Leeson without proper inquiry as to why such funding was necessary. The court found that there were effectively no internal management controls and stated that 'where delegation has taken place the board (and the individual directors) will remain responsible for the delegated function or functions and will retain a residual duty of supervision and control'. These principles have been incorporated into Irish law.[416]

238. In addition the duties of skill and care which a director owes to his or her company have now been codified in section 228 Companies Act 2014 where section 228(1)(g) states that a director must:

> exercise the care, skill and diligence which would be exercised in the same circumstances by a reasonable person having both–
>
> (i) the knowledge and experience that may reasonably be expected of a person in the same position as the director; and
> (ii) the knowledge and experience which the director has.

H. Nominal Director

239. There is no such thing in law as a nominal director: One is either a company director or not, and each director owes independent duties of care and loyalty to the company. For example, in *Re Hunting Lodges Ltd*,[417] Carroll J. made some observations in relation to the role of a nominal or non-executive director that were criticized at the time but that were prescient in terms of standards largely accepted in modern company law. In that case the court held that a director, regardless of whether he or she was executive or non-executive director, had a minimum set of obligations to which he or she must adhere. The Court cautioned that a person 'who continues as a director but abdicates all responsibility is not lightly to be excused'.[418] Keeping abreast of financial matters and ensuring that one is informed of financial statements was clearly a primary obligation. The courts have not always rigorously adhered to the logic of Carroll J.'s comments.[419]

---

415. *Re Barings PLC* (No. 5) [2000] 1 BCLC 523.
416. See N. Cahill & I. Lynch Fannon. In *Bloomsbury Professional's Guide to the Companies Act 2014* (Courtney ed., Bloomsbury 2015). See also the discussion in the Irish case law arising from the decisions in *Re Tralee Beef and Lamb Ltd.* [2008] 3 IR 347 and *Re Mitek Holdings*.[2010] IESC 31.
417. *Re Hunting Lodges Ltd* [1985] ILRM 75.
418. *Ibid.*, 85.
419. *Re Wood Products (Longford) Ltd; Director of Corporate Enforcement v. McGowan* [2008] 4 IR 598.

240. It is important to keep in mind that these standards were developed originally in the context of insolvency law and related statutory provisions. For example, the *Barings Bank PLC* case is a directors' disqualification case. The most usual outcome in these cases is a period of disqualification, whereas in suits regarding an actual breach of director's duties, personal liability will be the outcome as it was in *Dorchester Finance* or the *Munster Bank* case. In the early 1990s the incorporation of an objective element into the common law duties of care of a director, began in earnest. In *Re d'Jan of London Ltd*[420] and *Norman v. Theodore Goddard*,[421] Lord Hoffman, or Hoffman J. as he then was, introduced an objective element into the duty of skill and care owed by directors to their companies in common law. It is not clear whether, aside from similar pronouncements made in the context of restriction and disqualification, these standards have been incorporated into Irish law. Therefore, the duty of skill and care as it is owed to a company may be quite subjective in character. However, in advising a director how to act or make decisions in an Irish context, decisions must and should be informed by the standards developed in the context of restriction and disqualification applications, which are discussed *infra.*

241. Finally, in the context of insolvency and approaching insolvency, the Irish Supreme Court has acknowledged and approved a line of reasoning beginning with some cases from Australian and New Zealand which provide that at times when the company is insolvent but not in an insolvency process, the directors must act with the interests of the creditors in mind; in fact, this line of reasoning goes further to provide that the duties of the directors that are always owed to the company, which normally indicates the interests of the shareholders in a general meeting, are at times owed to the company, which in the context of insolvency indicates the interests of the creditors rather than the shareholders.[422] However, these duties have not been expressly codified in Irish law unlike the references regarding the consideration of the interests of employees in section 224 and the interests of members in section 228.

VIII. Enforcement of Obligations and Duties

242. In general and in the normal course of events – that is, most of the time other than insolvency events – the duties of a director are owed to the company. As described above this is now stated in section 227 of the Companies Act 2014. The company is therefore the proper plaintiff in enforcing such duties, a position that is not without its difficulties. A key issue regarding whether alleged breaches of directors' duties may be pursued is the possibility of ratification. Where an alleged breach is disclosed, the company can either absolve the director from liability by approving the breach, or it can choose to pursue the breach as the proper plaintiff to whom

420. *Re d'Jan of London Ltd* [1994] 1 BCLC 561.

421. *Norman v. Theodore Goddard* [1991] BCLC 1028.

422. *Re Frederick Inns Ltd* [1991] ILRM 582 (citing *Nicholson v. Permakraft (NZ) Ltd (in liq)* [1985] 1 NZLR 242, affirmed by the Supreme Court [1994] ILRM 387. *Kinsela v. Russell Kinsela Pty Ltd* (1986) 10 ACLR 395 and *Walker v. Wimbourne* [1976] CLR 1); see, for example, *Hughes v. Hitachi Koki Imaging Solutions Europe* [2006] 3 IR 457, 463–464.

the duties are owed. If the company chooses to adopt the breach, the company, its board and its shareholders are bound by that. This raises the additional question of whether a breach is ratifiable by the company in this manner. Under Irish company law as with English company law, most breaches will be considered ratifiable – that is, capable of being approved once disclosed to the company. However, certain categories of actions are not ratifiable. In such instances, the company's cause of action against the director remains, regardless of whether the company purports to adopt or ratify the breach. Thus, a company cannot ratify an action of a director, which is a breach of duty and which also amounts to a criminal act.[423] Similarly, acts that were ultra vires the company were not ratifiable for the obvious technical reason that it was not within the company's legal capacity to adopt such an act. It would seem that this principle is now moot given the new position regarding statements of objects in PLCs or activities in DACs where such statements are not to affect questions of the company's capacity. Beyond acts that are criminal and ultra vires, it becomes more difficult to identify what other conduct is not capable of ratification. It is relatively clear, however, that where an action of the director amounts to an expropriation of corporate property, these actions are not ratifiable, not capable of adoption by the company and therefore can be acted on.[424] Where the actions of directors are not ratifiable but where the majority of the shareholders and the board seek to adopt actions of the directors, a minority shareholder may have a remedy under the derivative action. Alternatively, an action under the Companies Act 2014, section 212, formerly section 205 of the 1963 Companies Act may provide redress for a shareholder.

A. *Derivative Actions*

243. The derivative action, referred to *supra*, has roots stretching through case law to the eighteenth century,[425] but the doctrine as it currently stands in Ireland is principally drawn from a series of decisions from 1843 to 1901, of which the two most important are *Foss v. Harbottle*[426] and *Burland v. Earle*.[427] In *Foss*, the plaintiffs sued on behalf of themselves and all other shareholders in the company, except the defendants, alleging (among other things) that the defendants had purchased certain lands near Manchester, then formed a company and sold the land to that company at 'greatly increased and exorbitant prices'.[428] In addition to benefiting themselves, the suit alleged that the defendants had 'wasted and misapplied a considerable part of the monies belonging to the company'.[429] The defendants argued that the plaintiffs lacked standing to sue on behalf of the company. The Court thus had to consider 'whether the facts alleged in this case justify a departure from the

423. *Cockburn v. Newbridge Sanitary Steam Laundry* [1915] 1 IR 237.
424. *Cook v. Deeks* [1916] 1 AC 554; *Regal (Hastings) v. Gulliver* [1942] All ER 378.
425. *Charitable Corporation v. Sutton* (1742) 2 Atk. 400, 26 ER 642. See also *Hitchens v. Congreve* (1828) 4 Russ. 562, 38 ER 917.
426. *Foss v. Harbottle* (1843) 2 Hare 461; 67 ER 189.
427. *Burland v. Earle* [1902] 1 AC 83.
428. *Foss v. Harbottle* (1843) 2 Hare 461, 468; 67 ER 189, 193–194.
429. *Ibid.*, 471; 195.

rule which, prima facie, would require that the corporation should sue in its own and in its corporate character'.[430] Wigram V-C held that, '[i]f a case should arise of injury to a corporation by some of its members, for which no adequate remedy remained, except that of a suit by individual corporators in their private characters', then 'the claims of justice would be found superior to any difficulties arising out of technical rules respecting the mode in which corporations are required to sue'. The Court would, however, look for 'reasons of a very urgent character', before departing from the standard rule. In the present case, the plaintiffs lacked standing, because the general meeting, being the corporation's supreme governing body, had not addressed the question of whether to sue.

244. *Burland* involved a claim brought by minority shareholders to compel the directors to distribute as dividends a reserve fund that had accumulated over time. The plaintiffs contended that they had standing to bring the suit 'under the circumstances of an improper and oppressive use of their powers by the majority'.[431] Giving the judgment of the Privy Council, Lord Davey re-affirmed the rule that 'in order to redress a wrong done to the company or to recover moneys or damages alleged to be due to the company, the action should prima facie be brought by the company itself'.[432] However, 'where the persons against whom the relief is sought themselves hold and control the majority of the shares in the company, and will not permit an action to be brought in the name of the company', 'the Courts allow the shareholders complaining to bring an action in their own names'.[433] But because in such an action the plaintiffs cannot have a larger right to relief than the company itself would have if it were plaintiff, they cannot complain of 'acts which are valid if done with the approval of the majority of the shareholders, or are capable of being confirmed by the majority'.[434] Lord Davey added that the cases in which shareholders were allowed to bring such actions were 'confined to those in which the acts complained of are of a fraudulent character or beyond the powers of the company'. An example of this, said Lord Davey, citing *Menier v. Hooper's Telegraph Works*,[435] was 'where the majority are endeavouring directly or indirectly to appropriate to themselves money, property, or advantages which belong to the company, or in which the other shareholders are entitled to participate'.

245. The Irish Supreme Court[436] has approved the law as set out in *Burland* and reflected in more modern decisions of the English Court of Appeal.[437] Thus in *Balkanbank v. Taher*, the Supreme Court (*per* Hamilton C.J.) noted that the rule in *Foss v. Harbottle* 'is concerned with answering the question of who is the proper

430. *Ibid.*, 490–491, 202.
431. *Burland v. Earle* [1902] 1 AC 83, 89.
432. *Ibid.*, 93.
433. *Ibid.*
434. *Ibid.*
435. *Menier v. Hooper's Telegraph Works* (1874) LR 9 Ch App 350.
436. *O'Neill v. Ryan* [1995] ILRM 557; *Balkanbank v. Taher* (unreported, Supreme Court, 19 Jan. 1995).
437. *Edwards v. Halliwell* [1950] 2 All ER 1064, 1066; *Prudential Assurance Co. Ltd v. Newman Industries Ltd* (No. 2) [1982] 2 WLR 31.

person to bring an action in respect of damage suffered by a Company. It states that the proper person is the Company itself'.[438] Irish company law textbooks refer to four (or perhaps five) 'exceptions to the rule in *Foss v. Harbottle*'.[439] The principal 'exception' (properly so called) was stated as follows by the Court in *Balkanbank*: 'If a majority who are in control of a company commit a fraud on the minority, the minority, or an individual member acting on their behalf may maintain proceedings in respect of the fraud.'[440] As the Court noted, the word 'fraud' in this context does not necessarily connote dishonesty, let alone criminality, but rather is used 'more in the sense in which courts of equity were traditionally prone to use it'– that is, exercise of a power for a purpose other than the purposes for which it was entrusted, such conduct being described as 'a fraud on the power'.[441] Gross negligence is almost certainly sufficient to make out a case under this heading,[442] as too is ordinary negligence, at least where accompanied by an element of self-dealing.[443]

246. The other possible exception referred to in some authorities is that a derivative action should be permitted 'in the interests of justice'. In *O'Neill v. Ryan*,[444] the Supreme Court left open the question of whether an 'interests of justice' exception existed, but in *Glynn v. Owen*, Finlay Geoghegan J agreed with the extra-judicial view of Keane C.J. that 'the rule should not be applied in so rigorous a fashion ... as to lead to injustice', adding that it should not 'too broadly or liberally' be set aside, but only when 'a very strong case' has been made.[445] It is not clear that the Court advances matters by permitting such a nebulous exception. The derivative action is intended to avoid the injustice that may ensue when aggrieved shareholders have no other means to seek redress for breaches of fiduciary duties owed by directors to the company. To say this is to identify the *reason* for making an exception to the rule in *Foss v. Harbottle* does not specify the scope of that exception.

247. The case law suggests that a plaintiff seeking leave to proceed by way of derivative action must show that alleged wrongdoers control the voting power of the company in a general meeting and that it is accordingly futile to put the matter of whether the company should enforce the cause of action that the plaintiffs say exists.[446] The Irish High Court (Finlay Geoghegan J.) recently accepted a relatively broad understanding of the term 'control' in this context, as spanning 'a broad spectrum extending from an overall absolute majority of votes at one end, to a majority of votes at the other end made up of those likely to be cast by the [alleged] delinquent himself plus those voting with him as a result of influence or apathy'.[447] The

438. *Balkanbank v. Taher* (unreported, Supreme Court, 19 Jan. 1995), 36.
439. Courtney, *The Law of Private Companies* 1144–1156 (3rd edn., Butterworths, 2012).
440. *Balkanbank* (*supra*), 36.
441. *Balkanbank* (*supra*), 36–37.
442. *Pavlides v. Jensen* [1956] Ch 565.
443. *Daniels v. Daniels* [1978] Ch 408, as approved by Finlay Geoghegan J. in *Glynn v. Owen* [2007] IEHC 328.
444. *O'Neill v. Ryan* [1993] ILRM 557.
445. *Glynn v. Owen* [2007] IEHC 328.
446. *Prudential Assurance Co. Ltd v. Newman Industries Ltd* (No. 2) [1982] 2 WLR 31.
447. *Glynn v. Owen* [2007] IEHC 328. See also *Glynn v. Owen* [2012] IESC 15.

Court held that leave must be denied, because the third defendant did not form a part of a cohesive or consistent controlling majority, but rather stood neutral as between the two factions.

248. The exceptions to the rule in *Foss v. Harbottle* were also considered by Irvine J. in *Fanning v. Murtagh*[448] which cited the extra judicial view of the former Chief Justice Keane in Company Law:[449]

> *While the view was advanced in earlier editions of this book that the Irish courts might be reluctant to extend the exceptions to the rule, that is probably to err on the side of caution. While it is true that the wide import of the term 'fraud' enables most deserving cases to avail of the third exception where the other two are not available, there is probably no good reason why the courts should not carve out further exceptions if justice so requires. Not only should the judicial comments in support of that view already cited be borne in mind; it is also worth noting that in the two seminal cases of Foss v. Harbottle itself and Edwards v. Halliwell, Wigram V-C and Jenkins LJ both observed that the rule should not be applied in so rigorous a fashion in any case as to lead to injustice.*

249. The exceptional cases where a derivative action is available to a shareholder enabling him or her to sue on behalf of the company are enumerated as follows by Irvine J. in *Fanning v. Murtagh and Ors*:

(a) An act which is illegal or ultra vires to the company.
(b) An irregularity in the passing of a resolution which requires a qualified majority.
(c) An act purporting to abridge or abolish the individual rights of a member.
(d) An act which constitutes a fraud against the minority and the wrongdoers are themselves in control of the company.

250. There is a significant disincentive for potential plaintiffs to proceed by way of derivative action, since the benefit from any such action will flow to the company, not directly to the plaintiffs, and the plaintiff will carry the risk of incurring costs for himself and the company, as well as those of the defendant if he were to lose. As noted by O'Donnell J in *Glynn v. Owen* above, the issue of costs is a very significant problem in these kinds of cases. Recognizing this difficulty, the courts have held that plaintiffs may apply to the Court for an order that the company must indemnify them against the costs of pursuing a corporate cause of action.[450]

---

448. *Fanning v. Murtagh* [2008] IEHC 277.
449. (4th Edition, 2007).
450. *Wallersteiner v. Moir (No. 2)* [1975] QB 373; *Glynn v. Owen* [2007] IEHC 452 *Fanning v. Murtagh* [2008] IEHC 277. See further *Tomran Inc. William M. Passano Jr. et al., Baltimore City Circuit*, Matriacciani J.

Court of Appeals of Maryland, 13 Dec. 2005. I. Lynch-Fannon, *A Transatlantic Case: The Derivative Action as a Corporate Governance Tool* 27 DULJ (2005) 1–27.

IX. Obligations of Directors under Modern Legislation and Public Enforcement

251. As with most common law jurisdictions, considerable change has been made to the enforcement of directors' obligations and more generally standards of behaviour of directors and officers of companies by the enhancement of public law enforcement strategies. Beginning with the Companies Act 1990, extending through the McDowell Report of 1998 (the Working Group on Company Law Compliance and Enforcement) and the Company Law Enforcement Act 2001, Irish company law saw the introduction of disqualification procedures similar to those in the UK and Australia. In addition Ireland followed the recommendations of the Cork Committee and introduced a restriction provision. These provisions are now contained in Part 14 of the 2014 Act.[451]

252. Applications for restriction and disqualification orders under the provisions now enacted as Chapters 3 and 4 respectively of Part 14 of the Companies Act 2014 have generated considerable litigation in the Irish High Court and the following sections provide a brief summary of the principles involved. Chapter 4 of Part 14 provides a mechanism by which a director of a company may be disqualified from acting as director of any other company. Chapter 3 of Part 14 provides for the making of restriction orders against directors of insolvent companies and sets out certain conditions to be satisfied by the respondent director before s/he may become a company director, but does not represent an outright ban. However, it should also be borne in mind that the Court is free to attach such conditions as it sees fit to an order under Chapter 4 (a 'disqualification order'), with the result that a modified disqualification order may not be all that different from a restriction order.[452]

253. Chapter 4 Section 838 envisages circumstances in which disqualification automatically follows certain events, including conviction of 'any indictable offence in relation to a company, or offences involving fraud or dishonesty'[453] and failure of a person disqualified in another State to inform the Registrar of Companies of that fact upon his or her appointment as director of an Irish company.[454] Apart from automatic disqualifications, Chapter 4 section 842 allows certain persons to apply to the Court in various circumstances for the Court in its discretion to decide whether to order disqualification. Applications may be made for disqualification on the grounds listed in section 842 viz. that the respondent:

(a) while promoter, officer, auditor, receiver, liquidator or examiner of the company, committed a fraud in relation to the company;
(b) while acting in any such capacity breached his duty to the company;

451. See generally, I. Lynch Fannon & G. Murphy, *Corporate Insolvency and Rescue* (Bloomsbury Professional, Dublin 2012) Chs 10 and 11. See Cahill N, in Courtney (Ed) *Bloomsbury Professional's Guide to the Companies Act 2014* (Bloomsbury 2015) Ch. 8
452. Consider the order made in *Cahill v. Grimes* [2002] 1 IR 372.
453. Companies Act 2014, s. 838(1)(a) and (b) (for five years).
454. Companies Act 2014 s. 839.

(c) has been the subject of a declaration of civil liability in respect of fraudulent or reckless trading;
(d) has, while promoter, officer, auditor, receiver, liquidator or examiner of the company, engaged in conduct making him unfit to be concerned in the management of a company;
(e) in consequences of a report of inspectors appointed by the Court, has engaged in conduct making him unfit to be concerned in the management of a company;
(f) has been persistently in default of statutory provisions requiring accounts, returns and documents to be sent to the Registrar of Companies;
(g) has been guilty of two offences in respect of failure to ensure compliance with section 286 of the 2014 Act (regarding books and accounts);
(h) was a director of a company at the date of sending to the company of a letter indicating intention of the Registrar of Companies under section 727 to strike the company off the Register for failure to file annual returns for three consecutive years and which was subsequently struck off under s. 733, or
(i) has been disqualified under the law of another State, and the Court finds that such conduct would have merited disqualification in this State, had it occurred here.

The Court, where satisfied on any of these matters, may, either on an application made to it or of its own motion, make a disqualification order against such person for such as it sees fit.[455] Most of the above categories of potential respondents – director, liquidator, receiver, etc. – are self-explanatory, but the term 'officer' has been held by the High Court to include a range of individuals who might be regarded as being in 'senior management' positions. The High Court 'recogniz[ing] the reality of the power and responsibility of senior management in large public or private companies who have particular expertise and authority', held that the section applied to 'those in a superior position in a company who may encourage, direct or acquiesce in defrauding creditors, customers, shareholders'.[456]

254. As to who may apply to the Court for a disqualification order, the Director of Corporate Enforcement may apply under paragraphs (a)–(i) of section 842; the Director of Public Prosecutions may apply under paragraphs (a)–(g); the Registrar of Companies may apply under paragraph (f); and members, contributories, officers, employees, receivers, liquidators, examiners and creditors may apply under paragraphs (a)–(d).[457]

255. Many of the disqualification cases in Ireland have concerned the grounds under what was formerly section 160(2)(d) and (e) of the 1990 Act, now section 842(d) and (e), namely unfitness to be concerned in the management of a company.

455. Companies Act 2014, s. 842.
456. *Director of Corporate Enforcement v. Boner* [2008] IEHC 151 See also *DCE v. D'Arcy* [2006] 2 IR 163.
457. Companies Act 2014, s. 844.

It has been held, that, in order to demonstrate unfitness, an applicant must prove conduct displaying a lack of commercial probity, gross negligence or total incompetence.[458] This standard is similar to that pertaining in English law. Two important decisions in the Supreme Court[459] and Court of Appeal[460] respectively provide clear guidance on the criteria which ought to be applied to these cases in light of the considerable divergence of approaches which has emerged in the 20 years since the enactment of the original provisions.

256. As stated, Chapter 3 of Part 14 of the Companies Act 2014 provides for the making against a director of a restriction order, which amounts to a set of conditions that must be met before the respondent may act, or be appointed, as director of any company. Where such an application is made, the onus is, unusually, on the person resisting the application to persuade the Court that he or she acted 'honestly and responsibly in relation to the conduct of the affairs of the company, that he or she has co-operated to the extent reasonably expected with the liquidator of the company in relation to the conduct of the winding up of the company, and that there is no other reason why it would be just and equitable that he should be subject to [a restriction order]'.[461] The Supreme Court, albeit *obiter*, has expressed 'doubt as to whether this blanket reversal of the onus of proof, including a requirement to prove a negative proposition, is consistent with fundamental fairness and constitutional justice'.[462] The default condition attaching to a restriction is that any subsequent company of which the respondent is a director must have a minimum allotted share capital EUR 500,000 in the case of a public limited company and EUR 100,000 in the case of any other company, with such restriction to last for five years,[463] but it is open to the Court to vary these conditions. Further restrictions apply to the subsequent company including inability to avail of the private company exemption for financial assistance transactions under section 82 of the Companies Act 2014.

The Courts have adopted a range of criteria in deciding whether to impose a restriction order.

For some time criteria which had been enumerated by Shanley J. in *La Moselle Clothing Ltd v. Soualhi*[464] were often adopted and were described as having achieved almost 'canonical status' by the Supreme Court in the later decision in *Tralee Beef and Lamb Ltd.*[465] These criteria included the following:

(a) The extent to which a director has or has not complied with any obligation imposed on him by the Companies Acts.

---

458. *Re CB Readymix Ltd; Cahill v. Grimes* [2002] 1 IR 372; *Director of Corporate Enforcement v. D'Arcy* [2006] 2 IR 163 both citing with approval the English decision in *Re Lo-Line Electric Motors Co.* [1988] BCLC 698.
459. *Director of Corporate Enforcement v. McCann* [2010] IESC 59.
460. *Director of Corporate Enforcement v. Walsh* [2016] ICEA 2.
461. Companies Act 2014, s. 819(2)(a)-(c).
462. *Re Tralee Beef and Lamb Ltd (In Liquidation); Kavanagh v. Delaney* [2008] 3 IR 347.
463. Companies Act 2014, s. 819(3).
464. *La Moselle Clothing Ltd v. Soualhi* [1998] 2 ILRM 345; *Re Squash Ireland (Ltd)* [2001] 3 IR 35.
465. *Supra* n. 460.

(b) The extent to which his conduct could be regarded as so incompetent as to amount to irresponsibility.
(c) The extent of the director's responsibility for the insolvency of the company.
(d) The extent of the director's responsibility for the net deficiency in the assets of the company disclosed at the date of the winding up or thereafter.
(e) The extent to which a director, in his conduct of the affairs of the company, has displayed a lack of commercial probity or want of proper standards.

However, in *Tralee Beef and Lamb* an issue arose as to whether these criteria properly allowed for a consideration of the broader range of duties owed by directors. The High Court accepted the 'amplification', of this set of criteria by reference to directors' duties generally, namely, 'duties to the Company which are normally divided into duties of loyalty based on fiduciary principles, developed initially by the Courts of Equity, and duties of skill and care developed initially by the Common Law Courts from the principles in the law of negligence'. Though approving of this amplification in theory, the Supreme Court allowed an appeal in that case, because such amplification – or the respondent's compliance with his common law duties – had not been clearly part of the statutory scheme. In a subsequent decision the Supreme Court has made it clear that the full range of obligations owed by directors can properly be the subject matter of consideration in such cases.[466]

257. The procedure governing applications for restrictions is unusual; it has been described by the Supreme Court as 'unique' and 'draconian'.[467] Under section 683 of the Companies Act 2014 the liquidator of every insolvent company must, issue proceedings, seeking a restriction order against each director of the insolvent company, unless relieved of the need to do so by the Director.[468] Failure to do so is an offence.[469] The Director may decline to relieve him or her of his or her duty to apply to the Court, and in such a case the liquidator must nevertheless apply to Court seeking a restriction order. The potential incongruity of such a scenario was the subject of adverse comment by the Supreme Court in *Tralee Beef and Lamb Ltd*[470] but was passed over without comment by the Court in the later case of *Dublin Sports Café Ltd.*[471]

258. A person against whom a restriction order is made may apply to the Court for relief, in whole or in part, from the order, or any conditions attaching thereto.[472] In an unusual provision, the legislation requires that such application must be made

466. *Re Mitek Holdings Ltd.* [2010] IESC 31. See also *Re Swanpool: McLaghlen v. Lennon* [2006] 2 ILRM 217.
467. *Re Tralee Beef and Lamb Ltd (In Liquidation); Kavanagh v. Delaney* [2008] 3 IR 347.
468. Companies Act 2014 s. 683, s. 56(2).
469. Companies Act 2014 s. 683(5).
470. *Supra* n. 467.
471. *Re Dublin Sports Café Ltd; Fennell v. Long* [2008] IESC 66.
472. Companies Act 2014 s. 822. See *Re Ferngara Associates Limited: F & R Robinson v. Forrest* [1999] 1 IR 426; *Re CMC (Ireland) Ltd; Fennell v. Carolan* [2005] IEHC 340 (unreported, High Court, Finlay Geoghegan J., 1 Nov. 2005); *Re Xnet Information Systems Ltd; Stafford v. Higgins* [2006] IEHC 289 (unreported, High Court, O'Neill J., 10 Oct. 2006).

'not more than one year after a declaration has been made in respect of him'. Although the original capitalization requirement attaching to a restriction order was quite modest, this has been increased under the Companies Act 2014 as described above (paragraph 257). However, once the subsequent company in which a restricted director is involved reaches this capital requirement 'the public may be, in practical terms, relatively unprotected from restricted directors who happen to have access to modest levels of wealth',[473] although not all would agree that EUR 100,00 is a modest amount. There is certainly a stigma in business circles attaching to a restriction order, and this reputational matter has been commented on by the courts on several occasions.[474]

259. Following the debate described above regarding the relevant criteria to be applied, it would seem that as regards restriction orders the directors of companies must comply with a more clearly sketched set of criteria as outlined by Clarke J. in *Re* Swanpool: *McLaghlen v. Lennon*[475] which include the following:

(1) Compliance with Companies Acts.
(2) Compliance with other duties.
(3) Duties which may arise under *Re Frederick Inns Ltd*[476], namely duties owed to creditors as described *supra* in paragraph 242.

260. The Companies Act 2014 has introduced a new procedure whereby an individual director may submit to a restriction or disqualification through providing an undertaking that he or she agrees to the terms of a restriction order or disqualification order.[477] The undertaking process is designed to prevent a multiplicity of applications to the Irish High Court and has been welcomed for that reason. The process is provided for in Chapter 5 of Part 14 of the Companies Act 2014.[478]

X. Conclusion

261. At present the range of obligations owed by company directors to their companies are extensive under equitable principles and common law. In addition, as demonstrated by the discussion in paragraphs 251–261 under Irish law there is considerable jurisprudence regarding the enforcement of directorial standards under modern legislation, particularly since 2001.[479] In fact, this area has led to a great deal of litigation in recent years. This public method of the enforcement of directorial standards has far outpaced the setting of standards through pronouncements and decisions in private law enforcement. The reason for this state of affairs is that

473. *Re Xnet Information Systems Ltd; Stafford v. Higgins* [2006] IEHC 289 (unreported, High Court, O'Neill J., 10 Oct. 2006), 19.
474. See, for example, *Xnet* (*supra*), 23; *Tralee Beef and Lamb* (*supra*), 10–11.
475. [2006] 2 ILRM 217.
476. [1994] ILRM 87.
477. Companies Act 2014, Ch. 5 of Part 14.
478. See generally N. Cahill, *supra* n. 451 Ch. 8.
479. Company Law Enforcement Act 2001, now re-enacted as Part 14 of the Companies Act 2014.

the methods for privately enforcing directorial standards are limited to an action by the company or, in most unusual circumstances, an action by a minority shareholder. Actions against directors brought by the company as plaintiff are still fairly uncommon in Irish law, so there is a dearth of jurisprudence in this area. Nevertheless, lack of private enforcement is counterbalanced by the rigour of the approach in the area of public enforcement. The following quotation is apt:

> It is of the greatest importance that any individual who undertakes the statutory and fiduciary obligations of being a company director should realise that these are inescapable personal responsibilities.[480]

XI. Auditors

262. The principle role of the company auditor is to ensure that the company complies with the currently enforced accounting standards as set down by law. The auditor conducts his or her business with this obligation in mind. The principle mechanism to ensure adequate financial governance is through the auditors' report, which must be read at the AGM and should be made available to every member of the company as provided for in the Companies Act 2014, section 383. Under the Companies Act, shareholders are entitled to receive a report from an independent auditor as to whether the financial statements presented by the directors give a true and fair view of the state of affairs of the company and of its profits (or losses) for the period under review. The report also addresses whether these financial statements have been properly prepared in accordance with[481] the accounting provisions of the Companies Act. This obligation is subject to the exemptions which are now provided for in sections 370ff of the Companies Act 2014. These exemptions primarily apply to small and medium sized enterprises. In circumstances where a company no longer qualifies as small or medium enterprise for the purpose of these exemptions then the directors must cause the company to deliver a copy of the revised statements with a directors' and auditor's report to the Registrar within twenty-eight days. The auditor has access to all books, accounts and vouchers and is entitled to require from officers information and explanations that are within their knowledge.[482] Auditors are under a duty to carry out the audit with professional integrity.[483]

263. In addition to this primary role and obligation to the shareholders, the role of the company auditor under Irish company law has come under increasing scrutiny following adoption of the Company Law Enforcement Act 2001, which is now re-eancted in the Companies Act 2014. In this context auditors have a role in relation to public enforcement of company law standards. Where auditors form the opinion that the company being audited is contravening, or has contravened, its

480. *Re Westmid Packaging Services Ltd; Secretary of State for Trade and Industry v. Griffiths and ors* [1998] 2 BCLC 646, 653 per Lord Woolf M.R. (approved in *Director of Corporate Enforcement v. Brennan* [2008] IEHC 132.
481. Companies Act 2014, s. 377(1)-(3).
482. Companies Act 2014, s. 336.
483. Companies Act 2014, s. 390.

obligations to maintain proper books of account, they are obliged to serve a notice on the company informing it of that opinion. This obligation is required under the Companies Act 2014, section 392. Subsequently, the auditors may be required to share this opinion with the Registrar of Companies, who will in turn notify the Director of Corporate Enforcement. In addition, the auditors are required to make a report to the Director of Corporate Enforcement when, by virtue of carrying out an audit, information comes into their possession that leads them to form the opinion that the company, or an officer or agent of it, has committed an indictable offence under the Companies Acts. The use of auditors' reports has become a significant database on which to base activities relating to enforcement.[484]

264. A further issue that has arisen in modern company law is the extent of the obligations imposed on auditors where non-audit work is carried on by the same firm of which the auditor is a member or

XII. Company Secretary

265. Section 129(1) of the Companies Act 2014 provides that the company must have a company secretary who may be one of the directors. However where a particular transaction or act requires both the signature of a secretary and director the same person cannot perform both functions.[485] Section 129(4) of the Companies Act 2014 now provides that the directors of a company now have a duty to ensure that the person appointed as company secretary has the necessary skills and resources to discharge their statutory duties. Section 226(1) of the Companies Act 2014 also provides for the additional delegation of duties to the company secretary by the Board of Directors. Any such delegation shall be 'without derogation from the secretary's statutory or legal duties'. The Company Secretary is obliged to keep minutes of meetings of directors and any committees of directors. Any director can inspect minutes and copy in accordance with the Act. In addition the Company Secretary is obliged to maintain the share register; to notify shareholders of meetings, resolutions and so forth; to maintain all necessary information pertinent to the exercise by shareholders of their rights; and to ensure that this information is available for inspection.

§5. Liquidation of the Company[486]

I. Types of Winding Up

A. *Introduction*

266. The Companies Act 2014 maintains the distinction between voluntary liquidations and compulsory liquidations. However the new legislation has sought to

484. Companies Act 2014, s. 393.
485. Companies Act 2014, s. 134.
486. See generally, Thomas B. Courtney, (gen. ed.) et al. *The Professional's Guide to the Companies Act 2014* (Bloomsbury 2015). Chapters 7 and 8. See also Lynch Fannon & Murphy, *Corporate Insolvency and Rescue* (Bloomsbury 2012).

achieve a streamlining of how all liquidations are conducted and also to shift the focus of how liquidations are conducted from official or compulsory liquidations to voluntary liquidations. Liquidations are dealt with in Part 11 of the Companies Act 2014. The major changes in this area of law which have been introduced by the new legislation include the following:

(i) The applicability of the new Summary Approval Procedure to the commencement of a members' voluntary winding up.[487]
(ii) Insolvency practitioners are to be regulated in Ireland for the first time.[488] In addition new rules regarding remuneration of liquidators have been introduced.
(iii) Some changes have been made to the role of the creditors' committee of inspection.[489]
(iv) Liquidators' powers have been clarified.[490]
(v) Some changes have been made to avoidance provisions.[491]

B. Voluntary and Compulsory Liquidations

267. The distinction between voluntary liquidations (whether members' voluntary or creditors' voluntary liquidations) and official or compulsory liquidation rests on who exercises control over the process. A voluntary liquidation can either be a members' voluntary liquidation or a creditors' voluntary liquidation, depending on whether it is open to the directors to swear a declaration of solvency in accordance with the new procedure under the Summary Approval Procedure (SAP) described in the following paragraph. A voluntary liquidation will begin with passing a resolution pursuant to the constitution of the company.

268. A members' voluntary liquidation may be commenced using the SAP which is a new element in the Companies Act 2014. This involves the passing of a special resolution and the swearing of a declaration by the directors of the company. The SAP[492] relies on a variety of forms of declaration depending on the purpose of the procedure. In this case, the declaration is to the effect that the company can pay its debts. Accordingly, the format of the declaration is outlined in section 207 of the Act. In accordance with the provisions of section 207, the relevant declaration will include a statement of the total amount of company's assets and liabilities at the 'latest practicable date' but not more than three months before the date of making the declaration, and will also include a declaration that the company will be able to discharge its debts within period not exceeding twelve months after the

487. The Summary Approval Procedure is outlined in Part 4, Ch. 7 of the Companies Act 2014. *Supra*.
488. Companies Act 2014, ss 633–635.
489. Companies Act 2014, ss 646(2), 666 and 667.
490. Companies Act 2014, s. 646(2).
491. Companies Act 2014, ss 603–608.
492. See generally Companies Act 2014, ss 201–211.

commencement of the winding up.[493] Section 580 of the Companies Act 2014 provides that the company may specify in its articles that the company should be wound up on completion of a certain task, or period pursuant to the provisions of section 579(3).

269. A creditors' voluntary liquidation may commence *ab initio* under the provisions of section 586(2). This includes where the company resolves by ordinary resolution to wind up the company because it 'cannot by reason of its liabilities carry on its business'. Alternatively, a creditors' voluntary liquidation may commence through the conversion of a members' voluntary winding up to a creditors' voluntary winding up in the following three situations:

(1) where the court makes an order under section 582(2) of the Companies Act 2014 on foot of an application made by creditors to the court;
(2) where a creditors' meeting is held in accordance with section 584 of the Companies Act 2014 and a resolution is passed to so convert a members voluntary liquidation;
(3) where there is a default in the making of the statutory declaration of solvency or in the conduct of the SAP generally.[494]

270. In contrast, a compulsory or official liquidation begins with a petition to the High Court on the grounds described *infra*. If the petition is successful, the court will appoint a liquidator and the liquidation will proceed under the supervision of the High Court.

II. Grounds for Winding Up

271. Section 569 of the Companies Act 2014 provides for the grounds upon which an application can be made to the court for winding up a company. This is called an official or compulsory liquidation, once the order has been granted by the court. Thus, in a compulsory liquidation the High Court, in answer to a petition to wind up the company, initiates the liquidation, appoints a liquidator and controls the liquidation throughout the process. The most common ground on which the petition is based is section 569(1)(d) whereby the company is wound up because it is unable to pay its debts. The 2014 Act has increased the threshold level of indebtedness and provides that a company shall be deemed to be unable to pay its debts where a creditor makes a demand 'exceeding €10,000' and this has not been paid within the twenty-one day demand period. (This is ten times the existing threshold of EUR 1,269.74 which provides a creditor with locus standi to petition the court).[495]

493. Companies Act 2014, s. 210 which imposes a significant civil sanction of personal liability for statement made regarding opinion as to solvency without reasonable grounds.

494. Companies Act 2014, s. 586(3)(c).

495. Section 570(b) with 571(b) provides similarly that a company shall be deemed to be unable to pay its debts where two or more creditors representing in aggregate a value of indebtedness of at least EUR 20,000 make a demand for payment which is not met.

Section 569(1)f) allows a petitioner in an action for oppression action to petition the Court to wind up the company as a remedy, and section 569(1)(e) refers to the possibility of a petition to wind up the company on 'just and equitable' grounds. This provision has covered a range of cases on the spectrum, from an alternative ground for the petitioner/creditor who seeks payment and who has petitioned under section 569(1)(d), to a member petitioning to have the company wound up in cases where there is a deadlock in the running of the company. In a new provision, section 569(1)(g) the Director of Corporate Enforcement has been added as a potential petitioner with locus standi to petition to wind up a company where the public interest requires this. There is no statement in the legislation as to what the public interest might entail but at the very least the Director of Corporate Enforcement will petition to liquidate companies which have ceased to trade. Section 572(4) provides that the court may order that the company can be wound up as if it were a members' voluntary winding up where the order is made under paragraphs (a), (b), (c), (e) or (f) of section 569(1).

III. Effects of Winding Up

A. *Creditors' Rights*

272. The general principle is that debts owing on a winding up are paid *pari passu* out of the liquidated assets of the company.[496]

However, as described *infra*, statute has assigned preferential status to certain types of debts – principally those owed to the Revenue and to employees. In all liquidations, the priorities of payments are governed by the provisions of Chapter 7, Part 11 of the Companies Act 2014 and specifically sections 617–623. Section 617 deals with costs of the winding up. The following priorities apply:

> First – The costs of the petition, including the costs of any person appearing on the petition whose costs are allowed by the Court.
> Next – The costs and expenses of any person who makes or concurs in making the company's statement of affairs.
> Next – The necessary disbursements of the Official Liquidator, other than expenses properly incurred in preserving, realizing or getting in the assets herein before provided for.
> Next –The costs payable to the solicitor for the Official Liquidator.
> Next – The remuneration of the Official Liquidator.
> Next – The out-of-pocket expenses necessarily incurred by the committee of inspection (if any).

The first series of payments out of the company's assets will thus be the expenses of the liquidation procedure, which will include costs of realization of all the assets, fees of legal advisors and remuneration of the liquidator. When an examinership[497]

496. Companies Act 2014, s. 618.
497. *Infra* para. 295.

has occurred prior to a winding up, the fees of an examiner and certified expenses 'shall be paid in full and shall be paid before any other claim, secured or unsecured'.

Of course, this necessarily implies that the examinership has not been successful, and the situation can be quite difficult for this reason.

273. Once fees as described above are paid, the liquidator will distribute the assets in accordance with section 619 which provides that 'in the winding up of an insolvent company the same rules shall prevail and be observed ... as are in force for the time being under the law of bankruptcy ... ':

- Fixed charge holders are entitled to realize assets and to be paid in full from this realization.
- The preferential creditors, accorded this status under relevant legislation will be paid before any other classes of creditors.[498]
- Floating charge holders will then be paid.
- Finally, the unsecured creditors will be paid, usually on a pro rata basis as there are often insufficient assets for unsecured creditors.

The nature and priority of each such type of creditor will be discussed in the next section. A useful starting point in considering the position of creditors in Irish company law is the following statement in the seminal case of *Salomon v. Salomon & Co Ltd.*[499] Even as the House of Lords set down the robust principle of corporate personality, thus copper-fastening the effect of the statutory concept of limited liability, it also addressed the role of creditors and in doing so pinned the creditors' position on a robust commitment to freedom of contract: 'Every creditor is entitled to get and to hold the best security the law allows him to take.' Thus in Irish (as in English) law, the role of the commercial contract in securing the position of the creditor is extremely important. This is seen in relation to the extent to which a contract can be used to secure a broad range of assets, as we will see in our brief discussion of fixed charges on book debts and proceeds; in relation to the establishment of the receiver as an important insolvency process (see *infra*, paragraph 295); and in relation to the use of retention of title clauses and other types of agreements to support an unsecured creditor. In contrast, the role of statute in giving security to creditors is not as prevalent, except in relation to the implementation of the preferential category of creditor.

B. *Fixed Charges*

274. A charge is a contractual agreement that certain property be available as security to meet performance of a liability, usually the payment of money.[500] A fixed or specific charge is one taken over 'ascertained and definite property or property

498. Companies Act 2014, ss 621, 622.

499. *Salomon v. Salomon &Co. Ltd.* [1897] AC 22, 52 per Lord MacNaghten.

500. *Re Clare Textiles Ltd.,* [1992] NI 323 p. 2.

capable of being ascertained and defined'.[501] This will often be an asset such as real property. As has been noted, assets subject to a fixed charge are 'permanently appropriated to the payment of the sum charged in such a way as to give the chargee a proprietary interest in the assets and to impose restrictions on the chargor's use of the asset'.[502] Fixed charges, as with other charges taken on company property, must be registered in the company's file pursuant to section 409 of the 2014 Act. Failure to register the charge with the CRO renders it void as against the liquidator and any creditor of the company.[503] The Companies Act 2014 has changed Irish law by introducing the option of a two stage procedure regarding the registration of charges. Under this procedure a lender or company may deliver notice of their intention to register a charge which must then be registered within a twenty-one day notice period.[504]

C. *Floating Charges*

275. Floating charges are peculiar to the corporate world and are not available over the assets of individuals in bankruptcy. The floating charge was defined by Lord MacNaghten in *Illingworth v. Houldsworth*[505] as 'ambulatory and shifting in its nature, hovering over and so to speak floating with the property which it is intended to affect until some event occurs or some act is done which causes it to settle and fasten on the subject of the charge within its reach and grasp'. The charge is said to 'crystallize' over the class of assets it has been floating above on the occurrence of certain events, known as 'crystallizing events'.[506] These are the appointment of a receiver, the appointment of a liquidator or the commencement of a liquidation. It appears that a company's ceasing to carry on business is also a crystallizing event.[507] Under English law in particular, some credence has been given to the possibility of automatic crystallization – that is, the possibility of the lender specifying the occurrence of other events, essentially private in nature, that could cause the charge to crystallize.[508] Although attractive to lenders, there are serious concerns about the viability of automatic crystallization of charges when measured against some of the fundamental principles of insolvency law, such as the concept of public notification of creditors' rights to other creditors and to other stakeholders

501. *Illingworth v. Houldsworth* [1904] AC 355. 358.
502. *In Re Spectrum Plus Ltd. (in liquidation)* [2005] 2 AC 680. A point worth noting is that, although the terms 'charge' and 'mortgage' are sometimes used interchangeably, there is a technical difference between them, inasmuch as a mortgage involves conveyance of legal title to the property involved subject to a right of redemption, whereas a charge merely gives the chargee the right to look to the charged property in satisfaction of the debt secured.
503. Companies Act 2014, s. 409(1). See generally Part 7 of the Companies Act 2014 regarding Charges and Debentures.
504. Companies Act 2014, s. 409(4).
505. *Illingworth v. Houldsworth* [1904] AC 355.
506. *Re Woodroffes (Musical Instruments) Ltd.* [1985] BCLC 227; *Re The Real Meat Co. Ltd* [1996] BCC 254.
507. *Re Woodroffes (Musical Instruments) Ltd* [1985] BCLC 227; *In re Sperrin Textiles Ltd* [1992] NI 323.
508. *Re Brightlife Ltd* [1987] Ch. 200.

in the company.[509] Crystallization by notice is a variant of this practice and has been discussed extensively by the Irish courts in *Re J.D. Brian Ltd.*[510] In this case both the Irish High Court and subsequently the Supreme Court on appeal have approved the possibility of crystallization by notice. The effect of this kind of crystallization was also considered in this litigation and is considered *infra* (paragraph 281). De-crystallization is also a conceptual possibility enunciated and approved of in the Irish Supreme Court by *Re Holidair Ltd.*[511]

276. Floating charges face a particular challenge as to their validity in liquidations under the Companies Act 1963, section 288, as amended by Companies Act 1990, section 136 and now re-enacted in section 597 of the Companies Act 2014. Historically, floating charges were often created at the last minute to secure assets and, as such, can be specifically open to challenge under section 597 of the Companies Act 2014. Similarly, floating charges can be challenged under the fraudulent preference provisions now contained in section 604 of the Companies Act 2014. (Formerly, s. 286 of the Companies Act 1963, as amended by Companies Act 1990, section 135.) However, any transaction can be a fraudulent preference, so this is not a disadvantage peculiar to floating charges.

D. Preferential Creditors

277. Section 285 of the 1963 Companies Act created a class of preferential creditors, which has been increased by various amendments. Despite much discussion and consequent change in neighbouring jurisdictions, in particular in the UK[512] about the need to have classes of preferential creditors, these have been retained by section 621 of the Companies Act 2014 in Ireland. Preferential creditors will be paid in full after the fixed charge holders are paid and will be paid before any creditors with a floating charge. The conceptual underpinning seeks to protect vulnerable creditors such as employees in relation to outstanding wages and payments. A significant creditor protected under this legislation is the State in relation to unpaid taxes. At the current time there is a significant class of creditors who are categorized as preferential creditors. The effect of the growth of the categories and types of preferential creditors was to diminish the value of the floating charge because these creditors are given priority over floating charge holders. As a consequence lenders sought to extend the reach and flexibility of the fixed charge, hence the

509. Although English case law has inclined toward approval of such clauses (cf. *Re. Griffin Hotel Co.* [1940] Ch. 87 and *Re Brightlife Ltd* [1987] Ch. 200), reservations have been expressed regarding approval of such clauses under Irish law. See Keane, *Company Law* 251 (4th edn., Tottel, 2007).

510. In the matter of J.D. Brian Ltd [2011] 3 IR 244. Finlay Geoghegan J. delivered a judgment regarding the issue of priorities, but unusually, and on request from the liquidator who indicated an intention to appeal, a second judgment was delivered regarding the effect of crystallization. Both judgments are reported at [2011] 3 IR 244. In the matter of J.D. Brian Ltd t/a East Coast Print and Publicity and Re East Coast Car Parts Ltd [2015] IESC 62 (Laffoy J.). See further I. Lynch Fannon, *The Floating Charge Debate: The Path to Clarity in Irish Law* 22 [2015] CLP 187–195.

511. *Re Holidair Ltd* [1994] I ILRM 481.

512. The Enterprise Act (UK) 2002 effectively abolished preferential status for all revenue and other debts, with the exception of preferential status being retained for employees.

extension of the concept of a fixed charge to book debts. Broader issues regarding securitization are explored currently in commercial practice, such as the charging of intangible assets, for example and particularly, intellectual property rights such as patents.

E. *The Extension of Classes of Assets Which Could Be Subject to a Fixed Charge*

278. Because of the growth of classes of preferential creditors, it became common practice for lenders to seek to extend the range of assets over which they could take a fixed charge, as the floating charge became vulnerable to non-payment due to the extensive reach of the claims of preferential creditors. Thus, the creation of fixed charges over book debts became common in Ireland and England during the mid-1980s. This practise was the subject of significant litigation primarily because the underlying conceptualization of a fixed charge over the book debts of a company that is still actively trading is not without significant difficulties in the common law. The classic definition of book debts is 'debts owing to the company concerned with and arising out of the company's trade or business, which are entered, or commonly would be entered in the ordinary course of business, in well kept books of such trade or business'.[513]

279. During the extensive litigation arising out of this difficult concept, a significant feature became one of control.[514] The key question was whether the lender/creditor had obtained significant control over the disposal of the asset in question to render the charge a fixed charge or whether in fact, primarily due to the exigencies of the situation – namely the need for the company to have access to the asset to facilitate trading – control over the asset had rested with the borrower/debtor company. If the latter was the case, the fact that the company still exercised control over the asset presented difficulties in establishing the fixed nature of the charge. This question is played out in many of the Irish decisions.[515] Nevertheless, the possibility of having a fixed charge over book debts was countenanced by the Irish courts. A second issue evolved as to the asset which was actually charged, and here a distinction evolved between a charge over the book debts themselves and the proceeds collected from the book debts. Where the lender/creditor did not specifically create the charge over the book debts and proceeds, the latter were eventually deemed to be free of the fixed charge.[516] The original litigation was driven by the relative positions of the commercial lender with a fixed charge over an asset such as book debts

513. Schmitthoff (ed.), *Palmer's Company Law* 46-06 (24th edn., Sweet & Maxwell 1987).

514. *Re Keenan Bros Ltd* [1985] IR 401; *Siebe Gorman v. Barclays Bank Ltd* [1979] 2 Lloyds Reports 142; *Re Armagh Shoes Ltd* [1982] N.I. 59; *Re Wogan's (Drogheda) Ltd* (*under the Protection of the Court*) [1993] 1 IR 157; *Re Holidair Ltd* [1994] 1 IR 416; *In re Spectrum Plus Ltd (in liquidation)* [2005] 2 AC 680.

515. For example, *Re Keenan Bros Ltd* [1985] IR 401; *Re Wogan's (Drogheda) Ltd* (*under the Protection of the Court*); *Jenkins v. Hill Samuel (Ireland) Ltd* [1993] 1 IR 157.

516. *Re Wogan's (Drogheda) Ltd* (*under the Protection of the Court*) [1993] 1 IR 157; *Re Holidair Ltd* [1994] 1 IR 416.

and the preferential creditor, usually the Revenue authorities. In Ireland, however, the litigation became even more significant because of the interplay between the significance of having a valid fixed charge over book debts and the necessity to fund an examinership if this were to lead to a genuine possibility of the rescue of a company. In litigation arising in the latter context, the court recognized the possibility of a charge that had crystallized into a fixed charge on book debts or proceeds on foot of the appointment of a receiver, de-crystallizing on removal of the receiver following the appointment of an examiner.[517]

280. The decision of the House of Lords in *Re Spectrum Plus*,[518] held that although it is possible in law for a company to create a security consisting of a fixed charge over all its present and future book debts,[519] it would be extremely difficult to realistically exercise the necessary control over such an asset whilst still operating a trading company. This decision has cast considerable doubt over the efficacy of the fixed charge over book debts and/or proceeds and assets of this kind. It should be noted that the court specifically overruled the decision in *Siebe Gorman*[520] which is the basis for the creation of such a charge in both Irish and English law.

281. This area has been further litigated in Ireland with an important recent decision from the Irish Supreme Court in the case of *Re J.D. Brian Ltd t/a East Coast Print and Publicity* in July 2015.[521] This was an appeal from the decision of Finlay Geoghegan J.[522] in the High Court where it had been held that even though the concept of automatic crystallization[523] of a floating charge was permissible under Irish law, the consequences of such crystallization would not affect the priority of preferential creditors under section 285 of the Companies Act 1963 (the '1963 Act').[524] The Supreme Court allowed the appeal from the High Court and made two important and significant decisions. First, that the charge in question had been 'converted into a fixed charge over the property of each Company by virtue of the service of the Crystallisation Notice by the Bank, prior to the commencement of the winding up of each Company'; and second that accordingly, the 'claims of the Bank as debenture holder to the funds realised from the assets the subject of the floating charges … converted into fixed charges … shall rank in priority to the preferential debts due by the Company identified by reference to s. 285(1)-(6) of the Act of 1963'.

---

517. *Re Holidair Ltd* [1994] 1 IR 416.
518. *In re Spectrum Plus Ltd (in liquidation)* [2005] 2 AC 680.
519. *Ibid.*, 711–712.
520. *Supra n.* 511.
521. *In the matter of J.D. Brian Ltd t/a East Coast Print and Publicity and Re East Coast Car Parts Ltd* [2015] IESC 62 (Laffoy J.).
522. *In the matter of J.D. Brian Ltd* [2011] 3 IR 244. Finlay Geoghegan J. delivered a judgment regarding the issue of priorities, but unusually, and on request from the liquidator who indicated an intention to appeal, a second judgment was delivered regarding the effect of crystallization. Both judgments are reported at [2011] 3 IR 244.
523. Note that no real distinction was made between the concept of automatic crystallization and crystallization by notice in these decisions. However, the actual clauses were crystallization by notice clauses.
524. Now s. 621 of the Companies Act 2014.

282. Section 285(7) (re-enacted as section 621(7)(b) of the 2014 Act) provides that where the assets of the company available for payment of general creditors are insufficient to meet the preferential debts, these debts will 'have priority over the claims of holders of debentures under any floating charge created by the company, and be paid accordingly out of any property comprised in or subject to that charge'. The priority of preferential creditors over floating charges is therefore still a significant matter in Irish insolvency law, whereas it is much less significant in the neighbouring jurisdictions of the UK, where the preferential status of Crown debts has been abolished by the Enterprise Act 2002.[525]

On the other hand, and regarding the first part of the decision of the Supreme Court, the broader questions of how crystallization of a floating charge can occur and what exactly is the effect of crystallization on a floating charge, are questions of legal significance in all jurisdictions. Here the Supreme Court held that the effect of such crystallization was to change the priority of the original charge. This approach is certainly doubtful and was not the approach taken in the High Court.[526]

F. The Unsecured Creditor

283. This creditor often has little hope of being paid in full after the fixed charge holder, the preferential creditors and the floating charge holder(s) have been paid. Thus, the supplier and other kinds of unsecured creditors have invented their own devices to deal with the difficult problem of not getting paid by companies and consequences for their own solvency. Retention of title clauses are thus commonly found in supply contracts, but are not always enforceable depending on the nature of the asset. Similarly, the recognition of a trust device to protect certain kinds of creditors, such as those ordering through mail or Internet where deposits are paid for certain goods, is a possibility under Irish law, as it is under English law.

G. Unsecured Creditor Protection: Retention of Title Clauses; Liens

284. Retention of title clauses seek to retain title in goods supplied until these goods are paid for. Therefore, although the goods may be in the possession of the creditor company, the retention of title clause purports to permit recovery of the goods supplied or indeed recovery of mixed goods to the value of the goods supplied. In addition, retention of title clauses seeks to follow the proceeds arising from the sale of goods so supplied. The possible validity of such clauses was recognized in the English decision of *Aluminium Industrie Vassem v. Romalpa Aluminium*[527]

525. Enterprise Act 2002 (UK) s. 251– this provision abolished the Crown's status as a preferential creditor. In addition, the Enterprise Act 2002 also established a scheme which 'ring-fenced' a fund which is a proportion of a company's assets up to a maximum of GBP 123,000 for the benefit of unsecured creditors (not floating charge-holders). Section 4 of this article will consider some significant contextual differences in England and Wales.

526. See further I. Lynch Fannon, *The Floating Charge Debate in Irish Law: The Path to Clarity* [2015] 22 CLP 186–195.

527. *Aluminium Industrie Vassem v. Romalpa Aluminium* [1976] 1 WLR 676.

and in Ireland in *Frigoscandia (Contracting) Ltd v. Continental Irish Meats Ltd.*[528] However, over time, the conceptual difficulties inherent in these clauses from a common law perspective cast some doubt over the possibility of such clauses being valid once the clauses purported to follow mixed goods or proceeds.[529]

The decision in *Carroll Group Ltd v. G & J.F. Bourke Ltd*[530] represents a clear statement of the law of retention of title clauses as it applies in Ireland. While a simple retention of title clause over identifiable products in the possession of the liquidator or receiver will be enforceable in the majority of cases, difficulties may arise when the retention of title clause follows goods into manufactured or mixed goods or proceeds of the sale of goods.[531] It is worth noting that simple retention of title clauses do not create a registrable charge even though it has been suggested in the UK that all contracts containing retention of title clauses should be registrable as charges. A recent case worth noting where a simple retention of title clause was not enough is *Chaigley Farms Ltd. v. Crawford; Kay & Greyshire Ltd.*[532] Here, when an abbatoir went into receivership, the suppliers sought the return of their meat. Garland J. determined that the retention of title had been lost.

H. Unsecured Creditor Protection: Trust Devices

285. The *Quistclose* trust, called after the decision that validated it, allowed for an unsecured creditor to recover funds when such funds had been forwarded for a specific reason. In *Barclays Bank Ltd v. Quistclose Investments Ltd,*[533] a loan was made to a company on the agreed condition that it would be used to pay an already declared dividend. The loan was paid into a special bank account opened specially for the purpose. The bank knew that the money was borrowed and that the account would be used only for the purpose of paying the dividend. Before the dividend could be paid, the company went into voluntary liquidation. The lender sought to recover the amount of the loan on the basis that, where funds were forwarded for a sufficiently clear reason and where the reason could not be achieved, there was a resulting trust in favour of the creditor. As a result, the bank, being on notice, was a constructive trustee of the money. This claim was upheld by the House of Lords.

---

528. *Frigoscandia (Contracting) Ltd v. Continental Irish Meats Ltd* [1982] ILRM 396; cf. *Kruppstahl A.G. v. Quitman Products Ltd* [1982] ILRM 551.
529. *Re Peachdart Ltd* [1983] BCLC 225 (clause purporting to follow leather into manufactured handbags held to be invalid); *Carroll Group Ltd v. G & J.F. Bourke Ltd* [1990] ILRM 285 (clause held to be valid insofar as it purported to retain title over identifiable products, cigarettes, but invalid to the extent it purported to follow proceeds of sale); *Re Bond Worth* [1980] Ch. 228 (again, a clause purporting to follow mixed goods was held to be invalid). See further *Thyssen v. Armour Edelstahlwerke A.G.* [1991] 2 AC 339, in which the House of Lords limited the effectiveness of such clauses, and 'Bradgate: Retention of Title in the House of Lords' (1991) 54 LQR 726 for a commentary on the decision in *Armour*.
530. *Carroll Group Ltd v. G & J.F. Bourke Ltd* [1990] ILRM 285.
531. I. Lynch Fannon & N. Murphy, *Corporate Insolvency and Rescue* 356 (2nd edn., Bloomsbury 2012).
532. *Chaigley Farms Ltd. v. Crawford; Kay & Greyshire Ltd* [1996] BCC 957.
533. *Barclays Bank Ltd v. Quistclose Investments Ltd* [1970] AC 576.

An example of the consequences of this decision is to be seen in *Re Kayford Ltd*,[534] in which a court upheld the creation of a *Quistclose* trust in these circumstances: A mail order company paid money received from customers (either full payment in advance or deposits) into a particular account, withdrawing the money only if and when it later delivered the goods, with the intention of protecting the funds remaining in the account from general distribution in the event of insolvency. Such customers would normally be regarded as unsecured creditors in relation to such deposits and would not normally receive any money in most insolvent liquidations. As has been emphasized in more recent case law,[535] the key issue in relation to a *Quistclose* trust is whether the parties intended the money to be at the free disposal of the recipient or whether instead the parties came to an arrangement that the money be used exclusively for a stated purpose. The necessary implication of money being advanced for a sole or exclusive purpose is that otherwise the money is to be returned to the lender.

In *Re Farepak Food and Gifts Ltd*,[536] Mann J. considered whether a Quistclose trust had arisen where customers had prepaid for Christmas hampers. He decided that this type of trust had not arisen based on the facts of the case as there was no contract of loan between the parties. Mann J. stated that:

> crucially, there is no suggestion that the money ought to have been put on one side by Farepak pending the transmutation from credited money to goods or vouchers. If there were a Quistclose trust then that obligation would have been inherent in it, but the business model would have made no sense. It would have required Farepak to have kept all the customer moneys in a separate account from January until November, untouched until the time when the goods or vouchers were acquired and then sent out. That is completely implausible. It would turn Farepak into a very odd savings organisation. Even banks do not have to do that.

I. Transfer of Undertakings Regulations

286. The Transfer of Undertakings Regulations was introduced into Irish law by virtue of a EU Directive designed to protect the position of employees of an undertaking where part or the entirety of that undertaking was transferred to another. Essentially, the rights of the employees and the corresponding duties of the employer are transferred to the purchasing entity. The European Communities (Protection of Employees on Transfer of Undertakings) Regulations 2003 (S.I. 131 of 2003) apply to any legal transfer of an undertaking, business or part of a business from one employer to another employer. Such transfers includes mergers. The Regulations, which came into operation on 11 April 2003, revoke and replace the

---

534. *Re Kayford Ltd* [1975] 1 All ER 604; 'Bridge: The Quistclose Trust' (1992) *Current Issues in Insolvency Law* (London: Stevens and Sons, 1991); see Lynch, Marshall & O'Ferrall, *Corporate Insolvency, and Rescue* (Butterworths 1996), Chs 4 and 7.
535. *Twinsectra v. Yardley* [2002] 2 AC 164; *Cooper v. PRG Powerhouse Ltd* [2008] BCC 588.
536. *Re Farepak Food and Gifts Ltd* [2006] ALL ER 265.

Regulations of 1980 (S.I. 306 of 1980) and the amending Regulations of 2000 (S.I. 487 of 2000), which had been in operation since 3 November 1980 and 21 December 2000, respectively. The Regulations implement an EU Directive, currently Council Directive 2001/23/EC (12 March 2001). An issue arose in relation to insolvency proceedings in Ireland, particularly whether the Regulations were applicable to receiverships or examinerships. The essential principle is that the contractual rights of the employees do not transfer when the original employer is subject to proceedings whereby it may be adjudicated bankrupt, or wound up for reasons of insolvency, by order of the High Court. However, if the sole or main reason for the institution of bankruptcy or insolvency proceedings is the evasion of an employer's legal obligations under the Regulations, then the Regulations apply to a transfer concluded by such an employer.

J. Powers and Duties of the Liquidator

287. The main obligations of the liquidator are to pay all proven debts in accordance with the priorities described *supra*, to wind up the company and to dissolve it in an orderly fashion. Under the Companies Act 2014, section 596, the liquidator must 'take into his custody or under his control' all the property to which the company appears entitled.

Under the Companies Act 2014, section 627, the liquidator has the power to sell the company's property. A liquidator also has standing to institute legal proceedings on behalf of the company, with a view to swelling the assets available for distribution to creditors, including proceedings claiming that certain transactions amounted to either fraudulent preferences of creditors or fraudulent dispositions of corporate property. *Infra paragraph.*

288. The Companies Act 2014 has changed the position of the provisional liquidator, usually appointed pending a full hearing of the court to appoint a liquidator in an official or compulsory liquidation. The new legislation now provides for the restriction of the powers of provisional liquidator under section 627. Section 627(1) provides that where a provisional liquidator is appointed by the court, then 'subject to section 559(3) to (5)', the provisional liquidator has such powers as the court orders. The statutory purpose would seem to be to limit the ability of a provisional liquidator to take drastic steps regarding the assets of a company where there may be a possibility, even at that late stage of a restructuring.

289. There are some changes made to the liquidation process in the 2014 Companies Act. Most significantly there have been changes made to what were the Rules of Court governing the process of liquidation. Indeed some provisions have been included as statutory provisions. Thus, Ord 74 r 22 regarding the service of the order for winding up is enacted under section 591(1) and Ord 74, r 24 is enacted under section 593. Similarly, section 617 enacts Ord 74, r 128 regarding the costs and expenses of the liquidation. Section 618 enacts in statutory form provisions of what was the old Table A under the Companies Act 1963 regarding distribution of assets in a members' voluntary winding up and section 619 goes on to apply the rules of distribution on bankruptcy to the winding up of insolvent companies, re-enacting section 284 of the 1963 Acts. It is envisaged that new Rules of Court will be enacted and these are referred to in section 564 of the 2014 Act. In addition the role of the court examiner (not to be confused with the Examiner who conducts the rescue process described below) has been abandoned under section 564(5) which provides for changes in the rules of court to 'remove those of the functions of the court officer known as "the Examiner" as are stated in those rules to be performable for the purpose of a winding up'. Instead the creditors' Committees of Inspection has taken on a significant role as described in sections 646(2), 666 and 667 of the Companies Act 2014. So for example the remuneration of liquidators will be agreed with the creditors' committee of inspection as provided for under section 646(2).

290. Further changes have been made to the role of the committee of inspection, i.e., the creditors' representative committee in liquidations. It is difficult to predict what the full effect of these provisions is and practitioner are divided in their assessment of their significance. Section 666 is new and provides that the committee of inspection in an official or court-ordered liquidation will be established on the initiative of the liquidator or alternatively the liquidator can be directed to do so on the initiative of a minimum proportion of the creditors without court sanction.

Section 667 similarly empowers creditors, without recourse to the court, to appoint a committee of inspection in the case of a creditors' voluntary winding up. It is worth recalling that the purpose of some of these provisions is to align more closely the procedure in creditors' voluntary, members' voluntary and court liquidations.

291. Section 687 is a new provision, which provides that creditors or contributories may override the wishes of the committee of inspection. It is stated in the explanatory memorandum to parallel section 309 of the Companies Act 1963 but here it is the liquidator, not the court, who must have regard to the wishes of the creditors. Section 687(2) provides that where there is a conflict between the wishes of the committee of inspection and the creditors or contributories, the wishes of the latter will prevail. To this end section 687(3)(a) empowers the liquidator to convene meetings of the creditors and contributories to ascertain their wishes. Section 687(3)(b) goes on to provide that the liquidator must convene meetings of the creditors or contributories where they pass a resolution so directing the liquidator or where such a request is made in writing by not less than one tenth in value of the creditors or not less than one tenth in value of the contributories.

K. Liquidators' Report

292. Section 682 provides for the liquidator to make a report and further secondary legislation[537] has made certain directions regarding the content of the liquidators' report which requires, *inter alia*:

537. SI 221/2015. Companies Act 2014 (s. 682) Regulations 2015.

(i) Details regarding shadow directors and directors.
(ii) Details regarding the financial position of the company and accuracy of statement of affairs.
(iii) Details regarding the Committee of inspection.
(iv) Details regarding section 683 (restriction) and section 842 (disqualification) proceedings.[538]

L. Regulation of Liquidators

293. Section 633 of the Companies Act 2014 now requires for the first time in Ireland that certain qualifications are necessary for appointment as a liquidator or provisional liquidator. Section 633(1) therefore provides that 'subject to ss 635 and 636 a person shall not be qualified for appointment as a liquidator of a company unless he or she falls within a paragraph of the Table to this section'. Section 519 applies these requirements to those acting as examiners. The Table referred to in section 633 includes the following individuals:

- Members of a prescribed accountancy body.
- Practising solicitor.
- Members of 'other professional body recognised by the Supervisory Authority'.
- Persons qualified under the laws of another EEA State.
- A 'person with practical experience of windings-up and knowledge of relevant law'.

This last category is described as limited and will be closely supervised by the Supervisory Authority.

M. Transactional Avoidance: Swelling the Assets

294. Transactional avoidance provisions are provided for in section 602 of the Companies Act 2014 which re-enacts sections 218 and 255 of the 1963 Act concerning the invalidation of dispositions made after the commencement of the winding up. Section 604 invalidates what were called 'fraudulent preferences' but replaces the term 'fraudulent' with 'unfair preference'. Nevertheless, proof of an intention to prefer is still required. There is no mention of an over-arching anti-deprivation principle, despite the considerable discussion engendered about this since the English decision of Belmont Park.[539] However, readers' attention is drawn to the interesting use of what was section 139 of the 1990 Act, now re-enacted in section 443 in the decision of *Re Chatelaine Thudichum*[540] and where transactions

538. See also SI 222/2015 regarding new 'undertakings' form.
539. See *Belmont Park Investments Pty Ltd. v BNY Corporate Trustee Services Inc.* [2011] 3 WLR 521. R. Goode, *Principles of Insolvency Law* 703 (4th edn., Sweet and Maxwell 2011) for a discussion of this principle in English law.
540. *Re Chatelaine Thudichum* [2008] IEHC 58.

have been challenged on the grounds that these transactions have the effect of perpetrating a fraud on the creditors.

IV. Pre-insolvency Remedies

A. Receiverships

295. A receiver is normally appointed on foot of a debenture document. A receivership is generally based on a contractual relationship between lender and company. A number of events usually entitle a debenture holder to appoint a receiver:

- Where there is failure to pay the principal sum.
- Where there is a failure to pay an instalment on the loan.
- Where the company is otherwise unable to pay debts.
- Where the company ceases to trade.
- Where a winding up has commenced. – Where the company jeopardizes the security.
- Where there is a breach of the debenture agreement.

The powers of the receiver are now enumerated under section 437 of the Companies Act 2014. This section is modelled on section 420 of the Australian Corporations Act 2001 and gives certain specific powers to receivers in addition to any powers conferred by order or instrument. Section 439 repeats the existing obligation imposed on a receiver by section 316A of the 1963 Act as inserted by section 172 of the 1990 Act to 'exercise all reasonable care to obtain the best price reasonably obtainable as at the time of sale'.[541] Accordingly, the receiver is liable to the company for negligence in relation to the sale of assets where he or she fails to meet this standard of care. If surplus assets are generated, they should be paid to the company.

B. Examinerships

296. This insolvency process was introduced in Irish law under the Companies (Amendment) Act 1990. Between 1990 and the mid-1990s a series of decisions of the courts highlighted some unsatisfactory aspects to the legislation, which was changed and amended by the Companies (Amendment No. 2) Act 1999. In general, there was a view that the original legislation was over focussed on rescue rather than according due regard to properly negotiated rights between the company and its creditors entered into prior to insolvency or prior to the commencement of the process.[542]

541. I. Lynch-Fannon, *Bloomsbury Professional's Guide to the Companies Act 2014*, 204 (Bloomsbury, 2014), Ch. 7.

542. For a general discussion of both the early phase of the examinership legislation and its development through the 1990s and beyond see I. Lynch Fannon & G. Murphy, *Corporate Insolvency and Rescue* (Second Edition, Bloomsbury Professional, Dublin, 2012). Chs 12 and 13.

297. Part 10 of the Companies Act 2014 largely repeats existing examinership law. A recent development in examinership legislation has been reconsolidated in section 509(7)(b) of the Companies Act 2014. The Companies (Miscellaneous Provisions) Act, 2013, introduced a change to the law in order to facilitate the access by small private companies (as defined in section 350 of the Act) to the examinership process. Small private companies may apply directly to the Circuit Court (where according to the Dept. of Justice, legal fees are 30% less than the High Court) to have an examiner appointed, and not be required to apply to the High Court first, as is currently the case. This makes the process cheaper and more accessible to the SME sector. Some cases have been heard already under this legislation, the first concerning the appointment of an examiner to Cell Bridge Playzone in Naas in April 2014 leading to the rescue of the company which employed twenty-seven employees.[543]

Despite the significance of the examinership process as a rescue vehicle for certain kinds of Irish companies it transpires that during the recent recession, examinerships were not as successful as expected. There was a decrease in figures from 2009 to 2010 due to lack of investments available. Sixteen companies availed of the process in 2010 compared with thirty-seven in 2009. Nevertheless, it has been It reported that in 2012 alone, almost 1,000 jobs were saved in small and medium size companies due to successful examinership petitions. This was an increase of over 65% on 2011 figures. It does not account for the number of jobs saved in large companies in 2012 such as Eircom. In 2014, twenty-seven companies went into examinership. By year end, seventeen had returned to normal status, one had entered creditors liquidation, two entered receivership and seven companies were in examinership.[544]

298. Under section 519 of the 2014 Act, in order to be appointed as an examiner, one must be qualified to act as a company's liquidator. Section 542(6)(b) has been inserted on foot of the High Court decision in *Re McEnaney Construction Ltd [2008] IEHC 43*. Under this provision the court is now allowed to authorize a reduction in the capital of a scheme of arrangement or compromise.

299. The examinership process is commenced on application to the High Court by a petitioner which may be the company, the directors of the company, a creditor or prospective or contingent creditor of the company (including an employee), or members of the company holding not less than one-tenth of such of the paid-up capital of the company as carries voting rights at general meetings as per section 510 of the 2014 Act. The Court may make an order to appoint an examiner when it appears to the Court that the company is, or is likely to be, unable to pay its debts, where there is no winding up of the company and where the court is satisfied that there is a 'reasonable prospect of survival'. Following the appointment of an examiner, the company is under the protection of the Court from its creditors for seventy days, but the examiner may also apply to the Court for extensions of up to thirty further days, in order to finalize his report and any proposed scheme of arrangement

543. (2014) *Irish Independent* 3 April.
544. Companies Registration Office Report 2014.

aimed at ensuring the survival of the company. At the end of the period of examinership, if the examiner presents a scheme of arrangement, the Court must decide whether or not to confirm proposals put forward by the examiner and the Court may, of its own motion or on the application of the examiner, extend protection for a further period while it considers its decision. Generally, no enforcement proceedings may be brought against the company while the company is under the protection of the Court. As regards a receivership, a receiver may be removed, following the appointment of an examiner under the provisions of section 522 of the Act.

C. Issues Surrounding Examinerships

300. As noted previously, some particular issues regarding the operation of the examinership process came under scrutiny in the 1990s. These are outlined and considered in the first report of the Company Law Review Group, published in December 1994. Arising from the recommendation of that group, the following matters were addressed in the 1999 Act: the requirement that an application for the appointment of an examiner had to be supported by a financial report from an independent accountant; that in considering matters arising in relation to the appointment of an examiner, the court would have regard (*inter alia*) to this report; and that the court must consider that there is a reasonable prospect of the company and its business surviving before an examiner could be appointed. The term 'independent accountant' under the 1990 Act has been replaced with 'independent expert' as per section 511 of the current legislation. In addition, the length of the examination period was shortened to seventy days, and certain rights the examiner seemed to have under the original legislation to deal with assets that were charged were curtailed. In particular, it was not possible for the examiner to deal with assets subject to a fixed charge. Furthermore, the dramatic power the examiner seemed to have under the original legislation to repudiate any contract that was detrimental to the company under the provisions was confined to contracts entered into in the course of the examinership, thus rendering the effect of that particular legislative provision to be entirely different from what seemed to be originally envisaged.

D. Outcome of Examinership

301. Despite those amendments, the examinership continues, in situations where it is viable, to deliver on the original goals envisaged in the legislation, in that it can facilitate corporate rescue and turnaround. A most important feature of the legislation is that it provides a legislative framework to facilitate the deferral of payment of some creditor's claims or indeed a sensible settlement of creditor's claims for less. It also provides a breathing space for a company to facilitate the sourcing of additional investment. Throughout the examinership period and at its culmination, the creditors of all classes are protected by the legislative requirements regarding the Court's role in overseeing the final scheme of arrangement. When the examiner's report is placed before the Court, any creditor or member whose claim or interest would be impaired if the proposals were implemented may appear and be heard.

The Court shall not confirm any proposals, unless at least one class of creditors whose interests or claims would be impaired by implementation of the proposals has accepted the proposals, or if the sole or primary purpose of the proposals is avoidance of payment of tax due. The Court must also be satisfied (1) that the proposals are fair and equitable in relation to any class of creditors or members that has not accepted the proposals and whose interests would be impaired and (2) that the proposals are not unfairly prejudicial to the interests of any interested party. Objections may be raised, at a hearing for the Court's consideration of an examiner's report, by a member or creditor whose interest or claim would be impaired by the proposals before the Court, on the grounds that: (a) there was a material irregularity at a meeting held for consideration of the proposals by members or creditors; (b) acceptance of the proposals at such meeting was obtained by improper means; (c) the proposals were put forward for an improper purpose; and/or (d) that the proposals unfairly prejudice the interests of the objector. A person who voted in favour of the proposals may only object on the grounds that acceptance of the proposals at such meeting was obtained by improper means or that, subsequent to the vote, he or she became aware that the proposals were put forward for an improper purpose. The Court, having regard to such provisions and any to any objections raised, may confirm or reject the proposals in full or confirm the proposals subject to modifications.

§6. Reconstructions, Mergers and Takeovers

I. Compromises and Arrangements

A. Introduction

302. Chapter 1 of Part 9 of the Companies Act 2014 replaces sections 201–204 of the Companies Act 1963, (as amended) which is designed to facilitate compromises and arrangements – referred to as 'schemes of arrangement' or 'reconstructions'– between a company and either its members or its creditors or both.[545] Schemes of arrangement under sections 450–454 present an alternative to the type of restructuring which occurs in examinership,[546] and sometimes in receiverships. During the recent recessionary period, the equivalent provisions have been extremely popular in the United Kingdom and have proved to be an attractive restructuring device, not only for English companies, but also for non-English companies seeking to avail of schemes in England.[547] This has not been the case for the Irish provisions, the view being that in fact examinership is a more attractive

545. See generally L. MacCann, *Corporate Restructuring: Schemes, Mergers and Divisions*, in *Bloomsbury Professional's Guide to the Companies Act 2014* (Courtney ed., Bloomsbury Professional 2015). See also Lynch Fannon & Murphy, *Corporate Insolvency and Rescue* (Bloomsbury Professional 2012), Ch. 14.

546. *Supra* paras 296–301.

547. See generally J. Payne, *Schemes of Arrangement* (Cambridge University Press, 2013).

re-organization tool.[548] A scheme of arrangement may involve, for example, reorganization of capital or rescheduling of debt.[549] The structure of any scheme is not pre-determined and the sparsity of the legislative framework provides a great deal of flexibility in the type of rearrangement of interests which can occur which can include creditors agreeing to convert loan capital into share capital (i.e., debt into equity) or the deferral of enforcement of creditors' claims. In addition to examinerships, the scheme of arrangement process presents an alternative to a creditors' (or a members') voluntary winding up but is available in non-insolvent situations as well.

B. Constructing and Approving a Scheme

303. A proposed scheme must be approved by a majority in number 'representing three-fourths in value of the creditors or class of creditors or members or class of members, as the case may be', voting on the proposal either in person or by proxy at a duly called meeting.[550] The scheme must also be approved by the company in a general meeting or by its board or, where appropriate, by its liquidator or receiver.[551] When a meeting of creditors or members is summoned under section 450, section 452 provides that with every notice summoning such a meeting must be sent a statement explaining the effect of the proposed arrangement and stating any material interests of the directors, whether as directors, creditors, members or otherwise, and the effect thereon of the proposed arrangement. Furthermore, the Court may order meetings of creditors and/or members to be held to consider proposals; at any such meetings affected parties must be segregated into appropriate classes 'confined to those persons whose rights are not so dissimilar as to make it impossible for them to consult together with a view to their common interest'. Failure to do so may result in the Court refusing to sanction a proposed scheme.[552] A scheme proposed under section 450 must be sanctioned by the Court before it can take effect. Under existing case law, the Court will not approve a scheme that is ultra vires the company.[553] In light of changes to the issues of capacity of companies under Irish law,[554] it is probably that these principles will be adapted to address

548. See generally I. Lynch Fannon, *Insolvency and Rescue,* in *Bloomsbury Professional's Guide to the Companies Act 2014.* (Courtney ed., Bloomsbury Professional 2015) for a comparison of the two processes.

549. See, for example, *Re McEnaney Construction* [2008] IEHC 43 (unreported, High Court, 25 Feb. 2008) (scheme for reduction of capital in examinership.

550. Companies Act 2014, s. 450(1). Previously such meetings could only be called with court approval but now these meetings can be convened by directors of the company.

551. *Re Savoy Hotel Co.* [1981] 3 WLR 441; *Re Oceanic Steam Navigation Co. Ltd* [1938] 3 All ER 740.

552. As occurred in *Re Pye (Ireland) Ltd* (unreported, High Court, Costello J., 12 Nov. 1984 and Supreme Court, 11 Mar. 1985). See further Lynch, Marshall & O'Ferrall, *Corporate Insolvency* (Butterworths 1996), Ch. 12. See also McCann, *supra* n. 531 at p. 174 and Lynch Fannon & Murphy: *Supra* n. 531.

553. *Re Guardian Assurance Co.* [1917] 1 Ch. 431; *Re Savoy Hotel Co.* [1981] 3 WLR 441.

554. *Supra* Section.

questions surrounding the stated activities or objects of a company where that is relevant. The Court only approves schemes where: the applicable statutory provisions and procedures have been complied with; the prescribed majorities (of members or creditors, as the case may be) have held the necessary meetings and have bona fide approved the scheme; and the scheme is fair and equitable.[555] The Court will not intervene, however, merely on the basis that, applying its own business judgment, it would have come to a different conclusion as to whether to approve the scheme.[556] In approving a scheme, the Court may impose such conditions or modifications as it sees fit, in order to ensure that the scheme is fair and equitable.[557] Under section 451, the Court has more extensive powers to stay all proceedings in being against the company and restrain any further such proceedings for such period as it sees fit. An application for a stay may be made by the company, the directors, a member or creditor, or where the company is being wound up, the liquidator.[558] A scheme becomes binding once the provisions of sections 453 and 454 of the Companies Act 2014 are complied with. These conditions include approval by the Court under section 453 and registration under section 454. The scheme then becomes binding on all creditors or members or any particular class thereof, on the company and where relevant the liquidator and contributories of the company.[559]

C. Acquisition of a Minority

304. Where an offer has been made to acquire shares in a target company and at least 80% in value of the shares affected has been so acquired, a remaining minority shareholding may be compulsorily acquired, as permitted by and subject to the provisions of sections 457–459 of the Companies Act 2014. The provisions of section 457 set out the requirements underpinning the right of the offeror whose offer has 'become binding or been approved or accepted in respect of not less than 80 per cent in value of the shares affected' to acquire the remaining 20% shareholding and sets out a time limit of six months in which such an acquisition takes place. Section 459(5) the minority shareholding block to apply to the court for an order contrary to the compulsory acquisition order envisaged in the section.

305. Once the requirements are complied with section 457(3) states that:

> the offeror shall be entitled to acquire the beneficial ownership of all or any of the remaining shares affected from the dissenting shareholder or shareholders on–
>
> (a) the same terms as have become binding or been approved or accepted as mentioned in subsection (2),

555. *Re John Power and Sons Ltd* [1934] IR 412; *Re Dorman Long and Co. Ltd* [1934] Ch. 635; *Carruth v. Imperial Chemical Industries Ltd* [1937] 2 All ER 422.
556. *Re London Chartered Bank of Australia* [1893] 3 Ch. 540.
557. *Re Canning Jarrah Timber Co. (Western Australia) Ltd* [1900] 1 Ch. 708.
558. Companies Act 2014, s. 451.
559. Companies Act 2014, s. 453.

or

(c) where an application is made under section 459(5)(a), any different terms that the court specifies.

If no such application is made, the offeror then becomes entitled to acquire beneficial ownership of said shares. The Supreme Court has held that, where a dissenting shareholder applies to Court opposing compulsory acquisition, he or she bears the 'heavy' burden of persuading the Court that the proposed transaction is unfair.[560] The Court will pay 'great attention' to the views of the majority who have accepted the bid,[561] although such views will not carry as much weight where the approving shareholders are associated (whether directly or indirectly) with the offeror company as would acceptance by shareholders wholly independent of the offeror company. It is not enough for a dissenting shareholder to argue that a more attractive scheme, contract or offer could have been put forward; rather it appears that to succeed in persuading the Court to intervene, it must be shown that the proposal is 'obviously unfair, patently unfair, unfair to the meanest intelligence'.[562]

Under section 457(6) and 457(7)(4),an offeror company acquiring the beneficial ownership of not less than 80% in value of the shares in the offeree company is obliged to give notice of that fact within thirty days of the date of such acquisition to all other shareholders, and any such other shareholder may, within three months of such notice being given to him or her, require the transferee company to acquire his or her shares.

II. Reconstruction by Voluntary Liquidation

306. Section 601 of the Companies Act 2014 allows the liquidator of a company undergoing a members' voluntary winding up, who has obtained to general or specific authority to do so via a special resolution of the company, to transfer assets or interests of the company to another company, in exchange for shares in that other company. Shares thus acquired are then distributed among the members of the company in liquidation. This provision has the benefit, in contrast to section 450, of not requiring an application to the Court in order to take effect. However, there is the potential drawback that a reconstruction under section 601, unlike section 450, is not binding on dissenting shareholders. In addition, whereas creditors are bound by any arrangement sanctioned under section 450, the same does not apply under section 601. Creditors are not bound to look to the company to whom the business is transferred for payment. Instead, the liquidator must retain sufficient assets to meet any creditors' claims, or, in the alternative, he or she must obtain an adequate indemnity in respect of same from the transferee company, and failure to do so will render him or her personally liable for creditors' claims that as a result go fully or

560. *Walls v. PJ Walls Holdings Ltd* [2008] 1 ILRM 1; *Re Fitzwilton PLC* [2000] 2 ILRM 263.
561. *Duggan v. Stoneworth Investment Ltd* [2000] 1 IR 563.
562. *Walls v. PJ Walls Holdings Ltd* [2008] 1 ILRM 1.

partially unpaid.[563] Dissenting shareholders are not bound by a section 601 reconstruction and may (under section 601(5)) serve notice of dissent on the liquidator within seven days of the special resolution at the registered office of the company. The effect of such notice is either to require the liquidator to abstain from carrying out the proposed reconstruction or to buy out the dissenting shareholders at a price to be agreed. In default of such agreement, the statute provides for the possibility of arbitration under section 601(9) and (10).

III. Takeovers and Mergers

A. *Public Law Regulation of Takeovers and Mergers*

307. The Competition Acts 2002–2014[564] govern the public regulation of takeovers, mergers and other acquisitions. The Competition and Consumer Protection Act 2014 replaced the Competition Authority with the Competition and Consumer Protection Commission (hereinafter referred to as 'the Commission' in this section). Consequently, mergers and acquisitions meeting certain criteria must be notified to this Commission under the terms of the Competition Acts 2002–2014. Section 16 of the Competition Act 2002 (as amended)[565] provides that notification is required where a transaction involves:

- the merger of two or more previously independent undertakings; or
- a sole or joint acquisition of direct or indirect 'control' of the whole or part of an undertaking ('control' for the purpose of this definition existing where decisive influence is capable of being exercised with regard to the activities of an undertaking.); or
- an undertaking acquiring all or a substantial part of the assets, including goodwill, of another undertaking, with the result that the first undertaking effectively replaces the second undertaking in the business concerned.

Section 18 (as amended)[566] provides that, in order to require notification, it must be the case that:

- the aggregate turnover of two or more of the undertakings involved is not less than EUR 50 million;
- the turnover in the State of each of two or more of the undertakings involved is not less than EUR 3 million; In addition, under section 18(5) (as amended) the Minister for Enterprise, Trade and Employment, where he or she is of opinion that exigencies of the common good so require, may, after consultation with the

563. *Pulsford v. Devenish* [1903] 1 Ch. 331.
564. Section 1 of the Competition and Consumer Protection Act 2014 provides that the Competition Acts 2002–2012 and Parts 3 and 4 of the present act may be cited together as the Competition Acts 2002–2014.
565. Competition and Consumer Protection Act 2014, s. 1(5), 6 and 53(c).
566. Competition and Consumer Protection Act 2014, s. 55.

Commission, by order specify a class or classes of merger or acquisition to be subject to the requirement of notification. Receiver-ships, liquidations and intra-group transactions are exempted from the definition of qualifying mergers and acquisitions.

308. The previous Authority (now the Commission as described above) considers that an undertaking carries on business in the State where it (a) has a physical presence (such as by having an office or agency) and either makes sales or supplies services to customers on the island of Ireland or (b) has made sales into the island of Ireland of at least EUR 2 million in its most recent financial year. 'Turnover in the State' has been interpreted as referring to turnover generated through services supplied or sales made to customers within the jurisdiction. A qualifying merger or acquisition below the financial thresholds may be voluntarily notified to the Commission. One possible reason for voluntary notification would be to obtain advance clearance from the Commission, where a possible competition concern is envisaged. It also bears noting that, under section 18(9) of the 2002 Act, (as amended)[567] it is an offence to fail to notify a qualifying merger or to fail to supply required information. A person guilty of such an offence is liable to a fines of up to EUR 3,000 (on summary conviction) or EUR 250,000 (on indictment).

1. Notification

309. Notification, where made, must be in writing to the Commission within one month of the date of conclusion of the agreement or making of a formal public bid, and the notification must contain full details of the agreement or bid. It is open to parties involved in any such transaction to seek a meeting with Authority staff, prior to notification. Once notification is made, short details of same are published online, and third parties may make submissions. Section 19 (as amended)[568] provides that a merger or acquisition notified to the Commission may not be put into effect until (a) the Commission determines that it should be put into effect; (b) the Commission makes a conditional determination; or (c) specified time periods have elapsed without the Commission informing the notifying parties of a determination. Within thirty working days commencing on the date of notification (or the date of response to any formal request for information), the Commission must inform the notifying parties, and any third parties who made submissions, as to its determination – either to allow the transaction or to initiate a full investigation. The merger or acquisition is deemed to be cleared where the Commission does not meet this time limit. If approved, the merger or acquisition must take place within twelve months of receipt by the Commission of the notification (or receipt of further information). If it elects to initiate a full investigation, the Commission must within 120 working days from the date of notification (or request for further information) make a determination – that the merger or acquisition may proceed, that it should take effect, or that it should take effect subject to conditions.

567. Competition and Consumer Protection Act 2014, s. 56.
568. Competition and Consumer Protection Act 2014, ss 56 and 58.

310. The substantive test used by the Commission in its analysis is whether the merger or acquisition will have the effect of substantially lessening competition in markets for goods or services in the State. This is similar to the US standard and varies only slightly from the test used in the EC Merger Regulation (i.e., whether a transaction 'significantly impedes effective competition').

2. Appeal

311. A notifying undertaking may appeal a decision of the Commission that a merger or acquisition shall not take effect, or a decision that it shall take effect only subject to certain conditions, to the High Court. Issues of fact and law – to a degree – may be dealt with on appeal. As far as practicable, the Court shall rule on any such appeal within two months. The appeal process is described in section 24 of the Competition Act 2002 as amended.

3. Special Circumstances

312. Previously, the Competition Act of 2002, contained special provisions relating to 'media mergers'. These have been repealed by section 7 of the Competition and Consumer Protection Act 2014.

313. Where a merger or acquisition has been put in place otherwise than in accordance with the procedures outlined *supra*, it is open to the Commission or third parties to bring proceedings alleging breach of sections 4 and/or 5 of the Act, (as amended) which prohibit anti-competitive agreements and abuse of a dominant position, respectively.

B. EU-Wide Mergers: The Role of the European Commission

314. The above position in Irish law is similar to the jurisdiction exercised by the European Commission in respect of large EU-wide mergers and acquisitions under Council Regulation (EC) No. 139/2004 of 20 January 2004 on the control of concentrations between undertakings (the EC Merger Regulation), which summarized and recast the original 1989 Regulation and subsequent amendments. The EC Merger Regulation applies to transactions it terms as having 'a Community dimension', namely those where (a) the combined aggregate worldwide turnover of the undertakings involved exceeds EUR 5 billion, and (b) the aggregate Community-wide turnover of at least two of the undertakings exceeds EUR 250 million. In the alternative, where a transaction does not meet those criteria, it will be deemed to a Community dimension where: (a) the combined aggregate worldwide turnover of the undertakings involved exceeds EUR 2.5 billion; (b) in each of at least Member States the combined aggregate turnover of all the undertakings is at least EUR 250 million, provided that in each of those three or more Member States the combined aggregate turnover exceeds EUR 25 million; and (c) the aggregate Community-wide turnover of at least two of the undertakings concerned is more than EUR 100 million. The Commission appraises transactions having a Community dimension as thus defined. The Regulation, in Article 2(2), provides that, in order to be declared compatible with the common market, a proposed 'concentration' (i.e., merger) must 'not significantly impede effective competition in the common market or in a substantial part of it, in particular as a result of the creation or strengthening of a dominant position, shall be declared compatible with the common market'. There is not sufficient space here for detailed consideration of the Regulation, but it should be noted that the Regulation has been amended by Commission Regulation (EC) No. 1033/2008 (Official Journal L 279, 22 October 2008, 3–12).

C. The Role of the Irish Takeover Panel

315. In addition to the foregoing, the Irish Takeover Panel supervises takeovers and certain other 'relevant transactions' involving companies listed on the recognized Irish stock exchanges. The Panel was established by the Irish Takeover Panel Act 1997[569] and is incorporated as a company limited by guarantee. The Panel is designated as the competent authority under the European Communities (Takeover Bids (Directive 2004/25/EC)) Regulations 2006 (S.I. 255 of 2006) for the purposes of Article 4(1) of the EC Takeover Bids Directive. Nothing in sections 450–454 of the Companies Act 2014 regarding schemes of arrangement prejudices the jurisdiction of the panel with respect to a compromise or scheme of arrangement constituting a scheme of arrangement within the meaning of the 1997 Act, although the Court and the Panel are each required to have due regard to the exercise of the other's powers.[570] Indeed, Order 75, rule 24 of the Rules of the Superior Courts provides (see Rules of the Superior Courts (Takeover Schemes) 2005 (S.I. 688 of 2005)) that: (a) the Court may direct the Registrar to invite the Panel to provide to the Court 'such form as the Court may request, any report or other information which appears relevant to the exercise of the Court's jurisdiction' under sections 450–454; and (b) the applicant or moving party in any such court proceedings must promptly provide the Panel with copies of any motion or petition and details of the terms of any court order, including promptly upon perfection a true copy of same.

316. The Panel is responsible for making Rules to ensure that takeovers (including takeover bids as defined in the 2006 Regulations) and other relevant transactions comply with the General Principles set out in the Schedule to the 1997 Act. Under section 5 of the 1997 Act, the principal objects of the Panel are to monitor takeovers and other 'relevant transactions', so to ensure compliance with the 1997 Act and any Rules made by the Panel. Section 8 provides that rules made by the

569. See also European Communities (Cross Border Merger) Regulations 2008. Directive 2004/25/EC, a Directive of the European Parliament and the Council of 21 Apr. 2004 (on takeover bids) and subsequent European Communities (Takeover Bids (Directive 2004/25/EC)) Regulations 2006 (S.I. 255 of 2006).
570. Companies Act 2014 ss 450–454.

Panel may be for the purposes of: (a) specifying, by reference to matters such as the amount of securities acquired, offers, agreements or transactions as 'relevant transactions' for the purposes of the Act; (b) ensuring that takeovers and other relevant transactions comply with the scheduled principles and the rest of the Act; (c) providing, in the interests of shareholders, for the manner in which such transactions and related activities are to carried out; and (d) specifying circumstances in which a person shall be presumed, until the contrary is established to the satisfaction of the Panel, to be acting in concert with another person in regard to a takeover or other 'relevant transaction'.[571]

317. Under section 9(1) of the 1997 Act, the Panel may of its own volition or on the application of any interested person make a ruling as to whether any activity or proposed activity, as respects a takeover or other relevant transaction, complies with the scheduled principles and any Rules under section 8, and any such ruling shall have immediate effect. Section 9(2) allows the Panel, to ensure compliance with any Rules and with the scheduled principles, to direct any party to a takeover or relevant transaction to do, or refrain from doing, anything specified in the direction. Under section 12 the Panel may apply to the Court in a summary manner for enforcement of any such direction. Section 10 provides that the Panel may, on its own initiative or at the request of a party to a takeover or relevant transaction, enquire into the conduct of any person, where it has reasonable grounds for believing that a breach of the scheduled principles or any Rules made under section 8 has occurred or may occur. Following an enquiry into the conduct of any person under this section, if it so thinks fit, the Panel may (publicly or otherwise) advise, admonish or censure such person in relation to his or her conduct. A person whom the Panel advises, admonishes or censures may appeal to the Court, which may, as it sees fit, approve or annul the decision; if the latter, the Court may direct a fresh enquiry or publicize notice of its decision. Section 11 provides that, in exercise of the powers conferred on it by sections 9 and 10, the Panel may hold hearings; for the purpose of any such hearing, the Panel shall have the same powers as the Court in respect of: (a) enforcing attendance and their examination and (b) compelling the production of documents. Likewise, a witness before the Panel shall be entitled to the same immunities and privileges as if he or she were a witness before the Court.

Under Regulation 10 of the European Communities (Takeover Bids (Directive 2004/25/EC)) Regulations 2006 (S.I. 255 of 2006), the Panel may specify circumstances in which it is enabled to grant derogations from, or waive, any rules under that section.

§7. Holding Companies and Subsidiaries

318. The doctrine of corporate personality has been considered *supra* (see Part I, Chapter 1, §2, IV). One of the most significant effects of corporate personality in modern commercial life is, however, to be seen in relation to groups of companies. Once corporations had legal personality, it was inevitable that a corporation would

571. See further www.irishtakeoverpanel.ie.

be permitted to become the owner of shares in another company. As a result, groups of companies now include a parent or holding company and many subsidiaries and related companies. A firm commitment to the doctrine of corporate personality underpins these structures, but in Ireland, as in England, a line of case law recognizes the possibility that this doctrine can be set aside in certain circumstances concerning groups. These cases are usually described as cases where the courts have disregarded separate corporate entities in groups in 'the interests of justice' or where a 'single economic entity' is recognized. In *DHN Ltd v. London Borough of Tower Hamlets*,[572] the seminal case in the area, the companies were operated separately and the affairs of the group had been arranged in such a way as to maximize certain benefits arising from the group structure. However, the terms of a compulsory purchase order issued by the defendants precluded the company from receiving full compensation. The court did not wish to visit an injustice on the group and allowed the group to be treated as a single economic entity, thus enabling it to secure full compensation for the actions of a local authority when, if the separate corporate personalities had been maintained, the group would not have received full compensation for the losses incurred. As Shaw L.J. observed: 'Why then should this relationship be ignored in a situation in which to do so does not prevent abuse but would on the contrary result in what appears to be a denial of justice?' *DHN* was followed in Ireland in the cases of *Power Supermarkets Ltd v. Crumlin Investments Ltd*[573] and *State (McInerney & Co. Ltd) v. Dublin County Council.*[574] In the *Power Supermarkets* case, statements by Costello J. indicated that the relationship between the two companies was so close that they had not been regarded by the group as separate entities. Statements in the judgment support the view that, despite the particular facts of the case, a broader principle was being set out: 'It seems to me to be well established … that a court may, if the justice of the case so requires, treat two or more related companies as a single entity … if this conforms to the economic and commercial realities of the situation.'

319. In recent times the authority of this analysis has been doubted by the courts. The following two cases will (1) illustrate the orthodox position and the significance and advantages of corporate structures in the group format and (2) indicate how the courts have embraced the robustness of the principle of corporate personality and its operation in a group structure to maximize the effect of limited liability. In *Adams v. Cape Industries PLC*,[575] the plaintiffs sought to have the group structure disregarded in some of its parts, to enable the significant liabilities of one company in relation to injuries caused through the mining of asbestos to be met by the parent company of the group. This application was refused. Involuntary creditors who had obtained judgment in Texas could not enforce that judgment against the principal company in the group, which was incorporated in London. The Court did not dispute that the group structure had been created '[so] that Cape would have

572. *DHN Ltd v. London Borough of Tower Hamlets* [1976] 1 WLR 852.
573. *Power Supermarkets Ltd v. Crumlin Investments Ltd* (unreported, High Court, Costello J., 22 Jun. 1981).
574. *State (McInerney & Co. Ltd) v. Dublin County Council* [1985] ILRM 513.
575. *Adams v. Cape Industries PLC* [1990] Ch 433.

the practical benefit of the group's asbestos trade in the United States of America without the risks of tortious liability'.[576] The Court concluded as follows:

> [W]e do not accept as a matter of law that the court is entitled to lift the corporate veil as against a defendant company which is the member of a corporate group merely because the corporate structure has been used so as to ensure that the legal liability (if any) in respect of particular future activities of the group (and correspondingly the risk of enforcement of that liability) will fall on another member of the group rather than the defendant company. Whether or not this is desirable, the right to use a corporate structure in this manner is inherent in our corporate law.[577]

In doing so, the court referred to the statements of Templeman L.J. in *Re Southard and Co. Ltd*,[578] which neatly encapsulated the peculiarities of English company law, namely that companies are not liable for the debts of related companies, subsidiaries, associated companies or parent companies. As the court stated in *Re Southard*, if one of the companies turns out to be 'the runt of the litter and declines into insolvency to the dismay of its creditors, the parent company and the other subsidiary companies may prosper to the joy of their shareholders without any liability for the debts of the insolvent subsidiary'. Similarly, a return to orthodoxy is evidenced in the Irish Supreme Court in *Allied Irish Coal Supplies Ltd v. Powell Duffryn International Fuels Ltd*,[579] where Murphy J. had this to say regarding attempts by the plaintiff to have the first defendant identified with the PLC parent and the line of case law on which the plaintiff's case rested:

> However, apart from the distinctions which may be drawn between this and other cases, the crucial feature of *Power Supermarkets Limited v. Crumlin Investments Limited* is that Costello J. did not purport to question the authority of *Salomon v. Salomon and Company* [1897] A.C. 22. Indeed no reference was made to that case in the course of his judgment nor, as far as I am aware, the argument on which it was based. Again it is clear from the judgment in *Rex Pet Foods Limited v. Lamb Brothers (Ireland) Limited* (Unreported, High Court, Costello J. 5th December, 1985) that Costello J. had not intended in *Power Supermarkets Limited v. Crumlin Investments Limited* to lay down any revolutionary principle of law.

320. The question as to how the courts ought to approach corporate groups remains a relevant issue in Irish company law and has been considered by the High

576. *Ibid.*, 544.
577. *Ibid.*, 544.
578. *Re Southard & Co. Ltd* [1979] 3 All E R 556. Here the issue concerned an application to convert a voluntary winding up to a compulsory winding up. In the context of group structures, Templeman L.J. made his observations about the robustness of the corporate personality doctrine as a means of enhancing limited liability. He went on to observe that 'The anxiety of the creditors will be increased where, as in the present case, all the assets of the subsidiary company are claimed by another member of the group in right of a debenture.'.
579. *Allied Irish Coal Supplies Ltd v. Powell Duffryn International Fuels Ltd* [1998] 2 ILRM 61.

Court in *Fyffes PLC v. DCC PLC*.[580] In that case Laffoy J. reviewed the relevant authorities in this area, beginning with *DHN v. London Borough of Tower Hamlets*, described *supra*. In *Fyffes* the plaintiff sought to disregard the various group entities and regard the companies at issue in relation to the defendants as a single economic entity to underpin the alleged infringement of the rules on insider dealing and market abuse outlined at the time of the trades in question by Part V of the 1990 Companies Act.[581] Laffoy J. referred to the former Chief Justice Ronan Keane's text on company law, which states the approach to disregarding the corporate entity very clearly. In terms of the grounds outlined, however, clarity must be retained by considering questions of agency and question regarding a group as a single economic entity separately. In acceding to the plaintiff's argument in the *Fyffes* case that the companies involved should be regarded as a single economic entity, the court held that to do so would be consistent with a purposive interpretation to the legislation in question:

> The plaintiff did not contend that there was a factual basis for saying that Lotus Green was in reality DCC or that Lotus Green was the alter ego of DCC, so as generally to render Lotus Green's assets liable to meet the liabilities of DCC or for all purposes. In broad terms, the plaintiff's contention was that, against the factual background which existed in relation to the companies within the DCC Group at the date of the Share Sales, Part V[582] should be applied so as to prevent the statutory remedy available under s. 109(1) being rendered ineffective.

321. This decision, insofar as it dealt with the doctrine of corporate personality was appealed and affirmed in the Supreme Court.[583] In fact it was observed in the Supreme Court that the decision of the High Court was so thoroughly and clearly reasoned that only one aspect of the decision was appealed. The analysis of the corporate personality doctrine was further followed in a recent decision of the Supreme Court in *O'Donnell and Ors v. Bank of Ireland &Ors*.[584] This case is somewhat similar in its facts to the similarly authoritative restatement of the doctrine of corporate personality from the UK House of Lords in *Prest v. Petrodale*.[585] In conclusion, difficulties surround the application of the single entity argument relating to groups of companies still subsist. It should be noted that this is a separate concept from the application of an express or implied agency relationship. It is also separate from an argument that the commercial realities of the group are such that in fact no real separate entities exist (the facts of *Powers* fall into this more limited category). The exceptional nature of the principle as applied in *DHN* and *Fyffes* is that the

580. *Fyffes PLC v. DCC PLC* [2005] IEHC 477 (unreported, High Court, 21 Dec. 2005). This decision on the issue of liability for insider dealing was successfully appealed to the Supreme Court by Fyffes. The Supreme Court found that trading had occurred where the defendant was in possession of price sensitive information: [2007] IESC 36.
581. Since repealed and replaced by Ch. 1 of Part 23 of the Companies Act 2014.
582. [2013] UKSC 2013.
583. [2007] IESC 36.
584. [2014] IESC 77.
585. [2013] UKSC 2013.

courts have discretion to disregard the entities in a particular context, in both cases perhaps qualified by the context created by a statutory framework or scheme. If this perhaps is the principle, we could bear in mind the views of one commentator that it is difficult to identify any set pattern in these cases –'indeed in many instances they seem to contradict each other in the most baffling way'.[586]

Most importantly in the context of groups, the statutory provisions in sections 599 and 600 of the Companies Act 2014 (formerly sections 140 and 141 of the Companies Act 1990) also present some flexibility regarding the doctrine of corporate personality in insolvency situations.

I. Groups and the Agency Question

322. In *Firestone Tyre & Rubber Co. Ltd v. Lewellin*,[587] a US company, Akron, the parent of the appellant, had established the appellant company, Brentford, as a subsidiary in the UK. Brentford manufactured tyres for sale to distributors in Europe. Distribution contracts entered into by Akron with distributors and with Brentford were used to support a claim that, for tax purposes, Brentford did not carry on business as a separate entity in the UK. The House of Lords rejected this argument based on the facts of the case, holding that the appellant was carrying on the business in the UK as an agent of the US parent company and was therefore subject to taxation under UK law. In *Smith, Stone and Knight Ltd v. Birmingham Corporation*,[588] the plaintiff company operated a paper manufacturing business and subsequently acquired a paper waste management business. Although a subsidiary company was created, called the Birmingham Waste Co. Ltd with a view to operating the business, the plaintiff parent company retained ownership of the property held by the original business and retained ownership of the business from the date of acquisition. Atkinson J. held that the waste management business was still owned by the parent company and operated by its agent, the subsidiary, with the result that the parent company could claim compensation for both the loss of land and business on foot of a compulsory purchase order made by the defendant corporation.[589]

II. Groups and Liability for Debts

323. Real injustices are sometimes visited on plaintiffs where groups have organized themselves to avoid liability in the manner described in *Re Southard* and *Adams v. Cape Industries PLC*. These injustices are clear regarding creditors of one subsidiary who may not be paid on insolvency even as other companies in the group 'prosper to the joy of the shareholders'. The injustice is particularly aggravated

586. L.S Sealy, *Cases and Materials in Company Law* 53 (10th edn., Oxford University Press 2014).
587. *Firestone Tyre & Rubber Co. Ltd v. Lewellin* [1957] 1 WLR 464.
588. *Smith, Stone and Knight Ltd v. Birmingham Corporation* [1939] 4 All ER 116.
589. A similar result was achieved in *D.H.N. Food Distributors v. Tower Hamlets London Borough Council* [1976] 1 WLR 852.

when we consider the plight of the involuntary tort creditor left without an unsatisfied judgment, as occurred in *Adams*. Irish law has attempted to deal with this situation with the enactment of sections 599 and 600 of the Companies Act 2014 (formerly sections 140 and 141 of the Companies Act 1990).[590]

The sections provide for contribution orders to be made by the High Court whereby companies related, as defined in the legislation,[591] to the company in liquidation may be ordered to contribute to the debts of the company where it appears to the Court that it is just and equitable to issue such an order given the criteria outlined in the act. Similarly, where two or more related companies are in liquidation, the court may order that the assets of the companies are pooled if the criteria set out in the legislation are satisfied. There have been no cases – or at least no cases resulting in written judgments of the Court – where such orders have been made. Section 599 of the Companies Act 2014 (formerly section 140 of the Companies Act 1990) provides for the possibility that the court, on application from a liquidator, creditor or contributory of a company in liquidation, will grant a contribution order 'that any company that is or has been related to the company shall pay to the liquidator of that company an amount equivalent to the whole or part of all or any of the debts provable in that winding up'. The court can make this order where it appears 'just and equitable' to do so. Certain criteria are outlined in the provision to provide guidance to the Court. These include primarily the following considerations: (a) the extent to which the related company took part in the management of the company being wound up; (b) the conduct of the related company toward the creditors of the company being wound up; and (c) the effect such order would be likely to have on the creditors of the related company concerned. Similarly, section 600 of the Companies Act 2014 (formerly section 141 of the Companies Act 1990) provides for pooling orders where the High Court can again make an order pooling the assets of two or more related companies in a group. Effectively, the order will provide that 'the companies shall be wound up together as if they were one company'. The court may make such an order where it appears 'just and equitable' to do so, and again similar criteria are mentioned to which the Court shall have regard.[592]

590. Similar provisions are present in New Zealand law; cf. Companies Act (NZ) 1993, ss 271–272. See further *Re Frederick Inns Ltd.* [1994] IRLM 387.

591. Companies Act 2014 s. 2(10) and 2(11) provide a definition of relatedness for the purposes of ss 599 and 600 as follows: that other company is its holding company or subsidiary; or more than half in nominal value of its equity share capital (as defined in s. 7(11)) of the Companies Act 2014) is held by the other company and companies related to that other company (whether directly or indirectly, but other than in a fiduciary capacity); or more than half in nominal value of the equity share capital (as defined in s. 7(11)) of the Companies Act 2014) of each of them is held by members of the other (whether directly or indirectly, but other than in a fiduciary capacity); or that other company or a company or companies related to that other company or that other company together with a company or companies related to it are entitled to exercise or control the exercise of more than one half of the voting power at any general meeting of the company; or the businesses of the companies have been so carried on that the separate business of each company, or a substantial part thereof, is not readily identifiable; or there is another company to which both companies are related.

592. Companies Act 2014, s. 600(6) –'(a) the extent to which any of the companies took part in the management of any of the other companies; (b) the conduct of any of the companies towards the creditors of any of the other companies; (c) the extent to which the circumstances that gave rise to the

III. Groups and Accounts and Taxation

324. In the context of groups, one of the most significant features of Ireland's economy is the success of its policies in attracting significant Foreign Direct Investment (FDI) in terms of location of multinational subsidiaries. The taxation position of subsidiaries of multinationals is described in general *infra* on the principle that the taxation of a subsidiary is treated in much the same way as the taxation of a single Irish resident company. Some specific issues regarding groups are mentioned in the preceding section. Members of a group may surrender current year trading losses, excess charges on income, excess management expenses (in the case of investment companies) and excess capital allowances. In this context, the relevant definition is that two companies are members of a group if one is a 75% subsidiary of the other or both are 75% subsidiaries of a third company. Note that a company is a 75% subsidiary of another company where not less than 75% of the ordinary share capital is owned directly or indirectly by that company. Group relief is available to Irish companies, subject to certain conditions, in respect of trading losses incurred by their non-Irish subsidiary companies that are resident in EU Member States and European Economic Area (EEA) States with which Ireland has a double taxation treaty.

§8. Taxation

I. Introduction

325. In general a company will be subject to corporation tax regarding the taxation of corporate profits as calculated in accordance with the relevant accounting principles and taxation acts. It will also be subject to capital gains tax as described *infra*. In relation to the distribution of dividends, these will be taxed as income for those in receipt of the dividends, but also note the provisions regarding withholding tax as described *infra*. Provisions regarding the taxation of groups are described in the previous section in brief.

II. Corporate Income and Capital Gains

326. A company resident in Ireland is liable to pay corporation tax on its worldwide profits, not just its Irish source profits, whether or not these profits are repatriated into Ireland. In groups of companies the corporate personality principle will treat each company as a separate entity for these purposes. Accordingly, a non-resident company, such as a European or US multinational, trading in the State through a branch or agency is liable to pay Irish corporation tax on the profits of its

---

winding up of any of the companies are attributable to the actions or omissions of any of the other companies; (d) the extent to which the businesses of the companies have been intermingled'.

Irish subsidiary company wherever these profits arise. Foreign profits of Irish resident companies are subject to double taxation relief under Part 35 Taxes Consolidation Act, 1997. Ireland has a significant and extensive array of double taxation agreements, which have operated significantly to its advantage in relation to its attractiveness as a location for FDI.

327. During the 1990s Ireland operated a significantly advantageous tax regime for manufacturing and other companies as part of its successful mission of attracting significant multinational investment and location in Ireland, usually referred to as FDI policies. Companies engaged in manufacturing had their profits taxed at an effective rate of 10%. Although the corporate tax rate has been increased and the 'manufacturing rate' is in the process of being phased out, it remains in existence for some companies with regard to manufacturing activities that were carried on before 23 July 1998 (or grant approved on or before 31 July 1998) until it expires on 31 December 2010 – that is, for accounting periods ending on or before 31 December 2010 as provided for in Part 14 Taxes Consolidation Act, 1997. The current corporate tax rate is 12.5% which is applicable to all companies regardless of sectoral activity.

328. In recent years Ireland has become the focus of some concern regarding its corporate structure both from the United States, from the OECD and from the European Commission. In the case of the United States, the Obama administration sought to address the activities of US companies in utilizing particular jurisdictions to reduce their US tax liability. Ireland was one of the jurisdictions which became the subject of a US Senate enquiry. The OECD had also expressed concerns regarding the activities of certain multinational corporations.[593] In addition the EU Commission expressed concern about the nature of competitiveness in the EU and in particular the operation of very low corporate tax rates in certain jurisdictions, again Ireland was one such jurisdiction. Following various initiatives and investigations the Irish government made its strategy clear:

(i) Under EU law, member states have the right to set their own tax rates – a guarantee that was clarified during the Lisbon and Nice treaty debates in Ireland. Ireland clearly wishes to continue the low corporate tax rate of 12.5% – a matter which has full public support, but at the same time the government had to make it clear it would not tolerate manipulation of these rules by multinational corporations seeking to gain particularly favourable and undesirable outcomes.
(ii) In 2014 the Minister for Finance, Michael Noonan announced a government crack down on corporate schemes which were effectively being designed to evade global tax liabilities. A particular scheme described as the 'double Irish' was a particular target. Although the Government was described in the Irish media as responding to international pressure, in particular the opening of a

593. www.oecd.org. The OECD has launched its BEPS project in 2015. (Base Erosion and Profit Sharing Project). On 27 January 2016, thirty-three countries formally agreed to support this project including Ireland.

European Commission investigation into two specific tax rulings granted to Apple, there was a clear strategy on the part of the Government to pre-empt any pressure to increase the Irish corporate tax rate by demonstrating a robust attitude to existing tax provisions.[594]

There are currently in effect three rates of corporation tax as follows:

- 12.5% rate on trading companies. The relatively low rate of tax for Irish resident trading companies is still an important element in Ireland's FDI policy, although Ireland is coming under some pressure from certain fellow Euro-zone states to raise this tax rate;
- 25% rate for non-trading income and income from certain excepted trades. This rate applies to non-trading income including income chargeable under Case III (e.g., discounts, interest, foreign income), Case IV (patent royalties) and Case V (rental income from land and buildings in the State) of Schedule D of the Taxes Consolidation Act, 1997. Also included at this rate is income from activities that consist of working minerals, petroleum activities, and dealing in or developing land, other than construction operations;
- 20% rate for company capital gains and profits from dealing in residential development land. Companies' capital gains (other than gains from development land) are computed as capital gains tax to a corporation tax at the rate of 20%, which mirrors the general capital gains tax rate pursuant to section 21(3) and section 78 Taxes Consolidation Act 1997 (as amended by successive Finance Acts). Gains realized by companies from disposals of development land are chargeable to capital gains tax;
- Finally, the Irish Minister for Finance announced in October 2015 that a new corporate tax rate of 6.5% would be made available to corporations where the income was directly related to results of R &D conducted in Ireland. Known as the 'knowledge box' tax it seems that this initiative will come under review from the EU.[595]

III. Dividends and Other Distributions

329. Dividends and other distributions made by Irish resident companies are liable to Dividend Withholding Tax except where these are made to qualifying non-resident persons or excluded persons under section 172D Taxes Consolidation Act,

---

594. As described in the Irish Times:

> *The pre-emptive move arguably made sense in relation to the upcoming OECD rules on base erosion profit shifting (Beps) – Ireland would have had to bow to pressure on new standards sooner or later – but the controversy over Ireland's corporate tax regime opens up broader questions about the EU's jurisdiction over tax issues.*

Suzanne Lynch Controversy over 'double Irish' Raises Issues of EU's Power over Tax Regimes (Irish Times 17 Oct. 2014).

595. Irish Times (17 Oct. 2014, Dublin).

1997. Dividends received by Irish resident companies from other Irish resident companies are not chargeable to Corporation Tax, because such dividends are already subject to tax within the dividend paying company. In the group and multinational context, it is worth noting that section 43 of the Finance Act, 2008, made a change to the taxation of foreign dividends received by companies within the charge to Irish tax, where these dividends are received from companies that are resident for tax purposes in EU Member States or in countries with which Ireland has a tax treaty. Such dividends that are paid out of trading profits are now, on election, chargeable to tax here at the 12.5% rate of corporation tax (from the date of election) instead of at the 25% rate. Where dividends do not qualify to be charged at the 12.5% rate, they will continue to be charged at the 25% rate. Where a dividend is paid partly out of trading profits and partly out of other profits, the part of the dividend that is paid out of trading profits of the dividend paying company will be taxable at the 12.5% rate. The change applies as respects a dividend received on or after 31 January 2008.

Chapter 2. The Private Company

§1. Introduction

330. As described in Part I, Chapter 1, Irish company law applies to both public and private limited companies. There is no specific statute directed at the different circumstances of the smaller private company, which can often simply be a 'one-man' company or family-owned business. However, the new Companies Act 2014 which consolidates and, in some cases reforms, Irish company law has placed the legislative emphasis very clearly on the private company limited by shares as the main type of company used by Irish business. As described above the Act addresses private companies limited by shares in Parts 1–14. Further, Parts then tailor these provisions to fit the appropriate type of company. Of most relevance here is a PLC –public limited company.

Section 9 of the Act sets out the structure of the legislation stating the following:

> Subject to subsection (3) and(4) all of the law in this Act in relation to private companies limited by shares is to be found in Parts 1-14 (or instruments under them) and Schedules 1 to 6 … .

One of the much publicized features and heralded reforms of the new Irish private company limited by shares is that it has full legal capacity. A second type of private company limited by shares may continue to specify business activities. Such companies are now called designated activity companies or DACs. DACS are really a variant of the private company limited by shares. Following Parts 1–14 dealing with the standard form private company limited by shares, later Parts of the legislation deal with other types of companies. For example Part, 16 and Part 17 then deal with what are now called DACS – private companies limited by shares with designated activities- and PLCs-public companies limited by shares. Accordingly, in relation to DACs section 964(1) of the Companies Act 2014 states:

> The provisions of Parts 1 to 14 apply to a DAC except to the extent that they are
> disapplied or modified by–
>
> (a) this section; or
> (b) any other provision of this Part.

Similarly, section 1002 of the Companies Act 2014 states that:

> The provisions of Parts 1-14 apply to a PLC except to the extent that they are disapplied or modified by-
>
> (a) this section, or
> (b) any other provision of this Part.

A Table is provided for in this section for ease of reference.

There are two additional specific types of companies recognized by this new Companies Act 2014 which are perhaps worth mentioning for those practitioners with niche areas of practice. These are *External Companies* regulated in Part 21 of the 2014 Act and *Investment Companies* regulated in Part 24. In relation to the former, External Companies, the key distinction here is between a 'branch' of an external company and a 'place of business' of an external company. This distinction determines registration and filing obligations of the related enterprise, so that only a branch of a foreign registered company must be registered in Ireland under section 1302 of the Act. Investment Companies regulated in Part 24 are PLCs established for the collective investment of funds in property. Nevertheless, for the sake of consistency this monograph has adopted the structure adopted in monographs from other jurisdictions. Accordingly the Part 1 Chapter 1 deals with public limited companies and Part 1 Chapter 2, this chapter deals with private companies.

The previous chapter indicated, where relevant, when rules applied differently to private companies. This chapter focuses on these particular principles and notable exemptions.

§2. Formation

I. Incorporation

331. As described in Part I, Chapter 1, it is now possible to incorporate a limited liability company in Ireland with just one member under the European Communities (Single-Member Private Limited Companies) Regulations 1994.[596] This is a company limited by shares. The requirements as to incorporation and registration of this kind of company are set out in Part 2 of the Companies Act 2014. The number of members is set at a maximum of 149 under section 17(4). It is possible to have only one director in such a company under section 128(1) which states that 'A company shall have at least one director.' At least one director must be resident in the State, and the company must, under the requirements of the Companies (Act No. 2) 1999, carry on an activity in the State. A person must be over 18 to be appointed a director to a company.[597] of the Regardless of how many directors a company has, Irish law does not specifically distinguish between executive and non- executive directors. Each director will still be subject to a minimum standard of behaviour first adumbrated in Irish law in *Re Hunting Lodges Ltd.*[598] Although criticized at the time as over-stepping the very *de minimis* obligations normally expected of a nominal or non-executive director, these principles are now clearly part of Irish law as elucidated in the case law on director disqualification and restriction provisions. This latter series of cases is one of the most developed areas of modern Irish company law.[599]

596. See *supra*, paras 15 and 60.
597. Companies Act 2014, s. 131(1). This provision should be read in tandem with the new consent on appointment procedures which apply to directors.
598. *Re Hunting Lodges Ltd.* [1985] ILRM 75.
599. See *supra* Part 1, Ch. 1 s. 4, III, 6.

II. Establishing the Members and Their Contribution

A. *Numbers of Members Required, Minimum Capital Requirements*

332. Private companies' articles must limit the number of members to 149 or less, not including existing employees or former employees who, while in the employment of the company were, and still are, members of the company.[600] In addition, as described *supra*, the minimum number of members of a private company is one. The Companies Act 2014 has changed the rules in this regard relating to public companies which are now also permitted to have just one member. This is in keeping with further flexibility available regarding the formation of public limited companies whereby the minimum issued share capital requirement has been reduced to EUR 25,000.[601] There is no minimum capital requirement for private companies limited by shares. Perhaps the only exception to these permissive rules for private limited companies is where a company must comply with additional capitalization requirements as a result of taking onto its Board a restricted director pursuant to the provisions of Chapter 3 of Part 14 of the Companies Act 2014. The private company in this situation must have a minimum fully paid-up share capital of EUR 100,000. For PLCs in the same situation, the minimum capital is increased to EUR 500,000 and each share must be paid for in cash.[602]

B. *Consideration for Shares; Valuation; Fraudulent and Worthless Consideration*

333. In private companies, even though from a creditor's point of view the issues may be even more crucial, the 'adverse interest' is not apparent in terms of the shareholders themselves. Under Irish company law, this lack of regulation regarding the valuation of private company shares represents a considerable lacuna in the protection of creditors from asset or value stripping in private companies. For example, in a management buy-out of a company when the management, or indeed another interested party, receives ownership of the company in return for services rendered to the company or in return for an asset conveyed, there is no legislative provision for an independent valuation of such service or other asset. Accordingly, there is little to protect the overall wealth of the company from the creditors' point of view. In many respects, therefore, this legislation, designed as it is primarily to protect creditors as all capital maintenance provisions are, does nothing to protect the value of private companies, a crucial part of the Irish economy.

III. Formal Incorporation Documents

A. *The Objects Clause and the Ultra Vires Doctrine*

334. As noted in Part I, Chapter 1, §2, *supra*, the new Irish company which is a private company limited by shares will have full legal capacity. As stated this is

600. Companies Act 2014, s. 17.
601. Companies Act 2014, s. 1010.
602. Companies Act 2014, s. 819(3).

one of the key reforms heralded by this legislation. Now, this kind of company – a company limited by shares – will have full legal capacity as described in section 38 of the 2014 Act which states:

> 38(1)Subject to subsection (2), notwithstanding anything contained in this constitution a company shall have, whether acting inside or outside of the State –
>
> (a) full and unlimited capacity to carry on and undertake any business or activity, do any act or enter into any transaction; and
> (b) for the purposes of paragraph (a), full rights, powers and privileges.
>
> (2) Nothing in subsection(1) shall relieve a company from any duty or obligation under any enactment or the general law.

These companies will be described as limited liability companies (LTDs) and the company name will be followed by the suffix LTD. Alternatively, a company may wish to continue with a clause specifying its activities. Such a company will be described as a designated activity company (DAC) and the company name will be followed by the suffix DAC.

Section 38 does not apply to DACs nor to PLCs. The relevant provision in relation to DACs state section 972(1) of the Act provides that:

> A DAC shall have the capacity to do any act or thing stated in the objects set out in its memorandum.

A really important feature however, is that the statement of the company's activities in its objects clause will form the basis of a rule of internal discipline only and will not have any effect whatsoever on contracts or actions affecting the company's external relationships. Section 973(1) of the Act provides that:

> The validity of an act done by a DAC shall not be called into question on the ground of lack of capacity by reason of anything contained in the DAC's objects.

The internal discipline rule is described as follows:

> (2) A member of a DAC may bring proceedings to restrain the doing of an act which, but for subsection (1), would be beyond the DAC's capacity but no such proceedings shall lie in respect of any act to be done in fulfilment of a legal obligation arising from a previous act of the DAC.
> (3) Notwithstanding the enactment of subsection (1), it remains the duty of the directors to observe any limitations on their powers flowing from the DAC's objects and action by the directors which, but for subsection (1), would be beyond the DAC's capacity may only be ratified by the DAC by special resolution.
> (4) A resolution ratifying such action shall not affect any liability incurred by the directors or any other person; if relief from any such liability is to be

conferred by the DAC it must be agreed to separately by a special resolution of it.

(5) A party to a transaction with a DAC is not bound to enquire as to whether it is permitted by the DAC's objects.

Accordingly the principles and issues arising regarding the application of the ultra vires doctrine may still pertain to DACs and PLCs. However, because of the provisions described above as they apply to DACs it is safe to conclude that from now the issue of specified objects or activities and the consequent ultra vires doctrine will only apply to these companies as a rule of internal discipline.

As stated in the accompanying explanation, this section gives effect to the recommendation in the First Report of the CLRG that private companies limited by shares should be granted the legal capacity of a natural person with the consequent effect that the doctrine of ultra vires is disapplied. The note states that the section is modelled on subsection 16(1) of the New Zealand Companies Act, 1993. Stating that nearly 90% of Irish registered companies were private companies limited by shares and the majority of these were closely held companies, the review group arrived at a belief that such companies should not be required to set out any objects or powers and such companies should be empowered with the capacity of a natural person. However, there is a view that companies may actually prefer to retain a list of specified or designated activities. The transition period is eighteen months from the date of the commencement of the legislation, namely, 1 June 2015 and so it remains to be seen as to what the preferred option for companies will be. The position relating to PLCs is described in Part 1, Chapter 1.

1. Authority

335. An issue which has always been related to the issue of ultra vires in the past is the question of the authority of a company's agents. So regardless of whether the company has full legal capacity or not it is still possible that a third party may be caught by entering into a transaction with an agent of the company who does not have the authority to enter into such a transaction. Conversely, the company may suffer from being bound by the unauthorized actions of a particular person, holding him or herself out as an agent. The question is not one of legal capacity but one of authority of an agent and whether the authority of that agent is actual, ostensible, or held out authority and whether there is reliance on such authority. A fairly recent Irish decision in *Ulster Factors Ltd v. Entonglen Ltd.*[603] exemplifies these problems very well. Leaving aside the question then of capacity, the issue of authority of agents is also dealt with in the Companies Act 2014. Section 40 provides that the 'board of directors of the company; and b) any registered persons' shall be deemed to have authority to exercise any power of the company and to authorize others to do so. Any person who is authorized by the Board to bind the company must be registered. (This provision is similar to that which has pertained under the European Companies Regulation 1973 and complies with EU Regulations).

603. [1997] IEHC 34.

However, where a person is given limited authority by the Board to bind the company, for example to borrow on behalf of the company up to a particular limit, say EUR 100,000, that person is not registered or registrable.[604] These provisions seem to go only half way in addressing the sorts of difficulties which arise. The non-registration of the person with limited authority only indicates that this person has less than full authority, but the third party may still be exposed to misrepresentation of his or her actual authority by such a person and the company may still be exposed to liability on foot of such misrepresentation where there is reliance. Section 39(6) and section 40(9) to section 40(11) address this problem. Section 39(6) state that 'the provisions of a company's constitution with regard to a person's office or powers shall not, in themselves, be taken as an authorization by the board of the directors of the company of the person as a person entitled to bind the company'.

Section 40(9) provides that where a question of ostensible authority arises, no 'reference shall be made to the company's constitution'.

Section 40(11) states that the section is 'in addition to, and not in substitution for, the Rule in Royal British Bank v Turquand' otherwise known as the 'indoor management rule'. In the past a third party might have relied on the Articles of Association to create the appropriate authority for an agent, this is excluded from now on. In cases where an agent has some authority in relation to a particular transaction but not full authority to bind the company, it would seem that a third party will be on notice that a particular agent does not have full authority due to the lack of registration of that person. But the limitations on a person's authority will not be apparent. How the limitations of that authority are to be established is left unanswered except that the Rule in Turquand's case will still apply. The nature of the enquiries a third party might have to make is not clear. In other words the act does little or nothing to resolve the kinds of problems which have occurred in the extensively discussed case law on this issue.

B. *Articles of Association*

336. Apart from the issue of capacity and the abolition of the ultra vires doctrine for private companies limited by shares, a second much heralded reform is that private companies limited by shares will no longer have a Memorandum of Association nor a set of Articles of Association. Instead this company will have a 'constitution'.[605] This constitution shall state the company's name, that it is a private company limited by shares, that the liability of the member is limited and a statement as to capital. Section 19(2)(a) states that the constitution shall 'be in a form in accordance with the form set out in Schedule 1 or as near to it as circumstances permit'; Instead of having a document which was usually referred to as the Articles of

604. Companies Act 2014, s. 39(1) 'Where the board of directors of a company authorises any person as being a person entitled to bind the company (not being an entitlement to bind that is, expressly or impliedly, restricted to a particular transaction or class of transactions), the company may notify the Registrar in the prescribed form of the authorisation and the Registrar shall register the authorisation.'

605. Companies Act 2014, s. 19.

Association which set out the governing rules for each company, the Companies Act 2014 has 'created a series of statutory defaults so that companies will no longer be required to make provision for standard administrative matters.'[606]

Therefore, unless the constitution of a particular company opts out of particular statutory provisions, the rules governing the internal governance of a private company limited by shares will be found throughout the Companies Act 2014. Parts 3 and 4 of the Act will be particularly relevant in this regard. So for example provisions relating to basic governance matters such as the authority of the Board which were provided for in Article 80 of the standard form Articles of Association in Table A are now included as provisions of the Companies Bill, in this case section 158. The authority of the Managing Director which used to be provided for in standard form Articles of Association is now described in section 159. In contrast, section 967(1) of the Companies Act 2014 states that 'the constitution of a DAC shall be in the form of a memorandum of association and articles of association which together are referred to in this Part as a "constitution"'. Section 967(2) goes on to state that the memorandum of association shall state the name, that the company is a designated activity company, its objects, that the liability of its members is limited and a capital clause. Schedules 7 and 8 of the Act set out the form of this constitution for a DAC limited by shares or a DAC limited by guarantee respectively. The same situation applies however, in relation to the relationship between default provisions of the Companies Act 2014 and what would have hitherto been described as Articles of Association. Section 968 describes 'mandatory' and 'optional' provisions of Parts 1–14 of the Companies Act and goes on to state that the Articles of a DAC may contain regulations in relation to the DAC but so far as these regulations do not exclude or modify any optional provisions of the Companies Act 2014 these will apply. Finally, section 968(5) provides that articles of a DAC 'instead of containing any regulations in relation to the DAC, may consist solely of a statement to the effect that the provisions of the Companies Act 2014 are adopted'.

IV. Legal Personality and Constitutional Structures

337. In relation to lifting the corporate veil, all of the issues described *supra* (cf. Part I, Chapter 1, §2, IV, A) relating to larger companies apply also in principle to the smaller private company. However, on the facts of various cases, when a company is smaller, it may be easier to establish an agency relationship[607] or to draw close connections between the company and the individual controlling the mind and will of the company in the context of attributing criminal intent[608] or some other human attribute, such as residence. Nevertheless, it is important to bear in mind that the necessary facts must be proven and that there is no per se agency relationship between any company and its owner; nor should a company be considered to be the

606. See Courtney, *Companies Act 2014: The Anatomy of the Act*, in *Bloomsbury Professional's Guide to the Companies Act 2014* (Courtney ed., Bloomsbury Professional 2015).

607. *Lee v. Lee's Air Farming Ltd* [1961] AC 12.

608. *D.P.P. v. Kent & Sussex Contractors Ltd* [1944] 1 KB 146.

same legal entity as its owner simply because it is a smaller entity with few or no countervailing shareholders or directors. This is particularly relevant in relation to smaller private companies limited by shares which are formed as subsidiaries of holding companies.[609]

V. Promoters

338. Discussion of the law relating to the fiduciary obligations of promoters to their companies is applicable to private limited companies. However, one of the difficulties regarding private companies in relation to this area of law, a difficulty that arises equally in relation to the enforcement of directors' duties, is that the duties are owed to the company, and therefore the company is the proper plaintiff regarding enforcement of these obligations. As a small private company is usually controlled by its founders (promoters) or controllers (directors), the expectation that the company will act as plaintiff is, in most cases, unrealistic. A third-party intervention usually occurs before such cases are litigated; this third-party intervention is often a liquidation, receivership, examinership or restructuring. In the case of *Hopkins v. Shannon Transport Systems Ltd,*[610] the litigation arose due to the refusal of a government department to pay grant aid that had originally been made available to the company and the consequent action on the part of the plaintiff to secure such payment. The court held that the plaintiff had been in breach of fiduciary duties, which he owed as a promoter to the company, and that the transaction was voidable at the instance of the company. However, the second type of activity that typically gives rise to a consideration of the position of a company promoter – namely the raising of capital through the issuing of a prospectus – does not normally apply in the private company context as usually such shares are listed or issued on a public market.

§3. Capital and Shares

I. Concepts of Share Capital

339. Under Irish law the private company limited by shares may adopt a complex or straightforward structure as is considered appropriate. Thus, it is common to find in private companies that there may be two classes of shares, ordinary shares and preference shares, that are commonly made available to original subscribers, promoters, venture capitalist investors and so forth. The use of preferential shares is also common in a venture capital context. Private companies may issue redeemable shares unless prohibited from doing so in its constitution.[611]

---

609. *Fyffes plc v. DCC and Ors.* [2005] IEHC and [2009] IESC.

610. *Hopkins v. Shannon Transport Systems Ltd* (High Court, unreported, 10 Jan. 1972).

611. Companies Act 2014, s. 66(4). See further Companies Act 2014, s. 102(1)(d) and Companies Act 2014, ss 105–116.

II. Capital Movement

340. A discussion of pre-emption rights in the context of private companies is considered *infra* in the section on Share Transfer.

III. Capital Maintenance

A. Introduction

341. All of the capital maintenance provisions discussed in Part I, Chapter 1, apply in principle to private companies. However, to a great extent capital maintenance rules take on an air of unreality as they apply to smaller private limited companies due to the fact that there is no minimum capital requirement under Irish company law and many private limited companies have little issued capital. In fact, many are undercapitalized. Despite this reality the rules described in Part I, Chapter 1 still apply. One of the consequences of this fact is that some of the rules work in unusual ways. The financial assistance prohibition in section 82 of the Companies Act 2014 is a case in point.

B. Financial Assistance Transactions

342. The provision by a company of financial assistance in the acquisition of its own shares are generally prohibited under section 82(2) of the Companies Act 2014. Such financial assistance includes loans; guarantees from the company to potential purchasers; security from its assets to secure loans entered into between a bank and the purchaser, for example; and any other securitized transactions. These provisions will catch any transaction that displays these characteristics. For a PLC some limited exceptions address specific situations, covering such matters as payment of dividends, discharge of lawfully incurred debts, and lending by financial institutions in the ordinary course of business, but, generally, these transactions are prohibited. Accordingly, various kinds of transactions that might serve to facilitate restructuring in a private company may involve the acquisition of a controlling interest by a director or investor whether an existing shareholder or otherwise. When the acquisition of a controlling interest is financed in part or directly or indirectly through use of the company's assets, such transactions are in breach of section 82 of the Companies Act 2014, as described previously. Thus, for example, a simple guarantee secured by reference to the company's assets supporting personal borrowing on the part of such an investor will be a breach of section 82. However, section 82(5) permits financial assistance if this is only 'an incidental part of some larger purpose of the company.'[612]

612. See further Companies Act 2014, s. 211(2). See further W. Johnston, *Taking Security, the Summary Approval Procedure*, in *Bloomsbury Professional's Guide to the Companies Act 2014* 145–153 (Courtney (gen. ed.) Bloomsbury 2015). This 'larger purpose' exemption has been part of English law since 1985. See also *Wallersteiner v. Moir* [1974] 3 All E. R. 217.

It is possible, however, to provide financial assistance for the acquisition of shares if the Summary Approval Procedure (SAP) outlined in section 82(6)(a) as described in section 202 and 203 is followed. However, the SAP is only available to PLCs in limited circumstances and this provision is excluded by virtue of section 1002(3). Effectively and as described in Part 1 Chapter 1 there remains a blanket prohibition on such transactions for PLCs. What was hitherto been considered an exemption provided for private companies is now a default type or provision which is not extended to PLCs. The SAP in this context[613] requires the following consent process:

(i) The passing of a special or unanimous resolution as outlined in section 202(1)(a)(i) having been passed not more than twelve months prior to the activity.
(ii) Where the resolution is not unanimous the resolution must normally stand for a waiting period of thirty days before the transaction. However, if more than 90% in nominal value of each class of issued shares votes in favour of the resolution, this waiting period does not apply.[614]
(iii) A declaration made by the directors in accordance with the terms of section 203 of the Companies Act 2014.

343. The consequences for breaching the terms of the private company exemption are severe. The transaction will be voidable at the instance of the company against a party with notice of the nature of the transaction or with notice of the non-compliance. The meaning of notice is important. In *Bank of Ireland Ltd v. Rockfield Ltd*,[615] McWilliam J. in the High Court, citing Lindley L.J. in *Manchester Trust v. Furness*,[616] held that notice of the transaction or notice of non-compliance must be actual for the transaction to be held to be void against the third party. However, in applying this doctrine to the facts, the Court held that there must be a limit within this principle where the court would not condone what was described as 'wilful blindness'. On appeal to the Supreme Court, the Court reiterated the basic principle but applied it to the facts in hand in a stricter, more literal way, finding that as the plaintiff notice did not have actual notice, it was entitled to enforce the transaction. The Court observed that there was no room for any form of constructive notice in commercial transactions. Further consideration of similar notice issues was considered in later cases such as *Eddison v. Allied Irish Bank PLC*[617] and *Lombard and Ulster Bank v. Brookhouse School*.[618] In both cases the essential principles were reiterated, emphasizing that a transaction in breach of the section would be void as

613. Companies Act 2014, s. 203.
614. Companies Act 2014, s. 211(2). See further W. Johnston, *Taking Security, the Summary Approval Procedure,* in *Bloomsbury Professional's Guide to the Companies Act 2014* 145–153 (Courtney (gen. ed.) Bloomsbury 2015).
615. *Bank of Ireland Ltd v. Rockfield Ltd* [1979] IR 21.
616. *Manchester Trust v. Furness* [1895] 2 Q B 539.
617. *Eddison v. Allied Irish Bank PLC* (unreported, High Court, Costello J., 24 Jul. 1985).
618. *Lombard and Ulster Bank v. Brookhouse School* (unreported, High Court, Costello J., 2 Jun. 1987); cf. Lynch, *Financial Assistance in the purchase of its own shares by a Company –s. 60 of the 1963 Companies Act*, 1 Dublin U. L. J. 14 (1988).

against parties with *actual* notice of the breach.[619] When non-compliance with the terms of the private company exemption were found, the transaction would be similarly void. However, for the transaction to be void, the enforcing party would have to be fixed with *actual* notice of the non-compliance.

In more recent case law such as the decision in *CH (Ireland) Inc. v. Credit Suisse Canada*,[620] the courts have taken a slightly different approach to parties who failed to appreciate the significance of various pieces of information available in the course of the transaction. As observed by McCracken J. in that case, because a clear statement of fact directly informed CSC of the nature of transaction, the Court cannot protect parties who may not have appreciated the relevance of the statement that amounted to a breach of company law. Finally, where a company gives financial assistance in breach of section 82, there is a provision for criminal liability whereby 'every officer of the company who is in default' shall be liable to conviction of an offence.

IV. Shares and Share Transfer

344. As noted in Part I, Chapter 1, the free transferability of shares is an important feature of a PLC. In private limited companies some restrictions can be placed on the transfer of shares, and these are commonly found in the Articles of Association. Under the reform of the Companies Act 2014 these provisions will no longer be found in Articles of Association as such. As explained the constitution of the company will contain mandatory and optional provisions derived from the Act itself.

The following rules apply:

Unless the constitution of a private company provides otherwise (whether this is an ordinary private company, a LTD or a designated activity company, a DAC) the directors will have discretion to refuse to register share transfers.[621]

In addition, the creation of pre-emption rights that oblige shareholders to offer their shares to existing shareholders were commonly found in the Articles and Memoranda of Association.

Pre-emption rights on the allotment of shares in private companies are now contained in section 69(6) of the Companies Act 2014. Section 69(8) recognizes that the constitution of a company can make alternative provisions.[622]

---

619. *Eccles Hall Ltd. v. Bank of Nova Scotia, Paramount Enterprises Ltd and O'Keeffe* (3 Feb. 1995, unreported) HC.

620. *CH (Ireland) Inc. v. Credit Suisse Canada* [1999] 4 IR 542. A further point worth considering in this context is that in the original decision of *Bank of Ireland Finance v. Rockfield, supra* n. s. 539 the decision of McWilliam J might be more defensible considering this was not entirely a commercial transaction, but concerned the conveyance of a mortgage on property.

621. Companies Act 2014, s. 95(1).

622. However, the subsequent statement in s. 69(11) as to the relationship between these subsections is not entirely clear. The pre-existing provision was contained in s. 23(10) of the 1983 Act.

A. Directors' Refusal to Accept Registration

345. Traditionally in private companies the directors were entitled under the Articles of Association to refuse to register the transfer of shares. As indicated above this discretion is now provided for in section 95(1) of the Companies Act 2014. This provision states that 'save where the constitution of the company provides otherwise – (a) the directors of a company may, in their absolute discretion, and without assigning any reason for doing so, decline to register any transfer of any share'.

Over time, the courts have had occasion to scrutinize the exercise of this power by directors. The exercise of the director's power in this regard is subject to the normal principles applying to the exercise of any power by directors, namely that the power must be exercised in good faith, for its proper purpose and for the benefit of the company.[623] The statutory provision above which reflects standard form clauses in older Articles of Association clearly states that the directors are not obliged to give reasons for their decision, and the general wisdom is that they are best advised not to do so. It may be open to some doubt as to whether the right not to give reasons for a decision would find favour under Irish law generally. An important underlying principle in this area is the countervailing principle that a shareholder has a right to transfer his or her shares and the exercise of the director's power to refuse to register a transfer must be considered against the backdrop of preserving that right. See a discussion of these principles in *Re Copal Varnish Ltd,*[624] *Re Swaledale Cleaners Ltd*[625] and *Re Zinotty Properties Ltd.*[626]

B. Pre-emption Rights

346. Pre-emption rights were commonly found in Articles of Association of private companies, ensuring the closed nature of the company. Thus, the standard-form articles contained in the Companies Act 1963 provided the following: 'The company is a private company and accordingly – (a) the right to transfer shares is restricted in the manner hereinafter prescribed.'[627] Pre-emption rights are contained in s. 69 (6) of the Companies Act 2014.

§4. Shareholders, Management and Control

I. Shareholder Meetings

347. The law relating to shareholders' meetings is now completely codified in Irish law and is contained in Chapter 6 of Part 4 of the Companies Act 2014. The

623. See, for example, the judgment of Green M.R. in *Re Smith and Fawcett* [1942] Ch. 304, and see further *supra* paras 163–167 for a general discussion of these principles.
624. *Re Copal Varnish Ltd* [1917] 2 Ch. 349.
625. *Re Swaledale Cleaners Ltd* [1968] 3 All E. R. 619.
626. *Re Zinotty Properties Ltd* [1984] BCLC 375.
627. Companies Act 1963, First Schedule, Table A, Part II, Art. 2.

case law interpreting these rules which would have hitherto been contained in both legislation and provisions of the Articles of Association are still relevant. The normal rules described in Part I, Chapter 1, §4 regarding the conduct of meetings in principle apply equally to private companies. However, when there are significantly smaller numbers of shareholders, procedures will of necessity be less formal. It is thus possible for private companies to conduct their business through the informal consent procedures described in Part I, Chapter 1, paragraphs 187–188. The following principles now apply under the reforms in the Companies Act 2014:

i) Repeating the exemptions provided for under the European Communities Regulations of 1994 it continues to be possible for 'single-member' companies to dispense with holding an AGM.[628] This also applies to DACS[629] and to other types of private companies such as companies limited by guarantees (CLGs).[630] As described *supra*, common law decisions in England recognized the possibility of a resolution being validly passed if unanimously agreed to by all the shareholders in a situation where the resolution was circulated to each without a meeting being actually held. This possibility was also approved of under Irish law in the case of *Buchanan v. McVey*.[631] As with English company law, this principle has now been codified.[632] Section 193 of the Companies Act 2014 provides more detail on this provision, for example that the resolution can consist of several signed documents,[633] and when the resolution is deemed to be passed.[634]

II. Shareholder Rights

A. Shareholder Agreements

348. It is common for those investing in private companies to enter into shareholder agreements to substantiate understandings between particular shareholders. The purpose is to elucidate matters that might not be entirely addressed in the Articles of Association, to provide further detailed agreements and to ensure enforceability of arrangements between the shareholders. The courts will enforce contractually valid shareholder agreements, and the enforceability of shareholder agreements rests solely on principles of contract law as it applies to the particular circumstances surrounding the entering into of the particular agreement. In all cases the agreements are subject to the constitution of the company, the Companies Acts and principles of company law. Thus, in *Russell v. Northern Bank Development*

628. Companies Act 2014, s. 175(3) and (4).
629. Companies Act 2014, s. 988.
630. Companies Act 2014, s. 1202.
631. *Buchanan v. McVey* [1954] IR 89.
632. Companies Act 2014, s. 193.
633. Companies Act, 2014, s. 193(3).
634. Companies Act 2014, s. 194(4) – when the last member signs.

Corporation,[635] the shareholder agreement was held void to the extent that it purported to constrain the power to increase capital, which a company has under the provisions of the Companies Act and which is central to how companies function. Interestingly, the Court allowed for the severing of the provisions of the agreement that were considered to be void and upheld other parts of the agreement that it found did not contravene this principle. Finally, shareholders agreements are only normally used when there are a small number of shareholders as the enforceability issues become more complex where additional shareholders take up either existing shares or additional shares.

B. Shareholders' Remedies

349. The procedure under section 212 of the Companies Act 2014 regarding the protection of shareholders' rights, described *supra*,[636] becomes particularly relevant in smaller companies. Many of the cases reported in Irish company law reflect the difficulties experienced by minority shareholders in face of a controlling faction or group of shareholders. In *Re Murphs Restaurant Ltd*,[637] one shareholder sidelined by two others was in a position to invoke section 205 (now re-enacted as section 212 of the Companies Act 2014) and the related section 213(f) and 213(g) of the Companies Act 1963 (now section 569(1)(e) and section 569(1)(f) of the Companies Act 2014). to obtain a remedy for oppression and disregard of his interests as a member. Similarly, in *Re Clubman Shirts Ltd*,[638] a shareholder whose interests were disregarded in relation to information made available to him was also able to seek a remedy under section 205. In *Re Westwinds Holding Company Ltd*,[639] a share purchase conducted in breach of company law principles was also the subject matter of a successful action by a minority shareholder. The courts have, however, repeatedly observed that mere breaches of company law may be insufficient to a remedy under oppression. Conversely, it is possible for a case of oppression or disregard of interests to be made out when there are no breaches of company law. In these cases the court may recognize that section 205 may be used as a remedy to address the 'quasi-partnership' character of many smaller private company although more recent cases suggest a retreat from this broadly described discretionary approach, in English law at least.[640] In Ireland, the oppression remedy is confined by the application of the majority rule principle enunciated in *Foss v. Harbottle*, which was rigorously applied by the Supreme Court in *O'Neill v. Ryan*.[641] Section 212 now reverses the effect of the decision of the Supreme Court in *Irish Press PLC v. Ingersoll Irish Publications Ltd (No. 4)*,[642] where the remedy available had been held to be limited to the ending of the oppression complained of and consequently

635. *Russell v. Northern Bank Development Corporation* [1992] 3 All ER 161.
636. See *supra* Part I, Ch. 1, §4, II, F.
637. *Re Murphs Restaurant Ltd* [1979] ILRM 141.
638. *Re Clubman Shirts Ltd* [1983] ILRM 323.
639. *Re Westwinds Holding Company Ltd* (unreported, High Court, 21 May 1974).
640. *O'Neill v. Phillips* [1999] 1 WLR 1092.
641. *O'Neill v. Ryan* [1993] ILRM 557.
642. *Irish Press PLC v. Ingersoll Irish Publications Ltd* (No. 4) [1995] 2 IR 175.

the court found itself unable to award damages. Section 212(2) now states that the court may, 'with a view to bringing to an end the matters complained of, make such order or orders as it thinks fit'. Section 212(3) specifically mentions 'the payment of compensation' under subsection 212(3)(d).[643]

350. Winding up on 'just and equitable' grounds as provided in the Companies Act 1963 section 231(f) and now re-enacted in section 569(1)(e) of the Companies Act 2014 is of an older equitable provenance but is now codified and available to a minority shareholder as a last-resort remedy to address concerns regarding how companies are run. For obvious reasons, such a remedy is granted only in exceptional circumstances. In English law, it is settled law that this remedy is not available if the petitioner cannot show an interest in the outcome, specifically, for example, if the petitioner shareholder cannot show that a surplus will be generated in a liquidation that will be distributable to shareholders, following the decision in *Re Rica Gold Washing Company*.[644] However, it is not entirely clear whether this rule applies in Ireland. Similarly, section 659(1)(f) of the Companies Act 2014 provides for the winding up of a company on foot of a petition based on section 212 of the same Act. This was considered along with the section just and equitable procedure and applied in *Re Murph's Restaurant Ltd*.[645]

III. Directors and Other Executive Officers

A. *The Board of Directors*

351. Firstly, section 128(1) of the Companies Act 2014 allows a private limited company to have just one director. As described in this text the structure of Irish companies has now changed with most provisions which would have hitherto been contained in an Articles of Association are now contained in the legislation itself, i.e., the Companies Act 2014. Companies will have much shorter constitutions which will refer to the Companies Act 2014 which will contain provisions which are mandatory for the company to have in its constitution and default optional provisions. Accordingly section 158 of the Companies Act 2014 is a statutory default provision applying to all companies unless the constitution of the company provides otherwise. It states as follows:

> (1) The business of the company shall be managed by its directors … who may exercise all such powers of the company as are not, by this Act or by the constitution, required to be exercised by the company in general meeting, but subject to –
> (a) any regulations contained in the constitution;
> (b) the provisions of this Act; and

643. It might nevertheless be possible for an argument to be made that compensation would not bring an end to the matters complained of in a somewhat similar manner to the decision of the court in the Irish Press Case *ibid*.
644. *Re Rica Gold Washing Company* (1879) 11 Ch. D. 36.
645. *Re Murph's Restaurant Ltd* [1979] ILRM 141.

(c) such directions, not being inconsistent with the foregoing regulations or provisions, as the company in general meeting may (by special resolution) give … .

Section 158(2) goes on to provide that 'no direction given by the company in general meeting under subsection (1)(c) shall invalidate any prior act of the directors which would have been valid if that direction had not been given'.[646] It is the nature of small companies that the directors will frequently be the sole shareholders or the controlling shareholders. It is also common in start-up companies for a dominant director or shareholder to effectively control the company, even where there are a number of shareholders and directors. In this context the role of any second or other director can be quite insignificant in day-to-day terms. The new Companies Act 2014 does away with the need for a second director, which was often a nominal director, often the spouse or partner of the dominant director. Nevertheless, if the practice continues that companies will be usually formed with more than one director it is important to emphasize that even nominal directors face significant obligations under case law such as the standards set out in the decision of Carroll J. in *Re Hunting Lodges Ltd*,[647] and followed in *Re PSK Construction Ltd.*[648] These obligations have been extensively articulated in decisions arising following the enactment of the Company Law Enforcement Act 2001, which in its relevant parts has been re-enacted in Part 14 of the Companies Act.[649]

B. *Life Directors*

352. As described in Part I, Chapter 1, the balance of power in most companies favours control by the Directors, and this is true in private companies as well. However, certain matters must be reserved to the shareholders; in particular, shareholders can remove directors from the board. As described above,[650] section 146(1) of the Companies Act 2014 provides that the shareholders/the company 'may by ordinary resolution remove a director before the expiration of his or her period of office notwithstanding anything in its constitution or in any agreement between it and him or her.' However, section 146(2) goes on to state that this subsection shall not, 'authorise the removal of a director holding office for life'. Thus, Irish company law still allows for directors to be appointed for life in private companies which is now the default provision. This provision regarding life directors is disapplied to PLCs in section 1002(3).

646. These provisions repeat in effect what had been generally known as Art. 80 of the Standard form Articles of Association. See the now repealed Companies Act 1963, First Schedule, Table A, Regulation 80.
647. *Re Hunting Lodges Ltd* [1985] ILRM 75.
648. *Re PSK Construction Ltd.* [2009] IEHC 538.
649. See *supra* Part I, Ch. 1, s. 4, III, 6.
650. See, *supra* para. 200.

§5. LIQUIDATIONS

353. There are no particular rules regarding the liquidation process for private companies. In most liquidations, the grounds are the non-payment of debts as outlined under section 569(1)(d) (f)the Companies Act 2014. In private companies it is more common, but yet again not frequent, to find a petition for liquidation of a company by a shareholder on other grounds such as the 'oppression' ground under section 569(1)(f) of the Companies Act 2014. The final ground to note is section 569(1)(e) of the Companies Act 2014, which provides that the court may liquidate a company where it is 'just and equitable' to do so. This ground is usually mentioned in the alternative where creditors petition to have a company liquidated on the grounds that it is unable to pay its debts. However, the 'just and equitable' jurisdiction covers other situations where, for example, shareholders cannot agree and there is deadlock in the company,[651] or where shareholders are of the view that the original reasons for forming a company have been departed from ('failure of substratum').[652]

These cases have been decided under this kind of statutory provision, which mirrors a residual equitable jurisdiction the court had prior to the enactment of any legislation specifically providing for liquidation on 'just and equitable' grounds.

§6. RECONSTRUCTIONS

354. Again the provisions apply as with the public company. There are no significant exemptions regarding private companies in this part of the legislation. Naturally, however, provisions of the stock exchange rules regarding takeovers and mergers will not apply to private companies.

§7. TAX

355. See generally the provisions regarding taxation of income, gains, dividends and so forth that are set out in the previous chapter, paragraphs 324–329.

651. *Re Irish Tourist Promotions Ltd* (unreported, High Court, Kenny J., 22 Apr. 1974); *Re Yenidje Tobacco Co Ltd* [1916] 2 Ch 426.
652. *Re German Date Coffee Co.* (1882) 20 Ch D 169; *Re Almagamated Syndicate* [1897] 2 Ch 600.

Part II. Partnerships

Chapter 1. General Partnerships

§1. Introduction[653]

356. A partnership is a fiduciary relationship between two or more persons in business together. The firm thus created – we use the terms 'partnership' and 'firm' interchangeably, merely for the purpose of variation – remains in the eyes of the law a collection of individuals: Unlike a limited company, traditional partnerships have no separate legal personality. Whereas separate corporate personality for limited companies developed in the mid- to late nineteenth century, for a considerable time before that 'English law … always refused to see anything in a partnership, however large, beyond a mere aggregation of individuals.'[654] And, unlike limited company shareholders, partners do not enjoy financially limited liability. These are the most important consequences of distinguishing between whether a business has been incorporated as a company or is more properly regarded (by accident or design) as a partnership.

357. A partnership may arise intentionally or by default. Under Irish law, partnership is the default legal structure for a business venture or organization that does not operate under a defined legal framework, such as, for example, having been incorporated as a company. It is often more straightforward to infer a partnership where parties have given no express consideration to the terms of their business cooperation, as opposed to a case where such an inference would contradict express dealings or discussions between the parties, such as unfinished negotiations intended at forming a partnership.[655]

358. Partnership, 'although often called a contract, is more accurately described as a relationship *resulting from* a contract'.[656] The partners are bound by the terms

653. See generally, M. Twomey, *Partnership Law* (Butterworths 2000). This is the seminal Irish text on this area of law.
654. F.W. Clark, *A Treatise on the Law of Partnership and Joint-Stock Companies, According to the Law of Scotland* 3 (T & T Clark 1866).
655. *Greville v. Venables* [2007] EWCA Civ 878, para. 38, *per* Lloyd L.J.
656. R. C. I'Anson, *Lindley and Banks on Partnership* 2–13 (18th edn., Sweet & Maxwell 2002), cited by Arnold J. in *Hodson v. Hodson* [2009] EWHC 430 (Ch) (unreported, England and Wales High Court (Chancery Division), 12 Mar. 2009), para. 13.

(whether express or implied) of the underlying agreement, subject to the usual contractual doctrines of mistake and misrepresentation. The Partnership Act of 1890 sets out a number of default rules that may be excluded or modified by agreement. Such agreement may be expressly made between the parties, or it may be implied by the Court. The burden on a party seeking to exclude application of one of the default provisions has been said to be slight.[657]

359. The Partnership Act of 1890 remains the primary source of Irish law regarding traditional partnerships. The 1890 Act (still in force in the UK as well as in Ireland), which was drafted in large part by Sir Frederick Pollock, 'codified (though not exhaustively) the law of partnership and reflected the pre-existing principles of equity which had been developed by the Court of Chancery'.[658] Preceding rules of the common law and equity continued in force except where inconsistent with the Act.

360. Traditional partnerships are the main subject of our discussion, but later we briefly consider limited partnerships, which are less common business forms provided for in later statutes, the most important of which are the Limited Partnerships Act 1907 and the Investment Limited Partnership (ILP) Act 1994. See *infra*, Part II, Chapter 2. Until we come to that point, all uses of the word 'partnership' should be taken to relate only to traditional or general partnerships. Our brief discussion of the law relating to traditional partnerships mostly follows the layout of the 1890 Act. We first discuss the legal definition of a partnership, before going on to treat relations between partners *inter se*, the liability of partners to third parties, dissolution and winding up of a partnership, and finally, the tax implications of trading as a partnership.

I. Definition of a Partnership

361. The 1890 Act, section 1(1), defines partnership as 'the relation which subsists between persons carrying on a business in common with a view of profit'. Although it might be considered artificial to do so, breaking the definition in section 1(1) into its constituent parts permits greater analysis. A few preliminary points should be borne in mind, however. In interpreting the definition of partnership, the courts will look to the substance of the situation, rather than attach conclusive weight to the parties' understanding of the nature of their business relationship. Neither studious avoidance by parties in their dealings of the word 'partnership'[659] nor affirmative description by parties of their association as a partnership (or not) concludes the inquiry.[660] In a similar vein, the law does not require intention,

657. *Khan v. Miah* [2000] 1 WLR 2123, 2128 *per* Lord Millett.

658. *Hurst v. Bryk* [2002] 1 AC 185, 194 *per* Lord Millett.

659. *Greenham v. Gray* (1855) 4 IR CLR 501; *Hanna v. Barnes* (unreported, High Court of Northern Ireland, 26 Jun. 1992).

660. *Adam v. Newbigging* (1888) 13 App Cas. 308, 315; *Pilsworth v. Mosse* (1863) 14 IR Ch R 163. As has been said in a different context: 'The manufacture of a five-pronged implement for manual digging results in a fork even if the manufacturer, unfamiliar with the English language, insists that he intended to make and has made a spade.' (*Street v. Mountford* [1985] AC 809, 819).

knowledge or explicit consent; it may be that the parties in fact never directed their minds to the legal status of the business being carried on, and 'the lack of any express consideration by the parties as to whether or not they wished to be a partnership is wholly irrelevant to whether or not a partnership existed'.[661] That said, it should not be forgotten that the partnership relation is based on contract.[662] Accordingly, before a person may be held to be a partner, he or she must have consented to such a role.[663] Finally, it should be noted that there is no requirement that a partnership should necessarily be in writing; an oral agreement may suffice.[664] Indeed, it is not necessary that the parties ever addressed their minds to the nature of their business relationship.

A. *Relation Subsisting between Persons*

362. The relation between members of a company or association registered under the Companies Act 2014 (or any other statute apart from the Partnership Act 1890 and the Limited Partnership Act 1907) does not constitute a partnership within the meaning of the 1890 Act.[665] However, difficult questions sometimes arise when persons work together in the period immediately preceding formation of a company. For example, the English Court of Appeal has held that two parties who, while working together in preparation for the incorporation of a company ordered goods in the name of the proposed company, were not at that time carrying on a partnership so as to render one liable for goods ordered by the other.[666] The Court of Appeal took the view that, even though the parties apparently satisfied the literal definition, they did not constitute a partnership, because their association was merely for the purpose of putting in train the formation of a company.[667]

363. The word 'persons' has been interpreted as allowing a company to be a partner.[668] Likewise, it has been held a partnership may itself be a partner,[669] although that view jars somewhat with the theory that a partnership, being an unincorporated association, is not a separate legal entity, but a collection of individuals.

661. *Talbot v. Revenue & Customs* [2008] UKVAT V20665 (1 May 2008), at para. 8.
662. However, 'while partnership is a consensual arrangement based on agreement, it is more than a simple contract (to use the expression of Dixon J. in *McDonald v. Dennys Lascelles Ltd* 48 CLR 457, 476); it is a continuing personal as well as a commercial relationship'. *Hurst v. Bryk and others* [2002] 1 AC 185, 194.
663. *Hunter v. Stoney* (1831) Glasc 23 (mother signed partnership in the name of her son, who, on learning of this, disclaimed any such consent; *held*: the son was not a partner).
664. *Crowley v. O'Sullivan* (1884) 15 LR IR 431.
665. Partnership Act 1890, s. 1(2).
666. *Spicer v. Mansell* [1970] 1 WLR 333, [1970] 1 All ER 462.
667. See similarly *Forester v. Bell* (1847) 10 IR LR 555 ('The members of this provisional committee [of company promoters] were not partners, nor had any of them a right to bind the others; so that the defendant cannot be visited with liability by any analogy to the case of partners.').
668. *Williams v. Harris* [1980] ILRM 237; *MacCarthaigh (Inspector of Taxes) v. D.* [1985] IR 73.
669. *McCalmont v. Chaine* (1835) 3 IR Law Rec (ns) 215.

B. Carrying on a Business

364. An agreement to enter a partnership, never acted upon, does not render the parties to the agreement partners.[670] Put differently, intention to form a partnership is insufficient, where the putative partners never in fact carry on business in common. (Indeed, as noted *supra*, parties' intentions as to the legal structure of their business may be quite beside the point.) Likewise, there is no partnership where an agreed necessary pre-condition of its creation has not occurred.[671] Thus, for example, the holding of an option to enter a partnership does in itself create a partnership, where the grantee has not availed of the option.[672] Parties may validly agree that a partnership agreement is to be retroactive, provided the partnership commenced at the specified, earlier, pre-execution date specified in the agreement.[673] The fact that certain partners take a dormant, inactive or subservient role in the business being carried on is not per se adverse to the existence of a partnership in law.[674]

365. Although at first glance the expression 'carrying on' might appear to contemplate a concerted course of dealings, it has been held that a partnership may come into existence for the purpose of a single venture or for a pre-ordained, finite period.[675] However, the old case of *Robinson v. Anderson* is probably of doubtful authority, to the extent that it decides (or may be read as deciding) that two professionals jointly advising a client and sharing the profits have on such facts alone created a partnership beginning and ending with their advising of that client. It would certainly run counter to everyday practice: It is routine for business persons to be simultaneously in receipt of professional advice from various sources.[676] Outside the realm of professional advisers, it has been held that a series of separate, disconnected ventures is insufficient evidence of a partnership.[677]

366. The 1890 Act (section 45) defines 'business' to include 'every trade, occupation or profession'. Some of the cases appear to have taken an unduly narrow approach to the question of whether an activity amounts to a 'business' for this purpose and may be of doubtful authority.[678] Commerce, in the usual sense of being

670. *Macken v. Revenue Commissioners* [1962] IR 302.
671. *Milliken v. Milliken* (1845) 8 IR Eq. R. 16.
672. *Re Hall* (1864) IR Ch R 287.
673. *Best v. McKay* (1940) 74 ILTR 125; *Macken v. Revenue Commissioners* [1962] IR 302.
674. *Y v. O'Sullivan* [1949] IR 264 – shades here of *Salomon v. Salomon & Co Ltd* [1897] AC 22.
675. See the decision of the High Court of Australia in *Canny Gabriel Castle Jackson Advertising Pty Ltd v. Volume Sales (Finance) Pty Ltd* (1974) 131 CLR 321 (collaboration for the sole purpose of facilitating a particular concert tour amounted to a partnership).
676. M. Twomey, *Partnership Law* (Butterworths 2000), para. 2.51.
677. *Minister for Social Welfare v. Griffiths* [1992] ILRM 667.
678. See *French v. Styring* (1857) 3 Jur NS 670 (owning a racehorse and sharing its winnings was *held not* to amount to a business) and *Walsh v. Walsh* [1942] IR 403 (family members together working a farm 'for the sake of the family … the purpose of gain [being] incidental … were not, so far as the home farm was concerned, carrying on a "business" at all', 410). Courts have recently seen no obstacle to a finding of partnership in the case of a family business. See Twomey [2.48]–[2.49] and cases cited therein.

'for profit', is not a necessary aspect of business; thus, for example, a medical research centre operated on a for-profit basis may constitute a partnership.[679] Where what would otherwise be a partnership is carried on for unlawful purposes, or in an unlawful manner, the parties to the enterprise have none of the rights of partners against one another or against third parties. However, 'an innocent third party may be able to enforce his rights against an illegal partnership, if he was unaware of the illegality'.[680]

C. In Common

367. It is through the medium of this perhaps slightly vague phrase that a historical and purposive understanding of what we mean when speaking of a partnership has influenced the development of the law. The contiguity of the words 'in common' with the requirement that the business be pursued 'with a view to a profit', when taken together with the rule that profit sharing is prima facie evidence of partnership (see *infra*), militate against any conclusion that an employer-employee relationship could, without more, amount to a partnership. The logic of the case law is that partners are essentially co-owners of the business in which they are engaged. Despite the number of occasions on which this point has been argued in different cases, it may be that no more is required than an answer to the question: Were the parties *in business together*, particularly in the sense of sharing profits, liabilities and authority to bind the others?

368. Above all else, partners are agents of one another. In consequence, where it is clear that a party would not tolerate someone else acting as his or her agent, it is not open to the court to hold that the two constituted partners.[681] The agency relationship must be mutual.[682] Failure to deal with outsiders as if one were an agent may be evidence of lack of authority to do so.[683]

369. When a sole trader expands his or her business by including third parties, how is a court to decide whether a partnership is thereby created? The leading Irish text suggests that courts should look for 'perceptible differences in both the inner operations and outward appearance of the firm to support a finding that the business is now being carried on in common'.[684] This suggestion is based *Macken v. Revenue Commissioners*,[685] in which the High Court (Teevan J.) had to consider

679. *O'Kelly v. Darragh* [1988] ILRM 309.

680. G. Morse, *Partnership Law* 93 (6th edn., Oxford University Press 2006). The effect of illegality is considered further *infra*.

681. *Walsh v. Walsh* [1942] IR 403, 411. Total strangers, it has been held, could not have envisaged acting as one another's agent: *Smith v. Anderson* (1880) 15 Ch. D. 247.

682. *Re Boyle* [1947] IR 61. It is on this basis that the leading Irish text doubts the correctness of the finding of partnership in *Inspector of Taxes v. Cafolla & Co.* [1949] IR 210. See Twomey, 45.

683. *Re Hall* (1864) IR Ch R 287 (1865) ILTR 579, 580.

684. Twomey, 45.

685. *Macken v. Revenue Commissioners* [1962] IR 302.

whether, after a father agreed to admit his son and daughter into his painting business and began sharing profits with them, but before the written agreement between them was executed, the business was being carried on 'in common'.

370. As to the type of changes that would suggest partners had been admitted and the business was now being carried on in common, the Court had regard to the following factors: whether the name of the firm had changed; whether the firm bank accounts were now in the name of the purported partners; whether a notice had issued to parties who had been contracting with the business informing them of the change; whether debts had been transferred to the new arrangement; whether the statutory requirement that a partnership trading otherwise than under the name of all of the partners must register its name within one month of adopting such name had been complied with;[686] and the way in which the Revenue Commissioners treated the relationship between the parties for tax purposes. However, mere inclusion of a party in a firm's name does not necessarily make the named person a partner in the firm.[687] Similarly, a joint bank account in the firm's name might tend to suggest a partnership, but its absence will not necessarily preclude a finding of partnership.[688]

371. Partners need not necessarily make equal or equivalent contributions or inputs to be held to be carrying on business 'in common'. It may be that different partners contribute differently to the firm: One may contribute property or capital, while allowing another de facto control over trading operations.[689] Likewise a partnership may exist, even though some partners make greater contributions of talent, ability, time or effort to the running of the partnership than others.[690]

D. With a View to Profit

372. Profit must be the goal of the business, even if a loss is the result. The 1890 Act, section 2(3), makes the sharing of profits prima facie evidence of partnership and provides further, in section 35(e), that a partner may apply to the Court for dissolution of the partnership where the underlying business 'can only be carried on at a loss'. Therefore, it would seem that business ventures designed with the intention of creating losses cannot come within the definition of a partnership. However, on similar facts in the case of *MacCarthaigh (Inspector of Taxes) v. D.*,[691] *O'Hanlon*

686. Registration of Business Names Act of 1963, s. 1.
687. *Martin v. Sherry* [1905] 2 IR 62 (*Held*: John Peel not a partner in his father's firm, Joshua E Peel & Son. Several other factors weighed against John Peel being held a partner: no deed of partnership had been drawn up; he did not receive a division of the profits; and the business remained the sole property of his father.).
688. *Re Ferrar, ex p Ulster Banking Company* (1859) 9 IR Ch R 11 (Sims and Ferrar, who ran a newspaper together, but maintained separate bank accounts rather than open a firm account, were *held* to be partners).
689. *Greenham v. Gray* (1855) 4 IR CLR 501.
690. *Joyce v. Morrissey* [1998] TLR 707.
691. *MacCarthaigh (Inspector of Taxes) v. D.* [1985] IR 73.

J., though expressing 'some reservations ... [as to whether] the arrangement entered into ... should properly be regarded as a partnership at all', held that, since the case had come before him by way of a case stated by the Revenue Appeal Commissioner, he was bound by the Commissioner's finding that there had been a partnership, as this was 'a primary fact' that bound an appellate court. It must, with respect, be submitted that this conclusion is open to doubt: Surely the finding of the Appeal Commissioner was not purely a question of fact, such as one might expect to receive deference on appeal. In this instance, it would seem that the question as to whether a venture designed for tax reasons to be completely uneconomical amounted to a partnership was at least partially a question of *law*, and therefore reviewable on appeal. Had the Court reached the point, it seems that a vehicle created to sustain losses (for tax reasons) could well have failed to meet the prerequisite that a partnership is a business carried on '*with a view to profit*'.

373. If the definition in section 1 of the 1890 Act does not yield a clear answer, the Court, where relevant, shall have regard to certain evidentiary presumptions set out in section 2, which provides as follows:

> In determining whether a partnership does or does not exist, regard shall be had to the following rules:
>
> (1) Joint tenancy, tenancy in common, joint property, common property, or part ownership does not of itself create a partnership as to anything so held or owned, whether the tenants or owners do or do not share any profits made by the use thereof
>
> (2) The sharing of gross returns does not of itself create a partnership, whether the persons sharing such returns have or have not a joint or common right or interest in any property from which or from the use of which the returns are derived
>
> (3) The receipt by a person of a share of the profits of a business is prima facie evidence that he is a partner in the business, but the receipt of such a share, or of a payment contingent on or varying with the profits of a business, does not of itself make him a partner in the business; and in particular–
>
> (a) The receipt by a person of a debt or other liquidated amount by installments or otherwise out of the accruing profits of a business does not of itself make him a partner in the business or liable as such;
>
> (b) A contract for the remuneration of a servant or agent of a person engaged in a business by a share of the profits of a business does not of itself make the servant or agent a partner in the business or liable as such;
>
> (c) A person being a widow or child of a deceased partner, and receiving by way of annuity a portion of the profits made in the business in which the deceased person was a partner in the business or liable as such;
>
> (d) The advance of money by way of loan to a person engaged in any business on a contract with that person that the lender shall receive a rate

of interest varying with the profits, or shall receive a share of the profits arising from carrying on a business, does not of itself make the lender a partner with the person or persons carrying on the business or liable as such. Provided that the contract is in writing, and signed by or on behalf of all the parties thereto;

(e) A person receiving by way of annuity or otherwise a portion of the profits of a business in consideration of the sale by him of the goodwill of the business is not by reason only of such receipt a partner in the business or liable as such.

E. *Maximum Number of Partners*

374. It should also be noted that as a general rule a partnership may be made up of no more than twenty persons. Where a firm breaches this prohibition, it is illegal and automatically dissolved. There is an exception to this rule for partnerships engaged in the business of banking where the number of partners is limited to ten.[692] There is also a general exemption from this cap for firms in which all the partners are solicitors and firms in which all the partners are accountants.[693] In addition, the Minister for Enterprise, Trade and Employment may make an order exempting a particular firm or category of firm. Such orders have been made in respect of limited partnerships formed for the purpose of carrying on or promoting the business of thoroughbred horse breeding[694] and for limited partnerships 'consisting of not more than fifty partners which is formed for the purpose of, and whose main business consists of, the provision of investment and loan finance and ancillary facilities and services to persons engaged in industrial or commercial activities'.[695] In addition, it should be noted that this cap does not apply to partnerships formed under the ILP Act 1994.[696]

§2. Relations Between Partners *Inter Se*[697]

375. The relations of partners to one another are governed in the first instance by the partnership agreement. The 1890 Act provides a default template that applies 'only to the extent that its provisions have not been excluded or modified'.[698] Each partner is an agent of his fellow partners, and a principal for each of his fellow partners. Accordingly, it is unsurprising to find that statute provides that the firm must

692. Companies Act 2014, s. 1435. Section 1435(1) repeats the non-application of this provision to certain kinds of partnerships but provides in s. 1436 that the number of partners in a banking firm is limited to 10.
693. Companies Act 2014, s. 1435(1)(c) (ii) abd (ii).
694. Companies (Amendment) Act 1982 (s. 13(2)) Ord. 1988 (S.I. 54 of 1988).
695. Companies (Amendment) Act 1982 (s. 13(2)) Ord. 2004 (S.I. 506 of 2004).
696. ILP Act 1994, s. 4(4).
697. See Law Society of Ireland, *Business Law* 18–25 (2006).
698. H.R. Hahlo & M.J. Trebilcock, *Hahlo's Casebook on Company Law* 33 (Sweet & Maxwell 1977).

indemnify each partner in respect of payments made and personal liabilities incurred by him in the ordinary course of the business of the firm, or in 'anything necessarily done for the preservation of the business or property of the firm'.[699]

I. Fiduciary Duties

376. Partners must act with utmost good faith in their dealings with one another. A partnership agreement is a contract *uberrimae fidei*, irrespective of its terms.[700] This is a mandatory (and therefore exceptional) rule of partnership law.[701] The court will construe partnership agreements in light of this overarching duty.[702] This overarching duty of good faith founds the following aspects of fiduciary duty codified in sections 28–30 of the 1890 Act:

- Partners are bound to render true accounts and full information of all things affecting the partnership to any partner or his legal representatives.
- Every partner must account to the firm for any benefit derived by him without the consent of the other partners from any transaction concerning the partnership, or from any use by him of the partnership property, name or business connection, including transactions occurring after the dissolution of the firm by a partner's death or bankruptcy, up until the affairs of the firm have been completely wound up.[703] This duty extends to a liability to account to the firm for secret profits made in a personal capacity, in circumstances where no demonstrable harm has been done to the firm.[704]
- If a partner, without the consent of the other partners, carries on any business of the same nature as and competing with that of the firm, he must account for and pay over to the firm all profits made by him in that business.

377. At common law a *former* partner is free to compete with the partnership, provided he does not use the partnership's property, name or business connection. Therefore, partnership agreements often include no-competition clauses under which partners agree, in the event that they leave the firm, not to compete with it in

699. 1890 Act, s. 24(2).

700. *Const v. Harris* (1824) Turn & R 496, *per* Lord Eldon ('In all partnerships, whether it is expressed in the deed or not, the partners are bound to be true and faithful to each other.').

701. See, for example, *Lock v. Lynam* (1854) 4 IR Ch R 188.

702. *Green v. Howell* [1910] 1 Ch. D. 495 (C.A.) (power to expel a partner for breach of specified articles may not be exercised other than in good faith, such as where a partner is expelled in order to allow the purchase of his interest on unfavourable terms) and *Law v. Law* [1905] 1 Ch. D. 140 (C.A.) (where one partner negotiates with another to purchase the latter's share in the business, and the prospective purchaser knowingly enters the negotiations with greater knowledge regarding the partnership accounts, the prospective vendor must be put in possession of all material facts relating to partnership assets of which the prospective purchaser is aware).

703. See, for example, *Don King Productions Inc. v. Warren* [1999] 2 All ER 218 and *Taylor v. Masons* [2001] EWCA Civ 2106.

704. *Bentley v. Craven* (1853) 18 Beav 75 (partner bought sugar at discount and resold to company at market price; ordered to account to firm for profits so earned, despite the fact that the firm would have had to pay market price in any event) and *Boston Deep Sea Fishing & Ice Co v. Ansell* (1888) 39 Ch D 339.

a specified area and for a specified time. However, such clauses must not breach competition law.[705] Two years appears to be the outer temporal limit of such clauses, which is consistent with the dictates of competition law.[706]

II. Duty of Care

378. Partners owe each other a duty of care in the conduct of the firm's affairs. The baseline standard of care imposed on a partner is uncertain. The matter is not addressed in the 1890 Act. As a joint report of the English and Scottish Law Commissions has noted, nineteenth century cases adopted a variety of expressions, such as 'culpable negligence' and 'want of reasonable care', without closely analyzing the nature and extent of the duty.[707] In a more recent case, Woolf J. has spoken of a duty to act 'without culpable negligence' and 'not … below the standards of a reasonable businessman in the situation in which he found himself'.[708] The Law Commissions' report also found that there are 'few reported cases of partners attempting to sue each other in negligence'.[709] Recent Scottish authority has held that the standard of care must be objective rather than subjective.[710] In a later case, the New South Wales Supreme Court has held that the ordinary negligence standard does not apply between partners, holding that wilful misconduct or gross or culpable negligence before the partner at fault is liable,[711] but such a view has recently been rejected by the Chancery Division of the High Court of England and Wales, in favour of a duty to exercise reasonable care requiring compliance to an objective standard, albeit that a partner should not be liable for a failure due to want of a larger share of prudence or skill than he possesses.[712]

III. Management of the Firm

379. Subject to contrary (express or implied) agreement, every partner 'may take part in the management of the partnership business'.[713] Contrary agreement may permissibly locate powers of management of the firm in a subset of partners. A further default rule provides that 'difference[s] arising as to ordinary matters connected with the partnership business may be decided by a majority of the partners, but no change may be made in the nature of the partnership business without the

705. See Competition Acts 2002–2014.
706. See Law Society of Ireland, *Business Law*, 21–22.
707. The Law Commission and the Scottish Law Commission, Partnership Law (2003) (Law Com No. 283) (Scot Law Com No. 192), Ch 11.7, 183 (*Citing Bury v. Allen* (1845) 1 Coll 589, 604; 63 ER 556, 562; and *Thomas v. Atherton* (1878) 10 Ch D 185, 199 and 202).
708. *Winsor v. Schroeder* (1979) 129 NLJ 1266.
709. The Law Commission and the Scottish Law Commission, The Law Commission and the Scottish Law Commission (*supra*, n. 1), 183.
710. *Ross Harper & Murphy v. Banks* [2000] SLT 699.
711. *Lane v. Bushby* [2000] NSWSC 1029.
712. *Tann v. Herrington* [2009] EWHC (Ch) (unreported, Bernard Livesey QC sitting as a Judge in the Chancery Division, High Court of England and Wales, 10 Mar. 2009).
713. 1890 Act, s. 24(5).

consent of all existing partners'.[714] Unanimity is therefore required for any change in the partnership business; it is also required for the introduction of a new partner[715] and for an agreement permitting expulsion of a partner to be decided by a majority, rather than (as is otherwise the default position) unanimously.[716]

IV. Finances

380. In terms of finances, the following default rules apply, subject to contrary (express or implied) agreement between the partners:

- All partners are entitled to share equally (rather than in proportion to capital contributed) in the capital and profits of the business, and must also contribute equally toward losses, whether capital or otherwise, sustained by the firm.[717]
- Where partners agree to share profits unequally and make no specific provision, losses are shared in the same proportion.
- The rates of interest on a partner's capital contribution and on loans by a partner to the firm are, respectively, 0% and 5%.[718]
- No partner is entitled to remuneration for acting in the partnership business.[719]

  As has been noted, it is important 'not to confuse such a partner who receives a preferential appropriation of profit with a "salaried partner". The latter is simply an employee of the firm who is held out to the world as a partner. He is not "carrying on the business in common" with the partners but is employed by them'.[720]

In practice, partnership agreements typically provide that a partner may draw down money from the firm in anticipation of year-end profits, that at the end of the year that partner is entitled to (or if the amount is negative must repay) the entire profit to which he would have been entitled, *less* drawings.

V. Partnership Property

381. The question of whether property is owned by the partnership or owned by one or more of the partners is to be determined in accordance with the partners' intention and agreement. The 1890 Act creates two rebuttable presumptions, however:

714. 1890 Act, s. 24(8).
715. 1890 Act, s. 24(7).
716. 1890 Act, s. 25.
717. 1890 Act, s. 24(1). The reference in s. 24(1) to partners 'shar[ing] equally in the capital' of the business must be read to mean capital *profit*, due to s. 44(b)(3).
718. 1890 Act, s. 24(4) and 24(3).
719. 1890 Act, s. 24(6).
720. Law Society of Ireland, *Business Law*, 23.

- All rights and interests in property originally brought into the partnership stock, or acquired on account of the firm or for the purposes and in the course of the partnership business, are partnership property, and must be held and applied by the partners exclusively for the purposes of the partnership and in accordance with the partnership agreement.[721]
- Property purchased 'with money belonging to the firm' is presumed to be partnership property, unless contrary intention or agreement can be shown.[722]

§3. Liability of Partners to Third Parties

382. Section 5 of the 1890 Act stands for the following propositions: (1) A partnership is not a separate legal entity, but a collection of individuals. (2) A partner is an agent of the firm and all of his or her fellow partners. (3) The firm is liable for acts of all partners done as part of the ordinary course of the firm's business. Under section 9 of the 1890 Act, every partner in a firm is liable jointly with the other partners for all contractual debts and obligations of the firm incurred while he or she is a partner. The members of a firm are (jointly and severally) liable for any wrongful act or omission of any partner acting in the ordinary course of the business of the firm, or with the authority of his or her co-partners causing loss or injury to a third party.

383. Because partners' liability for acts of fellow partners is financially unlimited, it is important to consider the question: To precisely which acts does liability extend? As a general matter, liability extends to acts done by a partner *qua* partner 'in the ordinary course of the business of the firm'. Liability does not begin until the partnership (i.e., principals for which a partner may be said to be agent) has come into existence, but extends (under section 38) until after dissolution of the firm. The phrase 'in the course of the ordinary business of the firm', or a variant thereof, occurs in section 5 and the other specific instances of liability contained in the 1890 Act (in sections 5, 6, 10, 11, 13 and 15). This phrase covers much the same ground as debates over whether a partner acted with (express or implied) authority: The Court will not find an act to be impliedly authorized on behalf of the firm, unless it is within the ordinary course of the firm's business; and express authority makes it irrelevant whether an act would otherwise have been within the ordinary course of the firm's business. (Ostensible authority is different; it may be thought of as a form of estoppel. The same principles apply in determining whether a partner acted with the ostensible authority of his firm as applied to claims that a director acted with the ostensible authority of his company. See *supra*, paragraphs 219–220.) On one level, wrongful acts or omissions might be thought never to be within a firm's ordinary course of business. In answer to the conundrum thus posed, it might be said that while solicitors or surgeons do not in the ordinary course negligently conduct proceedings or operations, such activities (even if negligently carried out) constitute their ordinary business.

721. 1890 Act, s. 20(1).
722. 1890 Act, s. 21.

384. A partnership agreement frequently outlines the nature of the firm's business. This will be evidence of what is the firm's ordinary course of business, but such an agreement will not usually be exhaustive or treated in law as conclusive as to what constitutes the ordinary course of a firm's business, unless expressly stated as such. Partners – in trading and non-trading partnerships – have been held to have ostensible or implied authority to do the following things on the firm's behalf: conduct legal proceedings; open a bank account; sign cheques; enter contracts within the ordinary sphere of the firm's business; sell goods belonging to the firm or purchase; appoint, employ or remove employees or agents; receive payment of firm debts; and release firm debts.[723] The common law distinguishes between partners in trading firms from those in non-trading firms and holds that certain acts (such as borrowing) are within the implied authority of partners in trading firms, but not partners in non-trading firms.[724]

385. Under section 5 of the 1890 Act, where a partner acts in the ordinary course of the firm's business, but without authority, the firm is bound, unless the third party alleging a wrong either (a) knows the partner has no authority or (b) was not under the impression that he was dealing with a partner at all. Likewise, section 8 provides that, where partners agree on restrictions on the authority of one or more partners, no act done in contravention of such agreement binds the firm with respect to persons having notice of the agreement.

386. Although partners cannot escape liability solely on the basis that a wrong was primarily caused by a fellow partner, the case law suggests that partners do not have to contribute to losses where fellow partners' conduct amounts to recklessness, wilful misconduct or fraud, unless, of course, the former have authorized or ratified the conduct in question.[725]

387. As with company directors, acts of a partner done without authority may be retrospectively ratified by the principal on whose behalf the partner acted – that is, the firm. A firm may not retrospectively ratify an act by a partner before the firm came into existence, but, once in existence, the firm may prospectively adopt the transaction. Partners ratifying or adopting a transaction must have knowledge of the act.[726]

I. Other Instances of Agency

388. As well as general acts of a partner done in the ordinary course of the firm's business or with the express, implied or ostensible authority of the firm, a firm is also liable where a partner: executes acts or instruments (section 6 of the 1890 Act), misapplies property (section 11) or commits a breach of trust (section 13). Section

723. See Twomey, 220–221.
724. Twomey, 221–224.
725. Twomey, 324.
726. *Marsh v. Joseph* [1897] 1 Chs 213, 246.

13 is an interesting provision, in that it provides an exception to the general rule of vicarious liability, inasmuch as it exempts partners from liability where a co-partner, who happens to be a trustee, employs trust property 'in the business or on the account of the partnership' in breach of trust. The section provides that a partner will not be able to rely on this exemption if he or she had notice of the breach of trust. Section 16 provides that a firm is deemed to be on notice of a fact relating to 'partnership affairs' where one partner is deemed to be on notice of that fact. (This raises a question as to whether notice would be imputed automatically for the purposes of section 13 in the case of a breach of trust, but interpreting sections 13 and 16 together in that way would risk emptying section 13 of meaning, and normal principles of statutory interpretation would suggest that such an interpretation should be avoided.)

389. Another important provision is section 15 of the 1890 Act, which provides that an admission or representation made by any partner in the ordinary course of business concerning partnership affairs is evidence against the firm.

390. Finally, there is the issue of post-dissolution liability. Section 38 provides that 'the authority of each partner to bind the firm, and the other rights and obligations of the partners, continue notwithstanding the dissolution so far as may be necessary to wind up the affairs of the partnership, and to complete transactions begun but unfinished at the time of the dissolution, but not otherwise'.

§4. Dissolution and Winding Up[727]

I. Occurrence of Dissolution

391. A partnership is automatically dissolved, without the intervention of the Court, in the following circumstances (cf. sections 32–34 of the 1890 Act):

(a) If entered into for a fixed term, by the expiration of that term.
(b) If entered into for a single adventure or undertaking, by the termination of that adventure or undertaking.
(c) If entered into for an undefined time, by a partner giving notice to the others of his intention to dissolve the partnership. The partnership is dissolved from the date mentioned in such notice, or, if no date is specified, on receipt of notice, unless the articles provide for some other date.[728] (d) By the death of a partner, unless (as is often the case) the articles provide otherwise.
(d) By the bankruptcy of a partner, unless the articles provide otherwise.
(e) At the option of the other partners, if one partner suffers his share in the partnership property to be charged by the Court in respect of his separate debt.

727. See Law Society of Ireland, *Business Law*, 35–44.
728. See also 1890 Act, s. 26.

(f) By the happening of an event making it unlawful for the business of the firm to be carried on, or for the members of the firm to carry it on in partnership;[729] or where the partnership is formed to carry on intrinsically illegal activity, such as crime.

On the occurrence of any of these events, the partnership automatically dissolves. In circumstances such as the death or bankruptcy of a partner, though the partnership dissolves in theory, the remaining may in practice choose to carry on as before. This is known as a *technical* dissolution: the partnership is not in any real sense ended, but simply reforms and continues as before.[730] On the other hand, the parties may, on the occurrence of such an event, choose to wind up the partnership. This is a *general* dissolution. On the termination of a partnership, any surviving partner may apply to the Court to have the partnership wound up.[731] Winding up a partnership is the responsibility of the partners: The Act does not provide for an office holder to carry out such a function, but partners may apply to the Court for a receiver, if necessary, to preserve partnership assets.[732] The list of circumstances set out *supra* (taken from sections 32–34) are, with one exception (namely, illegal partnerships), default rules around which the firm may contract. Thus, written partnership agreements may provide, for example, that the death or bankruptcy of a partner (or dissolution by notice under section 26 and section 32(c)) will not trigger dissolution.

392. Further circumstances are set out in the 1890 Act, section 35, in which a partnership is not automatically dissolved, but in which a partner may apply to the Court for dissolution, namely:

(a) Where a partner is found lunatic by inquisition, or is shown to the satisfaction of the Court to be of permanently unsound mind.
(b) Where another partner becomes in any way incapable of performing his part of the partnership contract.
(c) Where another partner is in the opinion of the Court guilty of conduct that, having regard to the nature of the business, is calculated to pre-judicially affect the carrying on of the business.
(d) Where another partner wilfully or persistently breaches the partnership agreement, or otherwise so conducts himself in matters relating to the partnership that it is not reasonably practicable for the other partner(s) to carry on.
(e) When the business of the partnership can only be carried on at a loss.
(f) Whenever in any case circumstances have arisen, which, in the opinion of the Court, render it just and equitable that the partnership should be dissolved.

729. This provision has been strictly interpreted; thus, a solicitor's inadvertent failure to renew his practising certificate has been held to dissolve his partnership. See *Hudgell Yeates & Co. v. Watson* [1978] 2 All ER 363.

730. There can be no technical dissolution where an event occurs making it unlawful for the business of the firm to be carried on, or for the members of the firm to carry it on in partnership.

731. 1890 Act, s. 39.

732. *Hurst v. Bryk* [2002] 1 AC 185, 196 *per* Lord Millett.

§5. CONSEQUENCES OF DISSOLUTION

393. As noted *supra*, on the dissolution of a partnership any remaining partner is entitled to apply to have the firm's property applied in payment of the firm's debts and liabilities, or to have the firm wound up – and thereby instigate a general dissolution.[733] As also noted above, this is only a default rule. The partners may agree to exclude its application. Where a general dissolution occurs, the partners retain authority to bind one another, 'so far as may be necessary to wind up the affairs of the partnership, and to complete transactions begun but unfinished at the time of the dissolution, but not otherwise'.[734] Once the firm is in general dissolution, the firm's debts and liabilities will be ascertained and discharged, and the firm's assets will be sold as necessary to raise sufficient funds for that purpose. The assets of the firm, including the sums, if any, contributed by the partners to make up losses or deficiencies of capital, shall be applied in the following order: (1) in paying debts and liabilities of the firm to third parties; (2) in repaying advances made by partners to the firm; (3) in paying to each partner rateably what is due from the firm to him in respect of capital; and (4) the ultimate residue, if any, shall be divided among the partners in the proportion in which the profits are divisible.[735] Losses, including losses and deficiencies of capital, shall be paid first out of profits, next out of capital, and finally, if necessary, by the partners individually in the proportion in which they were entitled to share profits.[736] Partners may agree to share surplus assets and/or contribute to losses in a different ratio than the default ratio set out in the legislation (i.e., in the same proportion as their entitlement to profits),[737] but (predictably) may not by contract alter the rule that creditors are to be paid off first.[738]

I. Outsiders

394. Persons dealing with the firm are entitled to treat all apparent members of the firm as still being partners, unless and until they have notice of a change.[739] A public notice in *Iris Oifigiúil* (today's equivalent of the Dublin Gazette) shall be notice for persons who had not previously dealt with the firm,[740] but the remaining partners must individually notify existing customers.

II. Retirement

395. The 1890 Act does not provide a default mechanism that a partner may use to retire from a firm, other than by dissolving the partnership on notice.[741] As noted

733. 1890 Act, s. 39.
734. 1890 Act, s. 38.
735. 1890 Act, s. 44(b).
736. 1890 Act, s. 44(a).
737. 1890 Act, ss 24(1) and 44(b).
738. See Law Society of Ireland, *Business Law* (2006), 39.
739. 1890 Act, s. 36(1).
740. 1890 Act, s. 36(2).
741. 1890 Act, ss 26 and 32(c).

supra, such dissolution opens the prospect of an application for the winding up of the firm.[742] Therefore, retirement is an important and necessary subject of any written partnership agreement.

396. A partner who retires from a firm does not thereby cease to be liable for partnership debts or obligations incurred before his or her retirement.[743] The remaining partners may agree to indemnify the retiring partner in respect of such debts and obligations. A retiree is not liable for debts or obligations incurred by the partnership after his retirement, as the agency relationship has been ended.[744] (The same applies where a partner dies or becomes bankrupt.) However, there is an exception to this proposition in the case of existing customers or creditors – that is, persons who were aware of a partner's connection with the firm before that partner's retirement: They must have notice of the retirement, before the retiree is released from liability in respect of them.[745] The only other way a retiring partner may be liable for post-retirement debts is if he 'knowingly suffers himself to be represented' as a partner in the firm.[746] Where a person (by retirement, death or bankruptcy) ceases to be a partner, 'and the surviving or continuing partners carry on the business of the firm with its capital or assets without any final settlement of accounts as between the firm and the outgoing partner or his estate, then, in the absence of any agreement to the contrary, the outgoing partner or his estate is entitled at the option of himself or his representatives to such share of the profits made since the dissolution as the Court may find to be attributable to the use of his share of the partnership assets, or to interest at the rate of 5% per annum on the amount of his share of the partnership assets'.[747]

§6. TAXATION

397. Detailed treatment of the application of Irish tax law to partnerships is beyond the scope of this work. The following few points may, however, be of passing interest. Partnerships are tax-transparent: Tax is assessed on the partners separately and not on the firm,[748] unlike in a company where both the firm (on its profits) and its members (on their dividends) are taxed. This flows from the fact that a partnership is not a separate legal entity, but is rather a collection of individuals. So, too, do other tax advantages to the partnership as a form of business organization. For example, partners' social insurance contributions are less than the combined rate paid by employers and employees.[749] Structuring a business as a partnership so as

742. 1890 Act, s. 39.
743. 1890 Act, s. 17(2).
744. 1890 Act, s. 36(3).
745. 1890 Act, s. 36(1).
746. 1890 Act, s. 14(1).
747. 1890 Act, s. 42(1). See *Meagher v. Meagher* [1961] IR 96.
748. Taxes Consolidation Act (TCA) 1997, s. 1008(1). See, for example, TCA 1997, s. 30, as regards capital gains tax.
749. Social Welfare (Consolidation) Act 1993, ss 10 and 17.

to minimize tax liability is a legitimate and common practice,[750] but running a partnership at a deliberate loss, in order to set the same off against other tax liability, risks a finding that the business is not carried on 'with a view to a profit' and thus does not qualify as a partnership at all.[751]

398. Tax legislation provides that a firm's 'precedent partner'– defined as the first-named acting partner in the partnership agreement or, if there is no agreement, the partner who is named singly or with precedence over other partners in the usual name of the firm[752] – is responsible for filing a return of income and chargeable gains to the Revenue Commissioners,[753] and he or she is also the person to whom the Revenue gives notice of its determinations as to the partnership's tax affairs.[754] There are, in addition, certain other consequences of a person being a precedent partner. For example, in the event that profits for a given period are not exhausted (in the sense of being divided among the partners), the precedent partner is liable to an assessment in respect of such remaining balance, but if and when that balance (or part of it) is paid to the partner(s) entitled to it, the precedent partner may deduct therefrom the amount of such assessment paid by him or her.[755]

399. Finally, two miscellaneous points: First, a partnership may register collectively for Value Added Tax (VAT) and income tax by filing a form TR1 and is for this purpose included in a category with sole traders, trusts and unincorporated bodies. This is in effect an instance of the law treating a partnership as if it were a separate entity, which it is not. Secondly, the template Partnership Tax Return 2008, Form 1 (Firms), is a ten-page document readily available on the website of the Revenue Commissioners at www.revenue.ie.

750. *Inspector of Taxes v. Cafolla & Co.* [1949] IR 210.
751. This almost arose in *MacCarthaigh (Inspector of Taxes) v. D.* [1985] IR 73.
752. TCA 1997, s. 1007(1).
753. TCA 1997, ss 880 and 951(2). Any claim for a joint allowance must be made by the precedent partner: TCA 1997, s. 1010(9)(a).
754. TCA 1997, ss 1008(3), 1010(6), and 1012(1).
755. TCA 1997, s. 1008(4).

Chapter 2. Limited Partnerships

§1. Limited Partnerships Act

400. The Limited Partnerships Act 1907 for the first time under Irish law enabled a partnership to be formed that did not display three characteristics of a general or traditional partnership, namely: (1) the unlimited liability of every partner; (2) the implied authority of each partner to bind the firm and his or her fellow partners in all matters within the ordinary scope of the partnership business; and (3) the right of a partner, subject to contrary agreement, that each partner was entitled to participate in managing the business.[756] The Annual Report of the CRO stated that at the end of 2014 there were 1,049 limited partnerships registered with the CRO.[757] (It is not clear from the CRO Annual Report for 2014 whether this figure includes ILPs created under the 1994 Act, which are described *infra.*) There is no separate listing for ILPs in the Annual Report for 2014.

401. The 1907 Act did not create an internally complete, freestanding body of law. Rather, subject to the provisions of the 1907 Act, the law applicable to traditional, general partnerships (i.e., the 1890 Act and, to the extent that they are not inconsistent therewith, the rules of equity and common law relating to partnerships) apply to limited partnerships.[758] With that in mind, the following is a brief discussion of the modifications created by the 1907 Act.

I. Definition and Constitution; Management and Liability

402. A limited partnership established under the 1907 Act must consist of one or more persons called general partners and one or more persons to be called limited partners.[759] General partners manage the firm and have unlimited liability, whereas limited partners, like company shareholders, invest in the firm and enjoy limited liability (i.e., they are only liable for the firm's debts and obligations in the amount of their capital investment), but have no default right to take part in managing the firm.[760] (If a limited partner, notwithstanding that he or she does not have a right to do so, *does* take part in the management of the firm's business, he or she shall be liable for all debts and obligations of the firm incurred while so doing as though he were a general partner.[761]) A limited partner may, however, inspect the firm's books and 'examine into the state of the partnership business, and … advise with the partners thereon'.[762]

756. R.C. I'Anson Banks, *Lindley and Banks on Partnership* 842 (18th edn., Sweet & Maxwell 2002).
757. CRO Annual Report 2014 available on www.cro.ie.
758. Limited Partnerships Act 1907, s. 7.
759. Limited Partnerships Act 1907, s. 4(2).
760. Limited Partnerships Act 1907, ss 4(2) and 6(1).
761. Limited Partnerships Act 1907, s. 6(1).
762. Limited Partnerships Act 1907, s. 6(1).

403. The 1907 Act (by section 7 thereof) is, in effect, superimposed onto the 1890 Act and the common law, and so it follows that a limited partnership, to qualify as such, must meet the definition of a partnership contained in the 1890 Act and discussed *supra*: It must consist of two or more persons carrying on business in common with a view to a profit. Therefore, for example, a firm intentionally incurring losses for tax purposes could not in law be a limited partnership, just as it could not be a partnership under the 1890 Act.

404. As regards management of the company, the Act provides, as a default rule subject to contrary express or implied agreement between the partners, that: 'Any difference arising as to ordinary matters connected with the partnership business may be decided by a majority of the general partners.'[763] Likewise a limited partner has no right of veto over the introduction of a new partner into the firm.[764]

405. The 1907 Act expressly provides that a body corporate may be a limited partner. The Act is silent on whether a company may be a general partner in a limited partnership, and, therefore, it would appear that the principle applicable to traditional partnerships – that a company, because it is a legal person, may be a partner – would appear by virtue of section 7 to apply also to limited partnerships. Therefore, by incorporating a company (such as, for example, a de facto or de jure single-member private company) the person effectively acting as general partner may, subject to the rules of company law, cap his or her liability.

II. Registration

406. Every limited partnership must be registered with the Registrar of Companies, under pain of being regarded in default of that requirement as a general partnership and every limited partner being regarded as a general partner.[765] The following particulars (and a change in any of them) must be notified to the Registrar: the firm name; the general nature of the business; the principal place of business; the full name of each of the partners; the term, if any, for which the partnership is entered into and the commencement date thereof; a statement that the partnership is limited and a description of every partner as such; and the sum contributed by each limited partner and whether paid in cash or how otherwise.[766]

III. Dissolution

407. A limited partner is not entitled to dissolve the partnership by reason of any limited partner suffering his or her share to be charged for his or her separate debt

763. Limited Partnerships Act 1907, s. 6(5)(a).
764. Limited Partnerships Act 1907, s. 6(5)(d).
765. Limited Partnerships Act 1907, ss 5 and 15.
766. Limited Partnerships Act 1907, ss 8 and 9.

or to dissolve the partnership by notice.[767] In addition, a limited partnership shall not be dissolved by the death or bankruptcy of a limited partner, and the lunacy of a limited partner shall not be a ground for dissolution of the partnership by the Court, unless the lunatic's share cannot be otherwise ascertained and realized.[768]

IV. Taxation

408. All partnerships offer the benefit of being 'tax-transparent'. This means that the partnership, not having separate corporate personality, is not itself taxed, but rather income derived by partners from a partnership is subject only to the same taxation as income from any other source. (This is unlike the situation in a company where corporate profits are subject to corporation tax and any dividends declared out of those profits are then taxed again.) Limited partnerships' additional feature of not requiring limited partners to contribute to the debts and obligations of the firm beyond their capital contribution means that losses incurred by a limited partnership may be used for tax reduction purposes. For a time, a partner's share of the firm's trading losses could be set off against other taxable income, even when such losses exceeded (and sometimes far exceeded) that partner's capital contribution. The Revenue Commissioners unsuccessfully challenged that practice in *MacCarthaigh (Inspector of Taxes) v. D.*,[769] but shortly thereafter the legislature moved to limit the amount a partner could set off against other taxable income to the amount of his or her capital contribution, rather than his or her share of trading losses.[770]

§2. Investment Limited Partnerships Act

409. The ILP Act 1994 created a modified form of limited partnership for businesses principally engaged in the investment of funds in property.[771] Though they are a form of limited partnership, section 4(2) of the 1994 Act 'expressly disapplies' the provisions of the 1907 Act to ILPs.[772]

410. An ILP must have, and does not come into existence until it receives, a certificate of authorization from the Central Bank.[773] The Central Bank may impose such conditions on the authorization of an ILP as it considers appropriate and prudent.[774] Contravention of any such condition by the ILP is an offence, and any partner in default is liable to maximum penalties of a EUR 634,869 fine and fifteen

767. Limited Partnerships Act 1907, s. 6(5)(c) and (e).
768. Limited Partnerships Act 1907, s. 6(2).
769. Limited Partnerships Act 1907, s. 6(2).
770. Finance Act 1986, s. 46. See now Taxes Consolidation Act 1997, s. 1013.
771. ILP Act (ILPA) 1994, s. 5(1)(a). See generally, Murphy 'Investment Limited Partnerships', *Commercial Law Practitioner* 1 (1994): 287.
772. *Quigley v. Harris* [2008] IEHC 403 (unreported, High Court, 28 Nov. 2008) *per* Laffoy J.
773. ILPA 1994, s. 3.
774. ILPA 1994, s. 7.

years' imprisonment. The Central Bank may also apply to the Court for an order prohibiting contravention of such a condition[775] or decide to revoke an ILP's authorization.[776] Detailed consideration of the regulation of ILPs is beyond the scope of this work. The unusual structure of ILPs bears noting, however.

411. ILPs differ significantly from traditional partnerships, in that they 'consist of one or more general partners and one or more limited partners'.[777] The 1994 Act provides that management and conduct of the business of an ILP is a matter solely for general partners, inasmuch as that in order to maintain their limited liability status, limited partners in ILPs must not take part in the conduct of the business of the ILP, 'and in particular shall not have power to contract on behalf of the [ILP] and all letters, contracts, deeds, instruments and documents whatsoever shall be entered into by the general partner on behalf of the [ILP]'.[778] If a limited partner takes part in the conduct of the business of the ILP in its dealings with persons who are not partners, he or she 'shall be liable in the event of the insolvency of the [ILP] for debts of the [ILP] incurred during the period that he so participates' as if he or she were a general partner, but only in respect of debts or obligations incurred in favour of a person who reasonably believed, based upon the conduct of the partner, that he or she was a general partner.[779] Thus, from the point of view of limited partners, ILPs do not really resemble traditional partnerships regulated by the 1890 Act, or limited partnerships under the 1907 Act, but are better understood as arms-length investment vehicles.

775. ILPA 1994, s. 34.
776. ILPA 1994, s. 29.
777. ILPA 1994, s. 5(1)(b) as amended by S.I. No. 257 of 2013.
778. ILPA 1994, s. 6(1).
779. ILPA 1994, ss 6(2) and 6(3).

Selected Bibliography

Ahern, D. *Directors' Duties*. Dublin: Thomson Roundhall, 2009.

Byrne H. & L. McEntaggart. *The National Asset Management Agency Act 2009: Annotations and Commentary*. Dublin: Bloomsbury Professional, 2010.

Thomas B. Courtney, (General Editor) et al. *The Professional's Guide to the Companies Act 2014*. Dublin: Bloomsbury, 2015.

Courtney, T.B. *The Law of Companies*. 3rd edn. Dublin: Bloomsbury Professional, 2012.

Forde & Kennedy. *Company Law*. 4th edn. Dublin: Thomson Round Hall, 2007.

Keane, R. *Company Law in Ireland*. 4th edn. Tottel, 2006.

Lynch, Marshall & O'Ferrall. *Corporate Insolvency and Rescue*. 1st edn. Butterworths, 1996.

Lynch Fannon, I. & N. Murphy. *Corporate Insolvency and Rescue*. 2nd edn. Dublin: Bloomsbury, 2012.

Lynch-Fannon, I. *Working Within Two Kinds of Capitalism*. Oxford: Hart Publications, 2003.

McGrath, Sinead. *Company Law Essential Law Texts*. Dublin: Roundhall, 2003.

Twomey, M. *Partnership Law*. Dublin: Butterworths, 2000.

Ussher, P. *Company Law in Ireland*. London: Sweet & Maxwell, 1986.

Whelan, M., M. Kennedy & F. O'Raghallaigh. *The National Asset Management Agency Act 2009*. Dublin: Gill and MacMillan, 2011.

Other Useful Resources

British and Irish Legal Information Institute (BAILII) – www.bailii.org.

Irish Legal Information Initiative (IRLII) – www.irlii.org.

Irish Statute Book – www.irishstatutebook.ie.

Oireachtas – www.oireachtas.ie.

Office of the Director of Corporate Enforcement – www.odce.ie.

Companies Registration Office -www.cro.ie.

The Department of Enterprise, Trade and Employment.- www.djei.ie.

Company Law Review Group -www.clrg.org.

See the UK Government's Department for Business Innovation and Skills for comparative information on reform of Company Law. https://www.gov.uk/government/organisations/department-for-business-innovation-skills.

Enterprise Act (UK) 2002.

Companies (UK) Act 2006. As English decisions prior to 1922 form part of Irish law and since 1922 are considered to be of persuasive authority in Irish law, the following English texts are also referred.

Selected Bibliography

Clark, F.W. *A Treatise on the Law of Partnership and Joint-Stock Companies, According to the Law of Scotland*. Edinburgh: T & T Clark, 1866.
Davies, P.L. *Introduction to Company Law.* 2nd edn., Clarendon Law Series, Oxford: Oxford University Press, 2002.
Dignam, A. & J. Lowry. *Company Law*. Oxford: Oxford University Press, 2006.
Gower, L.C.B. & P.L. Davies. *Modern Company Law*. 8th edn. London: Sweet & Maxwell, 2008.
Grantham, R. & C. Rickett. *Corporate Personality in the 20th Century*. Oxford: Hart Publishing, 1998.
Gullifer, L. & J. Payne. *The Law of Corporate Finance: Principles and Policy*. 2nd edn., Oxford: Hart Publications, 2015.
Sealy, L.S. & S. Worthington. *Cases and Materials on Company Law*. 10th edn. Oxford: Oxford University Press, 20.
I'Anson, R.C. *Lindley and Banks on Partnership*. 18th edn. London: Sweet & Maxwell, 2002.
Morse, G. *Partnership Law*. 6th edn. Oxford: Oxford University Press, 2006.
Morse, G. (ed.). *Palmer's Company Law: Annotated Guide to the Companies Act 2006*. London: Sweet & Maxwell, 2007.
Moss, G., I. Fletcher & R. Isaacs. *The EC Regulation on Insolvency Proceedings: A Commentary and Annotated Guide*. (OUP 2002; second edition, 2009, third edition due to be published in 2016).
Pennington, R.R. *Company Law*. 8th edn. Oxford: Oxford University Press, 2001.
Pettet, B. *Company*. 2nd edn. Longman Law Series, 2005.
Wessels, B., B.A Markel, Judge & J. Kilborn. *International Co-operatioin in Bankruptcy and Insolvency Matters*. Oxford University Press, 2009.

Government Reports

The Report of the Company Law Review Group, December 1994.
Report of the Working Group on Company Law, Compliance and Enforcement, November 1998.
Central Statistics Office, This is Ireland, Highlights from Census 2011 Part 1 (CS0, Government of Ireland, March 2012). 978-1-4064-2650-2.
Department of Trade and Industry (UK) Consultative Document, Modern Company Law for a Competitive Economy. 200 … .

Index

The numbers here refer to paragraph numbers.

www.ingramcontent.com/pod-product-compliance
Lightning Source LLC
Chambersburg PA
CBHW071442230926
51846CB00001B/314
9789041168535